Reasoning Olympiad

Highly useful for all school students participating
in Various Olympiads & Competitions

Series Editor Keshav Mohan
Authors Amogh Goel, Sweta Rani

Class 6

arihant

ARIHANT PRAKASHAN, MEERUT

ARIHANT PRAKASHAN, MEERUT
All Rights Reserved

卐 Administrative & Production Offices

Corporate Office 'Ramchhaya' 4577/15, Agarwal Road, Darya Ganj New Delhi -110002
Tele: 011- 47630600, 43518550; Fax: 011- 23280316

Head Office Kalindi, TP Nagar, Meerut (UP) - 250002
Tele: 0121-2401479, 2512970, 4004199; Fax: 0121-2401648

All disputes subject to Meerut (UP) jurisdiction only.

卐 Sales & Support Offices

Agra, Ahmedabad, Bengaluru, Bhubaneswar, Bareilly, Chennai, Delhi, Guwahati, Haldwani, Hyderabad, Jaipur, Jalandhar, Jhansi, Kolkata, Kota, Lucknow, Meerut, Nagpur & Pune

卐 ISBN   978-93-5203-392-8

卐 Price   ₹90

Typeset by Arihant DTP Unit at Meerut
Printed & Bound by Arihant Publications (I) Ltd. (Press Unit)

Production Team

Publishing Manager	Mahendra Singh Rawat	Page Layouting	Krishna Kumar Saini
Project Head	Mana Yadav	DTP Operator	Shravan Pandey & Ravindar Rawat
Project Coordinator	Akanksha Jain	Cover Designer	Syed Darin Zaidi
Proof Reader	Sachin Kumar Prajapati, Gora Sharma	Inner Designer	Deepak Kumar

For further information about the products from Arihant
log on to www.arihantbooks.com or email to info@arihantbooks.com

Preface

Reasoning Olympiad Series for Class 6th-10th is a series of books, which will challenge the young inquisitive minds by the non-routine and exciting Reasoning or Logic based problems.

The main purpose of this series is to make the students ready for competitive exams, as Reasoning is an integral section of almost all competitive examinations. All the questions given in this series are objective in nature so, they will provide students a feel of competitive examinations as school/board exams are of qualifying nature, but not competitive, which mainly have Objective Questions.

Need of Olympiad Series

This series helps students, who are willing to sharpen their problem solving skills through logical thinking. Unlike typical assessment books, which emphasise on drilling practice, the focus of this series is on practising problem solving techniques.

Development of Logical Approach

The thought provoking questions given in this series will help students to attain a deeper understanding of the concepts and through, which students will be able to imbibe reasoning/Logical/Analytical skills in themselves.

Complement Your School Studies

This series complements the additional preparation needs of students for regular school/board exams. As most of the schools conduct aptitude test on a regular basis. Along with, it will also address all the requirements of the students, who are approaching National/State level competitions or Olympiads.

We shall welcome criticism from the students, teachers, educators and parents. We shall also like to hear from all of you about errors and short comings, which may have remained in this edition and the suggestions for their improvement the next edition.

Editor & Author

Contents

Verbal Reasoning

Chapter 1

Similar Pairs

'Similar Pairs' are the pairs in which there exists some relationship between the two elements of a pair and same relationship exists between the two elements of other pair.

For example, 'Milk' is related to 'White', in the same way as 'Orange' is related to
(a) Red   (b) Orange   (c) White   (d) Fruit

We know that the colour of milk is white; so in the first pair, the first member represents an object and the second represents the object's colour. Now, if we carefully observe the second pair, then we find that the first member represents the fruit orange, so the second member will represent the colour of this fruit, which is again orange.

Hence, option (b) is correct.

In similar pairs, following types of questions are generally asked

Direction (Ex. Nos. 1-3) Complete the second pair in the same way as the first pair.

EXAMPLE 1 5 is to 15, as 7 is to
     (a) 33   (b) 42   (c) 21   (d) 40

Think Try to find out the relation between both the numbers of first pair and follow similar relation to complete the next pair.

Sol. As , $5 \times 3 = 15$, similarly $7 \times 3 = 21$. So, 21 would replace the question mark.

Hence, option (c) is correct.

EXAMPLE 2 AD : BE :: CF : ?
     (a) DG   (b) DE   (c) EC   (d) FG

Think Analyse the both group of letters of first pair and relate each letter of first group with their respective letter of second group.

Sol. As, A D B E   (+1, +1)   Similarly, C F D G   (+1, +1)

Hence, option (a) is correct.

Note *Following letters position table in English alphabetical series will help the students to solve these type of questions*

Forward	1	2	3	4	5	6	7	8	9	10	11	12	13	14	15	16	17	18	19	20	21	22	23	24	25	26
Alphabet	A	B	C	D	E	F	G	H	I	J	K	L	M	N	O	P	Q	R	S	T	U	V	W	X	Y	Z
Backward	26	25	24	23	22	21	20	19	18	17	16	15	14	13	12	11	10	9	8	7	6	5	4	3	2	1

EXAMPLE 3 Petal : Flower :: ? : ?
     (a) Salt : Pepper   (b) Tyre : Bicycle   (c) Base : Ball   (d) Puppy : Dog

Sol. As petal is a part of flower. Similarly, tyre is a part of bicycle.

Hence, option (b) is correct.

Practice Centre

1. 17 is related to 32, in the same way as 11 is related to
   - **a** 26
   - **b** 31
   - **c** 24
   - **d** 28

2. 4 is to 9, as 7 is to
   - **a** 13
   - **b** 14
   - **c** 15
   - **d** 16

3. 14 is to 196, as 16 is to
   - **a** 289
   - **b** 255
   - **c** 284
   - **d** 256

4. 15 is related to 75, in the same way as 12 is related to
   - **a** 80
   - **b** 60
   - **c** 50
   - **d** 120

5. 5928 is related to 59, in the same way 7712 is related to
   - **a** 77
   - **b** 12
   - **c** 71
   - **d** 72

6. 6248 : 3124 : : 4024 : ?
   - **a** 2102
   - **b** 2201
   - **c** 2012
   - **d** 2210

7. 49 : 36 : : 64 : : ?
   - **a** 30
   - **b** 36
   - **c** 24
   - **d** 32

8. 24 : 14 : : 32 : ?
   - **a** 16
   - **b** 18
   - **c** 20
   - **d** 24

9. 423539 : 422539 : : 253682 : ?
   - **a** 251682
   - **b** 252682
   - **c** 252692
   - **d** 256282

10. (5 : 25) (6 : 36) (7 : ?)
    - **a** 49
    - **b** 37
    - **c** 50
    - **d** 94

11. (542 : 245) (368 : 863) (929 : ?)
    - **a** 928
    - **b** 929
    - **c** 930
    - **d** 939

12. XW : ZY : : DJ : ?
    - **a** FK
    - **b** EL
    - **c** FL
    - **d** LF

13. RQP : ONM : : KJI : ?
    - **a** GHF
    - **b** HGF
    - **c** HFG
    - **d** FGH

14. BAD : ABC : : CAT : ?
    - **a** BZS
    - **b** BBU
    - **c** DZU
    - **d** BBS

15. ABC : BDF : : ? : MOM
    - **a** LMJ
    - **b** LML
    - **c** LMN
    - **d** LNJ

16. Select the pair which shows similar relationship that is shown by the following pair.

    ABC : CDE
    - **a** LNM : NOO
    - **b** PDF : RFH
    - **c** PQR : QRS
    - **d** XYZ : ZAX

17. CARE : HFWJ
   a BOSS : GTXY
   b CROP : HXTU
   c GOAL : LTFQ
   d FEEL : KJKQ

18. G*M : 7*13
   a B*D : 4*2
   b L*O : 11*15
   c X*F : 25*6
   d P*T : 16*20

Direction (Q. Nos. 19-20) In each of the following questions, determine the missing term.

19. (A : Z) (C : X) (E : ?)
   a W   b V
   c T   d U

20. (AB : 3) (CD : 7) (EF : ?)
   a 11   b 10
   c 12   d 9

21. KLM is related to MLK in the same way HIJ is related to
   a JIH   b IJH
   c IHJ   d HJI

22. BD is related to 6, in the same way LK is related to
   a 22   b 23   c 24   d 25

Direction (Q. Nos. 23-26) In each of the following questions, there is a certain relationship between the pair of words on the left of ': :' and one word is given on the other side of ': :.' From amongst the four given alternatives, choose the word which completes the second pair in the same way as the first pair.

23. Helicopter : Aircraft : : Almond : ?
   a Expensive   b Nut
   c Fruit   d Cashew

24. Peacock : India : : Kangaroo : ?
   a Russia   b England
   c Australia   d America

25. Engine : Car : : Lens : ?
   a Convex
   b Transparent
   c Bifocal
   d Microscope

26. Optimist : Pessimist : : Filthy : ?
   a Clean   b Dirty
   c Muddy   d Airy

Direction (Q. Nos. 27-29) In each of the following questions, a pair of words is given. From amongst the four given alternatives, choose the pair which shows a relationship similar to the one expressed in the given pair.

27. Car : Automobile
   a Paper : Book
   b Vegetable : Potato
   c Cat : Animal
   d Game : Soccer

28. Mother : Parent
   a Uncle : Nephew
   b Sister : Sibling
   c Father : Son
   d Daughter : Sister

29. Fool : Wisdom
   a Wrestler : Strength
   b Teacher : Knowledge
   c Mother : Mercy
   d Liar : Honesty

30. Potato is related to vegetable, in the same way banana is related to
   a Animal   b Book
   c Fruit   d Yellow

31. Mind is related to think, in the same way teeth is related to
   a See
   b Chew
   c Walk
   d Tal

Chapter 2

What Comes Next ?

'What Comes Next' means finding the next term based on given arrangement.

It is also known as 'Series'. Student's are required to analyse the pattern followed by series and find the next term.

For example, Find the next term in the given series.

$$\boxed{1}\ \boxed{2}\ \boxed{4}\ \boxed{8}\ \boxed{?}$$

(a) 18   (b) 12   (c) 16   (d) 14

Here, we can see that the number in each step gets double of the previous one.

So, this process makes a series as $1 \xrightarrow{\times 2} 2 \xrightarrow{\times 2} 4 \xrightarrow{\times 2} 8 \xrightarrow{\times 2} \boxed{16}$

Therefore, the number in next step will be 8×2 i.e. 16.

Hence, option (c) is correct.

Series may be classified as

1. Letter series   2. Number series   3. Alpha-numeric series

Letter Series

In letter series, letters of the English alphabet are arranged in a specific pattern. The pattern is based on the position of letters in English alphabetical order.

In such type of problems, students are required to observe the given pattern and find out the next letter (or missing letter) to complete the series.

In letter series, following types of questions are generally asked

Direction (Ex. Nos. 1-3) What comes next in the series given below?

EXAMPLE 1 $\boxed{A}\ \boxed{B}\ \boxed{D}\ \boxed{G}\ \boxed{K}\ \boxed{?}$

       (a) P   (b) Q   (c) R   (d) L

Think
- Firstly, determine the difference between each successive letter and the previous letter to know the pattern of the series.
- Follow the same pattern to obtain the next letter.

Sol. The given series can be represented as $A \xrightarrow{+1} B \xrightarrow{+2} D \xrightarrow{+3} G \xrightarrow{+4} K \xrightarrow{+5} \boxed{P}$

Here, each letter is 1, 2, 3, 4, … steps ahead to its previous letter.

Therefore, the next letter will be K + 5 i.e. P, as shown above.

Hence, option (a) is correct.

EXAMPLE 2   (BT)   (ER)   (HP)   (KN)   (?)

(a) LM   (b) NL   (c) NP   (d) JM

Think Relate first and second letters of each term with the first and second letters of the next term, respectively to obtain the pattern of the series.

Sol. The given series can be represented as

$$B \xrightarrow{+3} E \xrightarrow{+3} H \xrightarrow{+3} K \xrightarrow{+3} \boxed{N}$$
$$T \xrightarrow{-2} R \xrightarrow{-2} P \xrightarrow{-2} N \xrightarrow{-2} \boxed{L}$$

Here, the first letter in each term is 3 steps ahead to its previous letter and the second letter in each term is 2 steps backward from its previous letter.

Therefore, the letters in next term will be K + 3 = N and N − 2 = L, as shown above.

Hence, option (b) is correct.

EXAMPLE 3   (EHJ)   (GJI)   (ILH)   (KNG)   (?)

(a) MPF   (b) LOH   (c) ILF   (d) MPI

Think Relate each letter of every term with their respective letter of successive term to obtain the pattern of the sequence.

Sol. The given series can be represented as

$$E \xrightarrow{+2} G \xrightarrow{+2} I \xrightarrow{+2} K \xrightarrow{+2} \boxed{M}$$
$$H \xrightarrow{+2} J \xrightarrow{+2} L \xrightarrow{+2} N \xrightarrow{+2} \boxed{P}$$
$$J \xrightarrow{-1} I \xrightarrow{-1} H \xrightarrow{-1} G \xrightarrow{-1} \boxed{F}$$

Here, first and second letters of each term is 2 steps ahead to its previous letter and third letter is 1 step backward from its previous letter.

Therefore, the letters in next term will be K + 2 = M, N + 2 = P and G − 1 = F, as shown above.

Hence, option (a) is correct.

Number Series

In number series, numbers are arranged in a specific pattern. The pattern can be based on addition, subtraction, multiplication or division.

In such type of questions, students are required to observe the given pattern and find out the next number (or missing number) to complete the series.

In number series, following types of questions are generally asked

✎ **Direction** (Ex. Nos. 4-7) Complete the following series.

EXAMPLE 4   (2) (3) (5) (8) (12) (?)

(a) 13   (b) 14   (c) 16   (d) 17

Think Determine the difference between each successive number and its previous number to know the pattern of the sequence.

Sol. In the given series, numbers are arranged in the following pattern $2 \xrightarrow{+1} 3 \xrightarrow{+2} 5 \xrightarrow{+3} 8 \xrightarrow{+4} 12 \xrightarrow{+5} \boxed{17}$

Therefore, the next number will be 12 + 5 i.e. 17, as shown above.

Hence, option (d) is correct.

EXAMPLE 5   (99) (95) (91) (87) (?)

(a) 82   (b) 86   (c) 93   (d) 83

Think Find out the rule used to obtain each successive number.

Sol. The given series can be represented as $99 \xrightarrow{-4} 95 \xrightarrow{-4} 91 \xrightarrow{-4} 87 \xrightarrow{-4} \boxed{83}$

Therefore, the next number will be 87 − 4 = 83, as shown above.

Hence, option (d) is correct.

EXAMPLE 6   (3) (6) (12) (24) (?)

    (a) 48   (b) 42   (c) 26   (d) 30

Think   Relate each successive number with its previous number to obtain the rule of the series.

Sol. In the given series, numbers are arranged in the following pattern $3 \xrightarrow{\times 2} 6 \xrightarrow{\times 2} 12 \xrightarrow{\times 2} 24 \xrightarrow{\times 2} \boxed{48}$

Therefore, the next number will be 24×2 i.e. 48, as shown above.
Hence, option (a) is correct.

EXAMPLE 7   (2) (4) (5) (10) (11) (22) (23) (?)

    (a) 24   (b) 25   (c) 40   (d) 46

Think   Find the relation of each successive number to its previous number to obtain the next number.

Sol. In the given series, numbers are arranged in the following pattern

$$2 \xrightarrow{\times 2} 4 \xrightarrow{+1} 5 \xrightarrow{\times 2} 10 \xrightarrow{+1} 11 \xrightarrow{\times 2} 22 \xrightarrow{+1} 23 \xrightarrow{+1} \boxed{46}$$

Therefore, the next number will be 23×2 i.e. 46, as shown above.
Hence, option (d) is correct.

Alpha-Numeric Series

In alpha-numeric series, letters and numbers together are arranged in a specific pattern.

In such type of questions, students are required to observe the given pattern and find out the next (or missing) term to complete the series.

In alpha-numeric series, following types of questions are generally asked

EXAMPLE 8   Find the next term in the given series.

A1	C3	E5	G7	?

    (a) F6   (b) G8   (c) I9   (d) 9I

Think   • Relate letters and numbers of each term separately to obtain the rule.
         • Follow the same rule to get the next letter and number.

Sol. The pattern of the series is as follows $A \xrightarrow{+2} C \xrightarrow{+2} E \xrightarrow{+2} G \xrightarrow{+2} \boxed{I}$, $1 \xrightarrow{+2} 3 \xrightarrow{+2} 5 \xrightarrow{+2} 7 \xrightarrow{+2} \boxed{9}$

Therefore, the next letter will be $G + 2$ i.e. I, next number will be $7 + 2$ i.e. 9 and next term will be I9.
Hence, option (c) is correct.

EXAMPLE 9   Find the next term in the given series.

AB3	DE9	GH15	?

    (a) KJ12   (b) JK21   (c) JK12   (d) KJ21

Think   Find the relation of each letter and number of a term with their respective letter and number of the next term to know the pattern.

Sol. The pattern of the series is as follows

$$A \xrightarrow{+3} D \xrightarrow{+3} G \xrightarrow{+3} \boxed{J}$$
$$B \xrightarrow{+3} E \xrightarrow{+3} H \xrightarrow{+3} \boxed{K}$$
$$3 \xrightarrow{+6} 9 \xrightarrow{+6} 15 \xrightarrow{+6} \boxed{21}$$

Therefore, the first letter of next term will be $G + 3$ i.e. J, second letter will be $H + 3$ i.e. K and number will be $15 + 6$ i.e. 21 as shown above.

Hence, option (b) is correct.

Practice Centre

Letter Series

1. C G K O ?

a T   **b** P
c S   **d** U

2. P N L J ?

a I   **b** E
c K   **d** H

3. B Z C Y D X ?

a W   **b** E
c F   **d** T

4. AB CE FI JN ?

a TO   **b** OS
c SO   **d** OT

5. AC DF GI JL ?

a LM   **b** MO
c NO   **d** KN

6. BC de FG hi ?

a jk   **b** LM
c JK   **d** HI

7. ABZ BDA CFB DHC ?

a EDJ   **b** DJE
c EJD   **d** EJE

8. Y S T O O K J ? ?

a K, J   **b** G, E
c E, F   **d** H, F

9.

BA	BA	CB	ED	HG	?	?

a KL, QP   **b** LK, PQ
c LK, QP   **d** KL, PQ

10.

ABD	EFH	IJL	MNP	QRT	?	?

a VUX, YZB   **b** UVX, ZYB
c UXV, YZB   **d** UVX, YZB

11.

YBI	XDH	WFG	VHF	?	?

a USA, UPA   **b** UAE, UPS
c UJE, TLD   **d** TJD, UAE

Number Series

12. 9 13 17 21 ?

a 25   **b** 26
c 23   **d** 19

13. 98 90 82 74 ?

a 70   **b** 60
c 69   **d** 66

14. 400 200 100 50 ?

a 25   **b** 40
c 15   **d** 30

15. 2 4 12 48 240 ?

a 1200   **b** 1680
c 1440   **d** 1848

16. 2 3 5 7 11 13 ?

a 14
b 15
c 16
d 17

17. 15 | 45 | 20 | 42 | 25 | 39 | ?

a 36 b 30
c 25 d 40

18. 100 | 98 | 94 | 86 | 70 | ?

a 83 b 07
c 38 d 89

19. 5 | 25 | 125 | 625 | ?

a 875 b 15625
c 3125 d 1125

20. 1 | 1 | 2 | 3 | 5 | 8 | 13 | ?

a 21 b 20
c 17 d 18

21. 68 | 56 | 46 | 38 | 32 | ?

a 24 b 26
c 28 d 30

22. 3 | 9 | 21 | 45 | ?

a 56 b 66
c 93 d 76

 Direction (Q. Nos. 23-29) Find the missing number in the given series.

23.

4	16	36	?	100

a 48 b 64
c 9 d 25

24.

8	64	216	512	?	1728

a 1331 b 729
c 999 d 1000

25.

2004	2009	2016	?	2036	?	2064

a 2008, 2036
b 2001, 2010
c 2025, 2094
d 2025, 2049

26.

8192	7283	6374	5465	?

a 5557 b 4556
c 3364 d 4565

27.

80000	88000	88800	88880	?

a 88888 b 880000
c 8888 d 88899

28. 6 | 14 | 24 | 36 | ? | 66

a 60 b 50
c 52 d 58

29. 1024 | 256 | 64 | ? | 4

a 16 b 2
c 8 d 32

Alpha-Numeric Series

Direction (Q. Nos. 30-32) Find the next term in the given series.

30. A01 | B11 | C21 | D22 | E23 | F33 | ?

a 34G b G34
c G31 d G30

31. A2C | D5F | G8I | J11L | M14O | ?

a P17R b Q20S
c Q18S d S18Q

32. AB9 | AC16 | AD25 | AE36 | AF49 | ?

a AG46 b AG50
c AG63 d AG64

Direction (Q. Nos. 33-35) Find the missing term.

33.

A100	B200	D400	G700	?

a K800 b K900
c K1000 d K1100

34.

B5C	D9E	F13G	?	J21K	?

a H71I, L25M b H17I, L25M
c H17I, L52M d HI17, LM25

35.

DE9	FG13	HI17	JK21	?

a LM25 b KL23
c LM26 d MN27

Chapter 3

Odd One Out

In 'Odd One Out', a group of some items is given. All these items, except one are similar in a certain way. The students are required to spot out this odd item, i.e. the one which does not fit into the given group of items.

For example, The set of 5 pencils is shown in adjacent figure.

Clearly, the second pencil from the right side, i.e. the one with a broken tip is different from others. So, this pencil is the odd one out from among the given pencils.

'Odd One Out' is also referred to as 'Classification'. Problems based on 'Odd One Out' aim to test a student's ability to classify various items into a group based on their common properties. The items given may be numbers, letters or words.

In Odd One Out, following types of questions are generally asked

EXAMPLE 1 Find the odd one out.

    (a) 31   (b) 45   (c) 34   (d) 41

Think • Look at the numbers and try to find out the common properties followed by all the numbers, except one.

• After careful observation, we find that the numbers follow odd and even numbers property.

Sol. We can see that numbers 31, 45 and 41 are odd numbers while 34 is an even number. So, 34 is odd one.

Hence, option (c) is correct.

EXAMPLE 2 Choose the odd one out.

    (a) BC   (b) KM   (c) GH   (d) WX

Think • Look at the groups of letters and try to find out the common pattern followed by all the groups, except one.

• After careful observation, we find that most of the groups follow consecutive letters' pattern.

Sol. We can see that, letters' group BC, GH and WX have consecutive letters while letters' group KM does not have consecutive letters. So, KM is different from others.

Hence, option (b) is correct.

EXAMPLE 3 Choose the odd one out.

    (a) Moon   (b) Jupiter   (c) Earth   (d) Mars

Think • Look at the words and try to find out the common characteristic contain by all the words, except one.

• After careful observation, we find that the words have planets and satellite property.

Sol. We can see that Jupiter, Earth and Mars are the planets while Moon is a satellite. So, Moon is odd one.

Hence, option (a) is correct.

Practice
Centre

Numbers Classification

1.

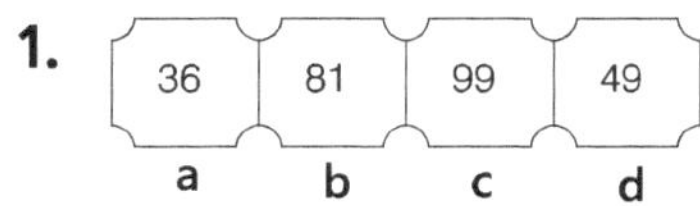

2.

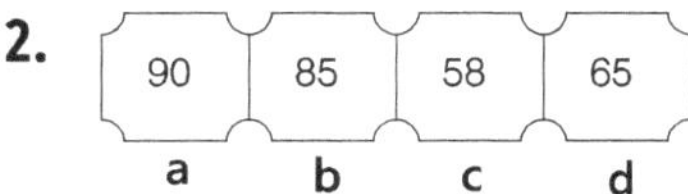

3.

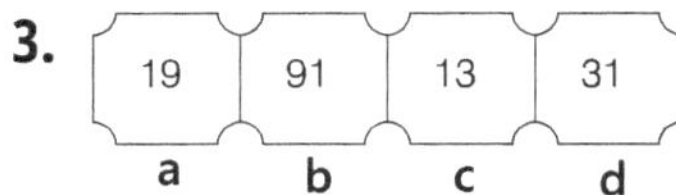

4.

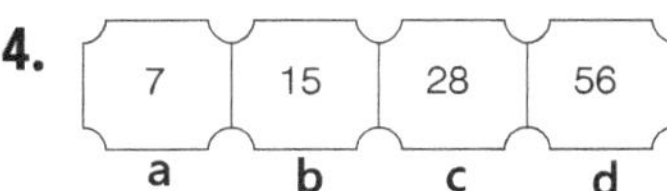

5.

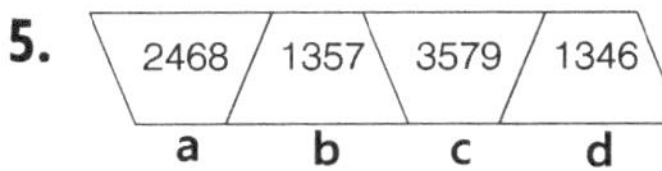

6.

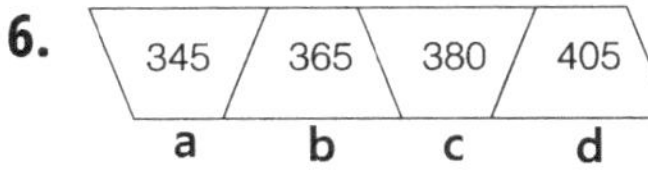

7.

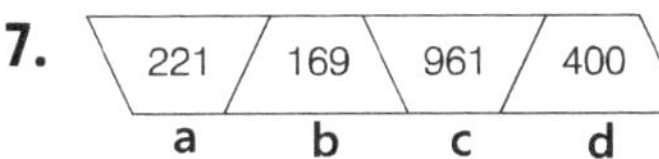

8.

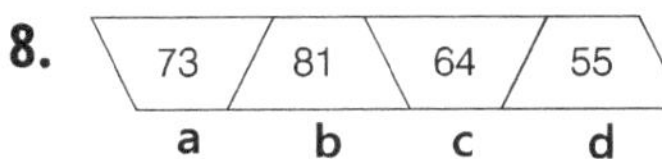

9.

10.

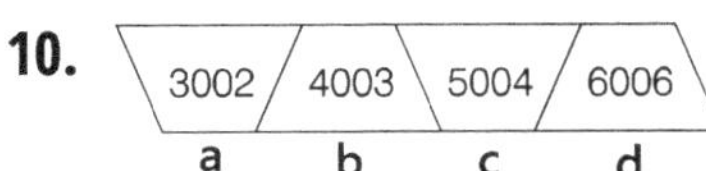

Letters Classification

11.

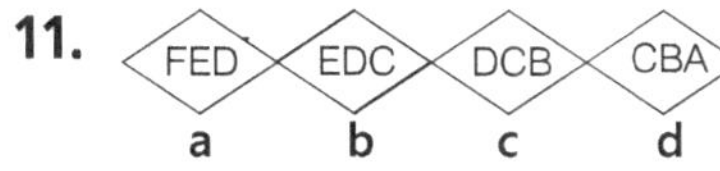

12.

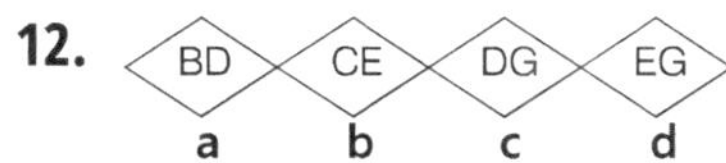

13.

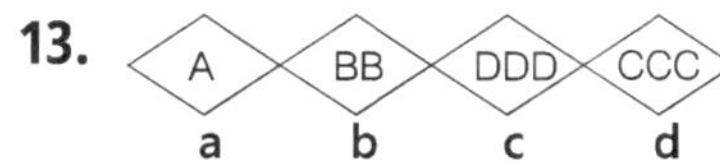

14.

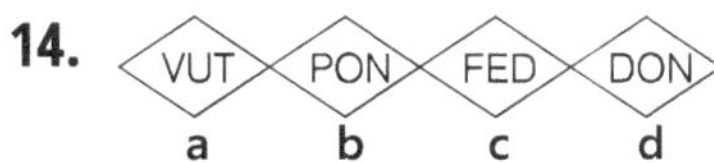

15.

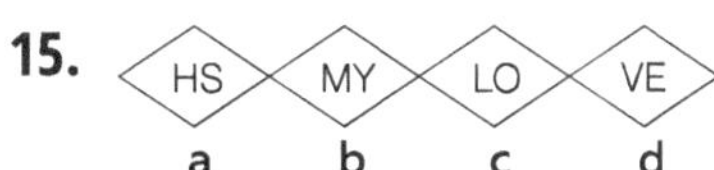

16.

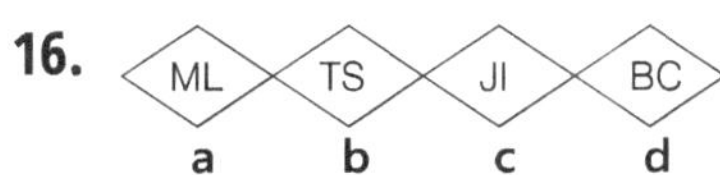

17.

21C	13D	33F	23G
a	b	c	d

18.

CDWX	EFVW	MNOP	IJRQ
a	b	c	d

19.

2C2	3F2	5O3	7G1
a	b	c	d

20.

FKP	HMR	LPU	DIN
a	b	c	d

21.

END	PUT	ARM	OWL
a	b	c	d

Words Classification

22.

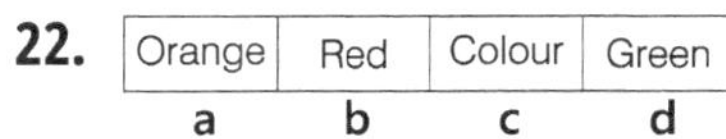

Orange	Red	Colour	Green
a	b	c	d

23.

Pants	Shirt	Umbrella	Socks
a	b	c	d

24.

June	March	July	January
a	b	c	d

25.

Tool	Rule	Cool	Fool
a	b	c	d

26.

Monday	Today	Tuesday	Sunday
a	b	c	d

27.

Turnip	Kiwi	Orange	Date
a	b	c	d

28.

Bulb	Fan	Tourch	Lamp
a	b	c	d

29.

Knife	Spoon	Plate	Fork
a	b	c	d

30.

Nose	Lungs	Hand	Knee
a	b	c	d

31.

Japan	Bhutan	Nepal	Beijing
a	b	c	d

32.

Bus	Motor-cycle	Bicycle	Car
a	b	c	d

33.

Rabbit	Lion	Cat	Fox
a	b	c	d

Chapter 4

Coding-Decoding

Coding 'Coding' is a method of conveying a message in secret way.

Decoding 'Decoding' is a process to break the code to understand the conveyed message.

By the following conversation one can easily understand coding-decoding.

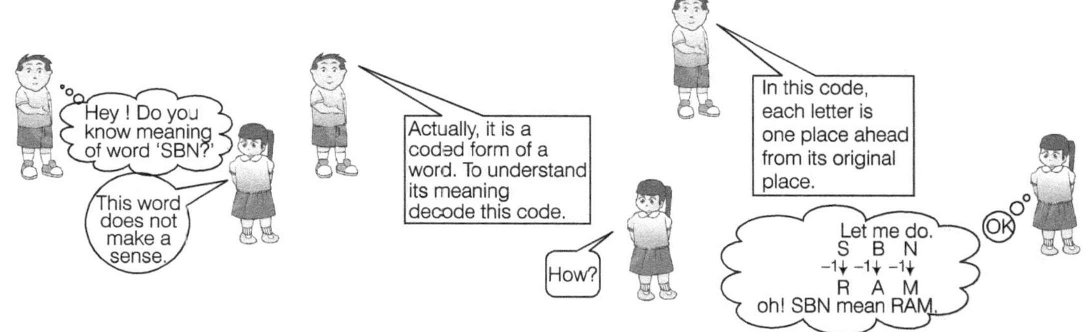

In coding-decoding, following types of questions are generally asked

EXAMPLE 1 In a certain code, GOAL is coded as HPBM, in the same way BEAR is coded as

   (a) SBFC   (b) FSBC   (c) CFBS   (d) BFSC

Think • Analyse the word and its code and try to find out the relation between letters of the basic word and coded word.

• After analysing we find that, each letter of the coded word is one place ahead to its corresponding letter in basic word in English alphabets.

Sol. As,

   G O A L   Similarly,   B E A R
   +1 +1 +1 +1   +1 +1 +1 +1
   H P B M   C F B S

Hence, option (c) is correct.

EXAMPLE 2 If NEWS is coded as *5#1, then ASLE is coded as

   (a) \$©*#   (b) 5*1#   (c) ©1\$5   (d) 5123

Think After observing we find that, first and third letters are coded by symbols and second and fourth letters are coded by numbers.

Sol. The code for E is 5 and for S is 1. And the code for first and third letters will be symbols.

Therefore, the code for ASLE will be ©1\$5.

Hence, option (c) is correct.

EXAMPLE 3 If BEAT is coded as ADZS, then how will you code TRACE?

    (a) USBDF   (b) SQZBD   (C) SQABD   (d) SQZDE

Think After analysing we find that, each letter of the original word is decreased by 1 to obtain the corresponding letter of the code.

Sol. As,

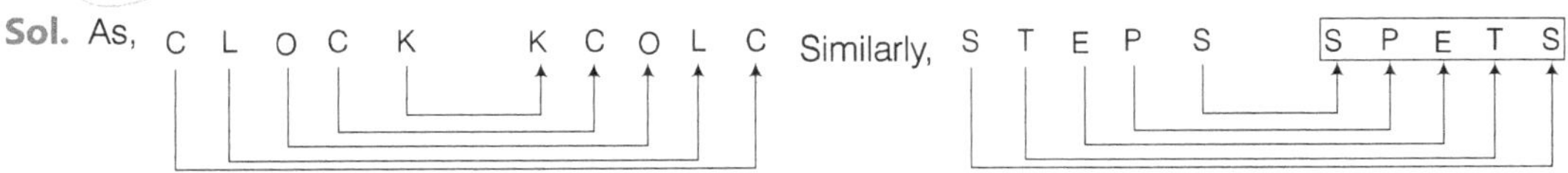

Hence, option (b) is correct.

EXAMPLE 4 If in a certain code, CLOCK is coded as KCOLC, how is STEPS coded in that code?

    (a) SPETS   (b) SPSET   (c) SPEST   (d) STEPS

Think After analysing we find that, the letters of the original word are reversed to obtain the code.

Sol. As, C L O C K → K C O L C   Similarly, S T E P S → S P E T S

Hence, option (a) is correct.

EXAMPLE 5 If blue is called red, red is called green, green is called yellow and yellow is called white, then the colour of grass is

    (a) white   (b) yellow   (c) red   (d) blue

Think · After observing we see that, some colours are replaced with other colours.

· Now, we have to determine the colour of the given object and interchange this colour with other colour according to the information given in the question.

Sol. We know that, the colour of grass is green, but in the given code, green is coded as yellow. So, the colour of grass is yellow.

Hence, option (b) is correct.

EXAMPLE 6 If in a certain code language, 'te ne' means 'good boy', 're ne se' means 'girls are good', 'he re na' means 'you are fool'. Then, find the code for 'girls' in that language.

    (a) se   (b) te   (c) ne   (d) re

Think · Write the words and their codes in the form of equation.

· Compare the equations to find out the words and their respective codes.

Sol.

$$te\ ne \to good\ boy \qquad ...(i)$$
$$re\ ne\ se \to girls\ are\ good \qquad ...(ii)$$
$$he\ re\ na \to you\ are\ fool \qquad ...(ii)$$

From Eqs. (i) and (ii),

$$ne \to good, te \to boy$$

From Eqs. (ii) and (iii),

$$re \to are, se \to girls$$

So, the code for girls is 'se'.

Hence, option (a) is correct.

Practice Centre

1. In a certain code, BEAN is coded as ABNE and SALE is coded as LSEA, then NEWS is coded as
   a SNEW   b SNWE   c WNES   d WNSE

2. If HEALTH is coded as GDZKSG, then code for NORTH is
   a OPSUI   b GSQNM   c FRPML   d MNQSG

3. If CORDIAL is coded as ENTCKZN, then code for SOMEDAY is
   a UNODFZA   b TNECKZN
   c DFZANOU   d DFZNOUA

4. If CALANDER is coded as CLANAEDR, then CIRCULAR is coded as
   a ICCRLURA   b CRIUCLRA
   c ICRCLUAR   d CRIUCALR

5. If BAKE is coded as 5796 and FIRE is coded as 3146, then FEAR is coded as
   a 6374   b 3674   c 4763   d 6347

6. If the code of AMONG is BKRJL then the code of SLEEP is
   a LEPSE   b TJHAU   c TMFGQ   d TJGBU

7. If STAR is coded as #8@7, then JRKT is coded as,
   a ★789   b ★7%8   c %8★9   d %7★#

8. If 1352 is coded as DEAR and 2693 is coded as ROPE, then 9352 is coded as
   a ARPE   b RAEP   c PEAR   d ERPA

9. If a certain code word BRAIN is coded as NIARB, then how is SLEEP coded in that code?
   a EPSLE   b SPLEE   c PEELS   d LEPSS

10. If RAID is written as %#©$ and RIPE is coded as %©@★, then DEAR is coded as
    a $★#%   b ★#%$ c $%★#   d #%$★

11. If RESANO is coded as S1T2O3, then MORALE is coded as
    a 3N2S1M   b NSM123
    c 123NSM   d N3S2M1

12. If GARDEN is coded as MgfvTS, then how will READ is coded?
    a fTgv   b TgSM   c gTMf   d vSgM

13. If A = 2, D = 8, K = 22 and TEN = 78, then BEL is coded as
    a 83   b 39   c 38   d 30

14. If MORALE is coded as 5 and CHARCOAL is coded as 7, then GOVERNMENT is coded as
    a 10   b 8   c 6   d 9

15. If 532 + 608 = 650382, then 230 + 891 = ?
    a 289310   b 310829   c 892013   d 829310

16. If 'red' is called 'pink', 'pink' is called 'black', 'black' is called 'white' and 'white' is called 'blue', then colour of milk is
    a black   b white   c blue   d pink

17. If 'water' is called 'food', 'food' is called 'tree', 'tree' is called 'sky', 'sky' is called 'wall', then on which of the following a fruit grows?
    a Water   b Food   c Sky   d Tree

Direction (Q. Nos. 18-19) In a certain code meaning of some words are as follows.

   (i) 'ho na ta' means 'food is good'.
   (ii) 'sa ta la' means 'eat food regularly'.
   (iii) 'da na ja' means 'keep good health'.

18. Which of the following means 'food' in that code language?
    a la   b ta   c na   d da

19. Which of the following means 'food is good' in that code language?
    a ta ho na   b sa ta la
    c ta na ho   d ja na da

20. In a certain code language, '256' means 'you are good'. 637 means 'we are bad' and '358' means 'good and bad'. Which of the following represents 'and' in that code?
    a 2   b 5   c 8   d 3

Jumbled Words

'Jumbled Words' is a kind of a word puzzle in which a clue is given, followed by a set of words, each of which is jumbled up by mixing its letters in a confused way. The students have to reconstruct the words and identify the one which is the answer to the given clue.

For example, You are given a clue below and a set of four words (a), (b), (c) and (d). All you need to do is to unjumble (reconstruct) the words and identify the word which is the answer to the given clue.

Upon reconstructing the words given in options (a) to (d), we get
(a) INKPOT   (b) TEAPOT   (c) SAUCER   (d) PENCIL

Now, upon carefully observing, we find that the word 'TEAPOT' starts with 'T', ends with 'T'. Also, a teapot holds tea, i.e. it is full of tea (T). Hence, the word given in option (b) is the correct answer to the clue.

In 'Jumbled Words', following types of questions are generally asked.

EXAMPLE 1 Capital of Japan
        (a) IEBINJG   (b) WOCSMO   (c) KYTOO   (d) LIHED

> **Think** • First of all, read the given clue carefully, and reach to the answer.
> • After this, rearrange the letters of the words given in options and choose a word which is suitable for the given clue.

Sol. We know that, the capital of Japan is 'TOKYO'.
Upon rearranging the letters in each of the given words, we get
Option (a) BEIJING, option (b) MOSCOW, option (c) TOKYO and option (d) DELHI.
Hence, option (c) is correct.

EXAMPLE 2 A kind of fruit
        (a) AAVUG   (b) OOINN   (c) TRPINU   (d) PTTOOA

> **Think** • We know that the kind of fruits are Apple, Guava, Orange, Banana etc.
> • Now, we will rearrange the letters of the words given in options.

Sol. Upon rearranging the letters in each of the given words, we get
Option (a) GUAVA, option (b) ONION, option (c) TURNIP and option (d) POTATO.
We know that, ONION, TURNIP and POTATO are all vegetables but 'GUAVA' is a fruit.
Hence, option (a) is correct.

Practice Centre

Direction (Q. Nos. 1-18) In each of the following questions, the letters of the words (given in the options) have been jumbled up. Reconstruct the words and identify the one which is the answer to the given clue.

1. A number
- a MSEUO
- b ANBAAN
- c PPRUEL
- d EVENLE

2. Three times
- a WIECT
- b HTIECR
- c SUQAER
- d BUODEL

3. A kind of vegetable
- a MOGAN
- b ISRAHD
- c RAEB
- d RONAEG

4. A unit of measurement for weight
- a AMGR　b UOHR　c RTEME　d YTEB

5. A body part
- a AYDUNS
- b LESIVR
- c IBNAR
- d LRLODA

6. A substance used for sticking objects
- a APPRE
- b BBRRUE
- c SLEAC
- d ULEG

7. A part of computer
- a BELAT　b SEUMO　c FFEETO　d EPN

8. A means of water transport
- a HSPI　b RTIAN　c NEAPL　d CKTUR

9. Opposite of dark
- a DIHE　b HTIWE　c RTGHIB　d CKLAB

10. A kind of an indoor game
- a TCEKRIC　b CYKHOE　c SEHSC　d NINEST

11. A name of a country
- a UMBIAM
- b NRAFEC
- c NDLOON
- d ARPIS

12. A name of a planet
- a DOMNDAI
- b AHCIN
- c RUJIPTE
- d RAOBD

13. Synonym of intelligent
- a LGUY
- b AWKE
- c HSOFOLI
- d LIBRATNIL

14. A name of a colour
- a AANBAN
- b KRDA
- c WLEYLO
- d NABLK

15. A name of a month
- a HCAMR
- b YUSNDA
- c ROANEG
- d ILGTH

16. A kind of season
- a ECOTOBR
- b NIRAY
- c ASUQER
- d AHSIML

17. One who teaches?
- a RUNSE
- b ECATERH
- c NEPO
- d OODCTR

18. A geometrical shape
- a LCSAE
- b NEPICL
- c LRCCIE
- d HWETI

Direction (Q. Nos. 19-20) Given below is a square having same letters. Using the letters of the square answer the question that follow.

G	P	B
A	V	A
U	T	O

19. A kind of fruit
- a GRAPE
- b BANANA
- c ORANGE
- d GUAVA

20. A name of a state
- a UTTAR PRADESH
- b GOA
- c BIHAR
- d PUNJAB

Chapter 6

Mathematical Reasoning

'Mathematical Reasoning' is all about playing with numbers. Problems based on this chapter test a student's ability to figure out the rule (or pattern), which exists in a given arrangement of numbers, letters or combination of letters and numbers.

Problems based on mathematical reasoning can be broadly divided into the following two categories

1. Matrix Based or Figure Based Problems
2. Mathematical Operations

Matrix Based or Figure Based Problems

In such type of problems, we deal with questions which have blocks/matrices. all follow a definite pattern. We are given numbers or characters associated with these blocks/sequences including one which is missing. The student is required to find this pattern and accordingly find the missing character.

For example, Following figures are arrangement of numbers. In which two figures have three numbers and third figure has 2 numbers. Find out the third number of third figure.

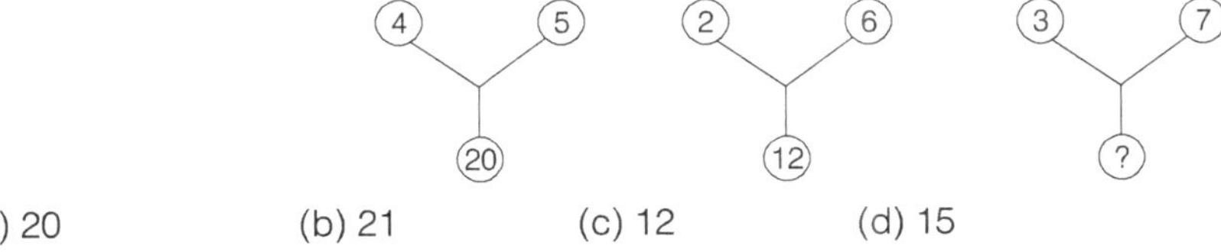

(a) 20   (b) 21   (c) 12   (d) 15

In each of above figures, the product of the numbers in upper two circles is given as

$$4 \times 5 = 20, \quad 2 \times 6 = 12$$

So, in third figure the product of 3 and 7 will come in bottom circle as shown below

$$3 \times 7 = 21$$

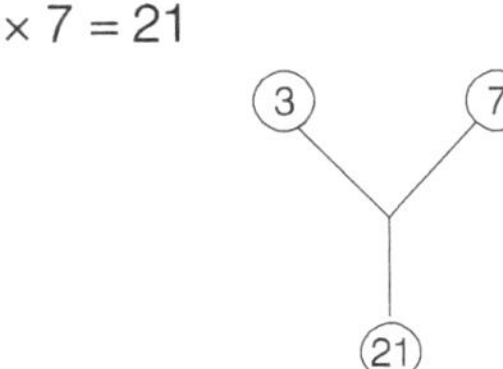

Hence, option (b) is correct.

In matrix based or figure based problems, following types of questions are generally asked

EXAMPLE 1 Which number will replace the question mark?

$\frac{1}{2}$	$\frac{1}{4}$	$\frac{1}{4}$
$\frac{1}{3}$	$\frac{1}{6}$	$\frac{1}{6}$
$\frac{1}{2}$	$\frac{1}{3}$	?

(a) $\frac{1}{2}$ (b) $\frac{1}{6}$ (c) $\frac{1}{9}$ (d) $\frac{5}{6}$

Think • Look at the matrix and try to find out the pattern, rowwise or columnwise.
• After observing we find that, the matrix follow rowwise pattern i.e. in each row.
• First term – Second term = Last Term.

Sol. Here, in row I, $\frac{1}{2} - \frac{1}{4} = \frac{1}{4}$ and in row II, $\frac{1}{3} - \frac{1}{6} = \frac{1}{6}$, Similarly, in row III, $\frac{1}{2} - \frac{1}{3} = \frac{1}{6}$

Hence, option (b) is correct.

EXAMPLE 2 Identify the rule that has been used to fill in the entries of the given square and then determine which one of the given options will replace the question mark?

K	L	M
O	P	Q
T	U	?

(a) Z (b) V (c) A (d) W

Think • After analysing rowwise we find that, in each row, consecutive letters are given.
• Considering columnwise, in each column, the first letter from the top is incremented by 4 to get the second letter and second letter is incremented by 5 to get the last letter.

Sol. Considering rowwise,

In row I, $K \xrightarrow{+1} L \xrightarrow{+1} M$, In row II, $O \xrightarrow{+1} P \xrightarrow{+1} Q$

Similarly, in row III, $T \xrightarrow{+1} U \xrightarrow{+1} \boxed{V}$

Considering columnwise,

In column I, $K \xrightarrow{+4} O \xrightarrow{+5} T$, In column II, $L \xrightarrow{+4} P \xrightarrow{+5} U$

Similarly, in column III, $M \xrightarrow{+4} Q \xrightarrow{+5} \boxed{V}$

So, 'V' will replace the question mark.
Hence, option (b) is correct.

EXAMPLE 3 Which number will replace the question mark?

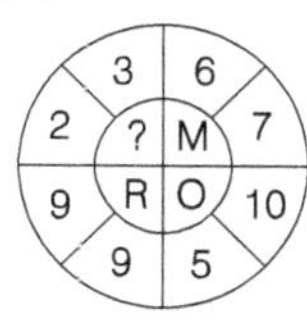

(a) Y (b) U (c) I (d) E

Think After observing, we see that in each quarter circle, the sum of the numbers gives the position of the alphabet written in that quarter circle.

Sol. As, $6 + 7 = 13 \rightarrow M$, $10 + 5 = 15 \rightarrow O$ and $9 + 9 = 18 \rightarrow R$. Similarly, $2 + 3 = 5 \rightarrow E$

Hence, option (d) is correct.

Mathematical Operations

Problems based on 'Mathematical Operations' involve simplification of a given arithmetic expression. But here, the mathematical operators like addition (+), subtraction (−), multiplication (×) and division (÷) are represented by symbols other than the actual ones and the students are required to substitute the actual symbols to reach the answer.

An important point to note here is that a mathematical expression should be simplified using the BODMAS rule.

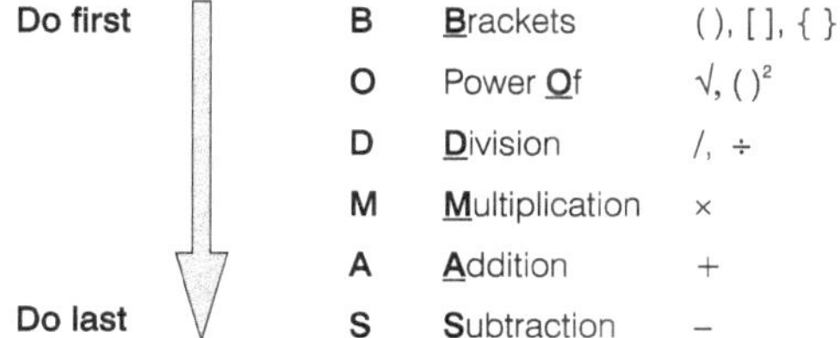

In mathematical operations, following types of questions are generally asked

EXAMPLE 4 If '+' means '÷', '−' means '×', '×' means '+' and '÷' means '−', then what is the value of $45 \div 40 + 8 \times 20 - 2$?

    (a) 100   (b) 80   (c) 120   (d) 90

Think Analyse the given signs substitution and substitute the signs of the expression according to the information given in question.

Sol. On substituting the signs as given in the question, we get

Expression $= 45 - 40 \div 8 + 20 \times 2$

Simplify the above expression using BODMAS rule,

$$45 - 40 \div 8 + 20 \times 2$$

$= 45 - 5 + 20 \times 2$	[division, $40 \div 8 = 5$]
$= 45 - 5 + 40$	[multiplication, $20 \times 2 = 40$]
$= 85 - 5$	[addition, $45 + 40 = 85$]
$= 80$	[subtraction, $85 - 5 = 80$]

Hence, option (b) is correct.

EXAMPLE 5 Which of the following signs, if changed, will make the equation correct?

$$50 \times 5 \div 4 + 4 = 44$$

    (a) ÷ and ×   (b) ÷ and +   (c) × and +   (d) None of these

Think After observing, we find that we have to interchange the signs as given in each option to balance the given equation.

Sol. After interchanging the signs as given in option (a),

$$\text{LHS} = 50 \div 5 \times 4 + 4 = 10 \times 4 + 4$$
$$= 40 + 4 = 44 = \text{RHS}$$
$$\therefore \quad \text{LHS} = \text{RHS}$$

Hence, option (a) is correct.

Practice Centre

1. Which number will replace the question mark?

6	7	8
10	16	22
8	?	6

a 7   b 10   c 14   d 12

2. Find the missing number.

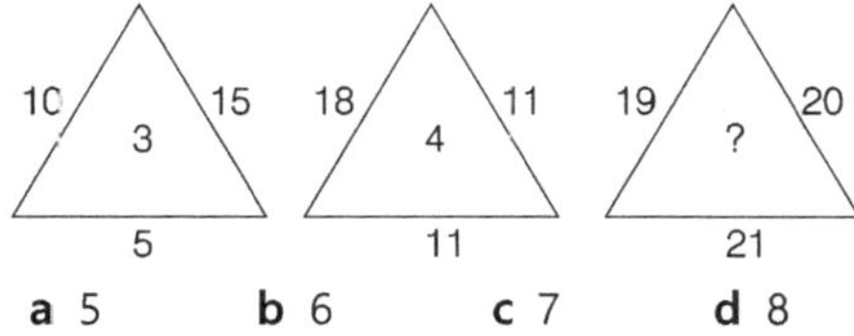

a 5   b 6   c 7   d 8

3. Which number will replace the question mark?

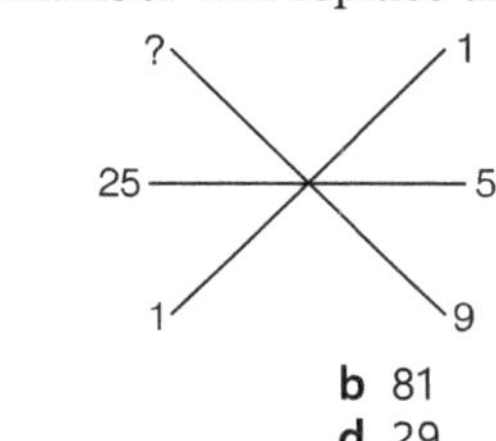

a 90   b 81
c 99   d 29

4. Which number will replace the question mark?

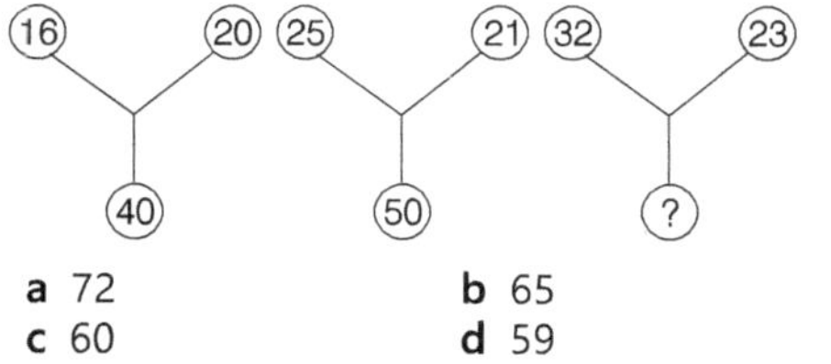

a 72   b 65
c 60   d 59

5. Find the missing number.

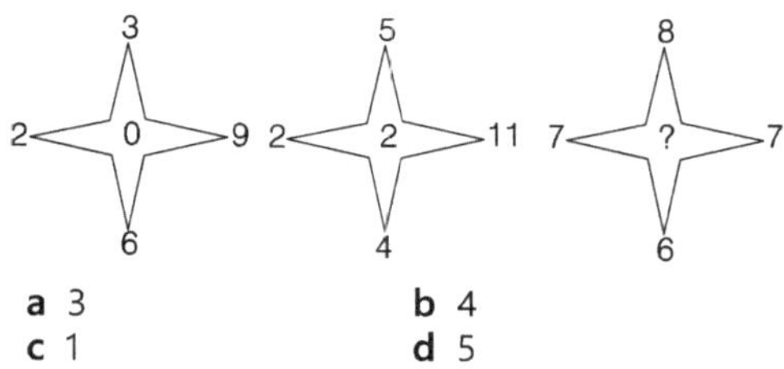

a 3   b 4
c 1   d 5

6. Find the missing letter.

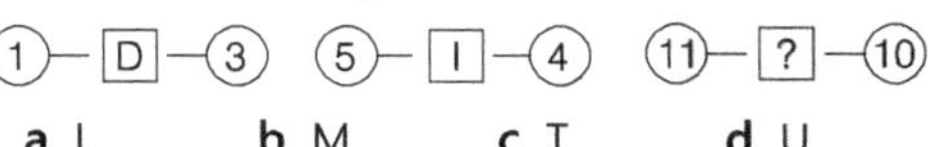

a L   b M   c T   d U

7. Which number will replace the question mark?

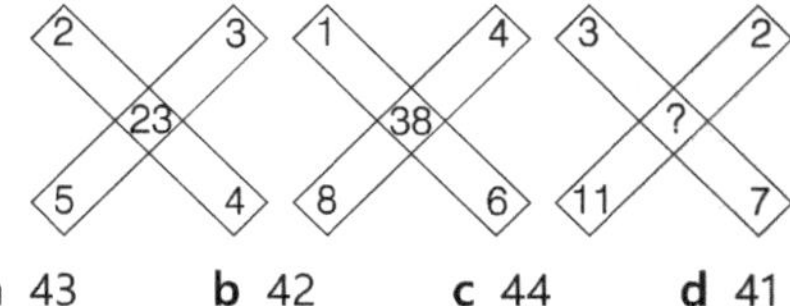

a 43   b 42   c 44   d 41

8. Which number will replace the question mark?

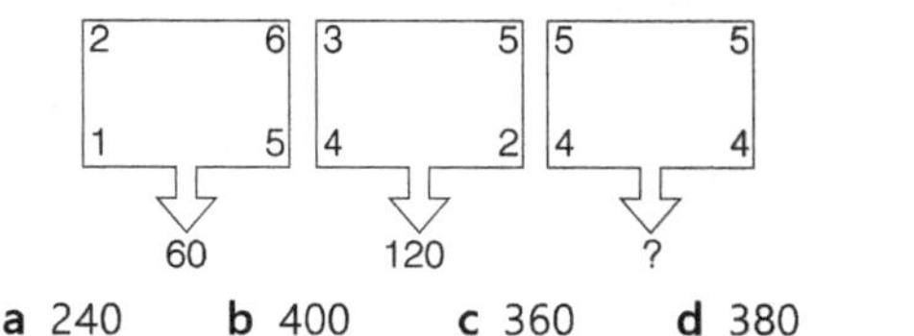

a 240   b 400   c 360   d 380

9. Find the missing letter.

A	G	M
C	I	?
E	K	Q

a O
b N
c P
d R

10. Find the missing entry.

11C	23A	2B
22A	67B	3C
?	34C	1A

a 11B
b 33C
c 11A
d None of the above

11. Based on the following figure, answer the question given below.

The value of $(X^2 - 1)$ is

a 195   b 399   c 999   d 933

12. Find the missing number.

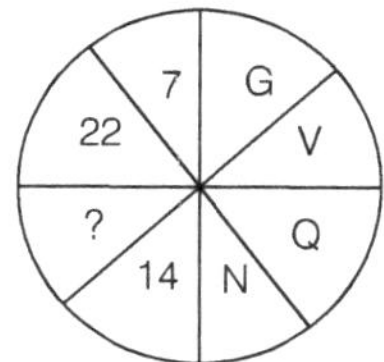

    a 12
    b 17
    c 14
    d 15

13. Complete the following matrix.

Z_2	X_{19}	V_{66}
A_3	C_{18}	?
T_4	R_{17}	P_{68}

    a E_6
    b F_{69}
    c E_{67}
    d E_{56}

14. Find the number that will replace the question mark.

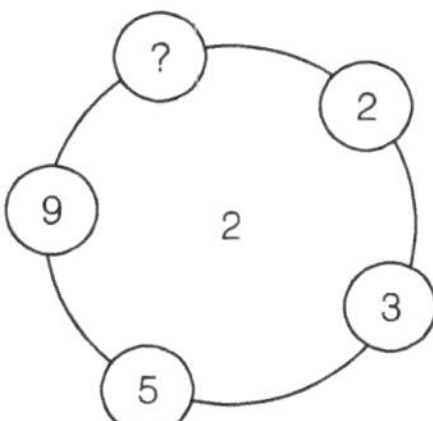

    a 79
    b 17
    c 15
    d 18

Direction (Q. Nos. 15-17) Read the information carefully and answer the questions given below. If '+' means '×', '−' means '÷', '×' means '−' and '÷' means '+', then find the value of the given expressions.

15. $24 + 2 \times 4 \div 6 - 3$

    a 50   **b** 46   **c** 48   **d** 52

16. $92 \times 12 + 7 - 4 \div 21$

    a 50.5   **b** 92   **c** 50   **d** 52.5

17. $5 \times 4 \div 6 + 5 - 4$

    a -6.5 **b** -5.5 **c** 8.5   **d** 6

18. If 'a' stands for '−', 'b' stands for '÷', 'c' stands for '×' and 'd' stands for '+', then find the value of 12d8c10a14b7.

    a 95   **b** 85   **c** 100   **d** 90

19. If ↑ means '+', ↓ means '−', ← means '×' and → means '÷', then what is the value of $1 \uparrow 41 \leftarrow 5 \uparrow 37 \downarrow 91 \rightarrow 7$?

    a 225   **b** 228   **c** 230   **d** 242

20. If $2 * 3 = 8, 3 * 2 = 9$ and $5 * 1 = 5$, then find the value of $4 * 3$.

    a 72   **b** 64   **c** 78   **d** 80

21. If $56 \# 14 = 4$ and $34 \sim 54 = 20$, then find the value of $98 \# (90 \sim 139)$.

    a 2   **b** 4   **c** 5   **d** 6

22. If $6 \star 5 = 31, 7 \star 8 = 57, 3 \star 4 = 13, 9 \star 10 = ?$

    a 90   **b** 91   **c** 81   **d** 19

23. If $18 + 6 = 3, 34 \div 14 = 20, 23 - 4 = 92$ and $13 \times 14 = 27$, then find the value of $4 \times 9 + 3 - 6 \div 10$.

    a 22   **b** 10   **c** 18   **d** 12

24. If $27 \oplus 19 = 8$ and $43 \oplus 29 = 14$, then find the value of $54 \oplus 56 \oplus 55$.

    a 57   **b** 55   **c** -57 **d** -56

25. Which of the following signs, if changed, will make the equation correct?

$$25 \times 5 - 50 \div 2 + 10 = 140$$

    a × and −   **b** + and −
    c ÷ and +   **d** + and ×

26. Which of the following interchanges of signs and numbers will make the equation correct?

$$4 + 5 \times 2 = 13$$

    a × and +, 5 and 2   **b** + and ×, 4 and 2
    c + and ×, 4 and 5   **d** None of these

27. If '+' means '−', '÷' means '+', '−' means '×' and '×' means '÷', then which of the following equation is correct?

    a $40 - 10 + 10 \times 5 = 92$
    b $66 \times 3 - 11 + 12 = 230$
    c $265 + 11 - 2 \times 14 = 22$
    d $2 - 14 \times 4 \div 11 = 16$

28. If signs '+' and '−' are interchange, and numbers '5' and '8' are interchanged, then which of the following expression is true?

    a $82 - 35 + 55 = 2$ **b** $82 - 35 + 55 = 102$
    c $85 - 38 + 85 = 132$ **d** $52 - 35 + 55 = 72$

29. If $P = 8, Q = 5, R = 14$ and $S = 7$, then $P \times Q + R \div S = ?$

    a 24   **b** 38   **c** 42   **d** 84

Chapter 7

Puzzle Test

'Puzzle' is a problem in which the information is not given as such, but in a confusing or jumbled manner.

Many a times, only a part of the whole information is given and the students are required to fill in the missing links in the given information.

For example, Four children A, B, C and D are sitting on a bench. A is to the left of C and B is third right of D. Who is sitting at the extreme right end?

Now, lets mark the position of children seating on a bench as per the given information shown as

D   A   C   B

From the above sitting arrangement, it is clear that on the extreme right end of the bench child B is seating.

In puzzle test, following types of questions are generally asked

EXAMPLE 1 Read the following information carefully and answer the questions given below.

Six friends A, B, C, D, E and F are sitting in a circle facing the centre. A is between B and E. C is between D and F. E is to the immediate right of D.

   (i) Who is between E and C?

      (a) D   (b) B   (c) A   (d) F

  (ii) Who is immediate right of A?

      (a) B   (b) D   (c) E   (d) C

Think • Read the given information carefully and relate each object/persons with other objects/persons.

       • Draw a circular arrangement diagram and place all the six persons.

Sol. A is sitting between B and E. Since, the positions of B and E are not clear, so the possible diagram will be

C is sitting between D and F. Here, again the positions of D and F are not clear, so the diagram will be

Now, E is to the immediate right of D.
Then,

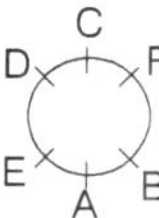

(i) As shown in the above diagram D, is between E and C.
   Hence, option (a) is correct.

(ii) As shown in the above diagram, B is immediate right of A.
   Hence, option (a) is correct.

EXAMPLE 2 Read the following information carefully and answer the questions given below.

Ravi and Kunal are good in Hockey and Volleyball, Sachin and Ravi are good in Hockey and Baseball, Gaurav and Kunal are good in Cricket and Volleyball. Sachin, Gaurav and Rohit are good in Football and Baseball.

(i) Who is good in Hockey, Cricket and Volleyball?
   (a) Sachin　　　(b) Kunal　　　(c) Ravi　　　(d) Gaurav

(ii) Who is good in Baseball, Cricket, Vollyball and Football?
   (a) Sachin　　　(b) Kunal　　　(c) Gaurav　　　(d) Ravi

Think · Draw a table showing the name of players and games in rows and columns, respectively.
· Now, read each statement and fill the table accordingly.

Sol. On the basis of given information, the table is drawn as shown below:

Players	Hockey	Volleyball	Baseball	Cricket	Football
Ravi	✓	✓	✓	✗	✗
Kunal	✓	✓	✗	✓	✗
Sachin	✓	✗	✓	✗	✓
Gaurav	✗	✓	✓	✓	✓
Rohit	✗	✗	✓	✗	✓

(i) Kunal is good in Hockey, Cricket and Volleyball.
   Hence, option (b) is correct.

(ii) Gaurav is good in Baseball, Cricket, Volleyball and Football.
   Hence, option (c) is correct.

Practice Centre

Direction (Q. Nos. 1-2) Read the following information carefully to answer the questions given below.

(i) Kailash, Govind and Harinder are intelligent.
(ii) Kailash, Rajesh and Jitendra are hard-working.
(iii) Rajesh, Harinder and Jitendra are honest.
(iv) Kailash, Govind and Jitendra are ambitious.

1. Which of the following persons is neither hard-working nor ambitious?
- **a** Kailash
- **b** Govind
- **c** Harinder
- **d** Rajesh

2. Which of the following persons is neither honest nor hard-working but is ambitious?
- **a** Kailash
- **b** Govind
- **c** Harinder
- **d** Rajesh

Direction (Q. Nos. 3-5) Study the information carefully, to answer the questions given below.
In a school, there were five teachers A, B, C, D and E. A and B were teaching Hindi and English. C and B were teaching English and Geography. D and A were teaching Mathematics and Hindi. E and B were teaching History and French.

3. Who among the following teachers was teaching maximum number of subjects?
- **a** A
- **b** B
- **c** C
- **d** D

4. More than two teachers were teaching which common subjects?
- **a** History
- **b** Hindi
- **c** English
- **d** Both (b) and (c)

5. D, B and A were teaching which of the following subjects?
- **a** English only
- **b** Hind and English
- **c** Hindi only
- **d** English and Geography

Direction (Q. Nos. 6-8) Read the following information and answer the questions given below.
Five girls are sitting on a bench to be photographed.

(i) Seema is to the left of Rani and to the right of Bindu.
(ii) Garima is to right of Rani.
(iii) Reeta is between Rani and Garima.

6. Who is in the middle of the photograph?
- **a** Bindu
- **b** Rani
- **c** Reeta
- **d** Seema

7. Who is second from the left in photograph?
- **a** Reeta
- **b** Garima
- **c** Bindu
- **d** Seema

8. Who is second from the right?
- **a** Garima
- **b** Rani
- **c** Reeta
- **d** Bindu

Direction (Q. Nos. 9-10) Read the following information and answer the questions given below.
A, B, C, D, E and F are sitting along a circle facing at the centre and are playing cards.

(i) E is the neighbour of A and D.
(ii) F is on the immediate right of A.
(iii) B is not the neighbour of D.

9. Who are the neighbours of B?
- **a** C and D
- **b** F and C
- **c** A and E
- **d** F and D

10. What is the position of F from E?
- **a** Immediate Left
- **b** Third to the right of E
- **c** Second to the right of E
- **d** Immediate right

Chapter 8

Number, Ranking and Alphabet Test

Ranking Test

In such type of problems, the rank (position) of a person from the top and bottom (from the left and right) is given and it is asked to determine the total number of persons.

In another variant, the total number of persons and the rank of a person from one of the ends is given, it is asked to determine the rank of the person from the other end.

EXAMPLE 1 In a class of 25 students, if Ram's rank is 16th from the bottom, then what is his rank from the top?

    (a) 13th   (b) 10th   (c) 9th   (d) 11th

Think Draw a diagram according to the given information or use formula to obtain the position.

Sol. According to the question,

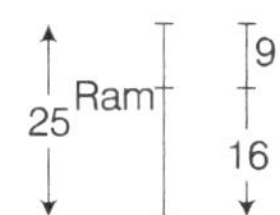

∴ Number of students at top of Ram $= 25 - 16 = 9$. Now, position of Ram from top $= 9 +$ Ram itself $= 9 + 1 = 10$th

Hence, option (b) is correct.

Alphabet Test

In such type of problems, a letter of the English alphabet is given and it is asked to determine the letter that is placed at certain number of positions to the left/right of the given letter. Before moving forward, let us revise the positional values of each of the letters in the English alphabet.

Forward alphabetical order

A	B	C	D	E	F	G	H	I	J	K	L	M	N	O	P	Q	R	S	T	U	V	W	X	Y	Z
1	2	3	4	5	6	7	8	9	10	11	12	13	14	15	16	17	18	19	20	21	23	23	24	25	26

Reverse alphabetical order

Z	Y	X	W	V	U	T	S	R	Q	P	O	N	M	L	K	J	I	H	G	F	E	D	C	B	A
26	25	24	23	22	21	20	19	18	17	16	15	14	13	12	11	10	9	8	7	6	5	4	3	2	1

EXAMPLE 2 Which letter is fourth to the right of M in English alphabetical order?

    (a) Q   (b) O   (c) P   (d) R

Think Add four to the positional value of M and then count the alphabet from the left.

Sol. As it can be seen from the table above (alphabetical order), the position of M in the English alphabet is 13.
Fourth to the right of M means (13 + 4), i.e. 17th position. Clearly, the letter Q is present at the 17th position.
Thus, the letter fourth to the right of M is Q.
Hence, option (a) is correct.

Number Test

In number test, a numerical sequence is given that follow a logical rule. Here, students are required to find the numbers based on the given situation asked in question.

EXAMPLE 3 In the following sequence find out the number of the 3's, which are neither preceded by 6 nor immediately followed by 9.

$$9\ 3\ 6\ 6\ 3\ 9\ 5\ 9\ 3\ 7\ 8\ 9\ 1\ 6\ 3\ 9\ 6\ 3\ 9$$

    (a) 3   (b) 2   (c) 4   (d) 1

Think Read the given condition carefully and then count the number of 3's.

Sol. Here, in the above sequence there are two 3's, which are neither preceded by 6 nor immediately followed by 9 as shown below

$$9\ \boxed{3}\ 6\ 6\ 3\ 9\ 5\ 9\ \boxed{3}\ 7\ 8\ 9\ 1\ 6\ 3\ 9\ 6\ 3\ 9$$

Hence, option (b) is correct.

Alpha-Numeric Sequence Test

In such type of problems, a jumbled sequence of letters and numbers is given and the students are required to count the number of occurrences of a particular letter/number following a certain rule (condition).

EXAMPLE 4 Which of the following would be the 4th element to the right of the 13th element from the left end? 8 C M @ N £ T 2 4 γ 6 5 £ Q $ 7 ★ W # Z

    (a) #   (b) W   (c) £   (d) ★

Think Read the given information carefully and then count the number of letters/numbers/ symbols of a sequence.

Sol. According to the question, the 4th element to the right of the 13th element from the left end is ★ shown in the series.
Hence, option (d) is correct.

Logical Sequence of Words

In logical sequence of words, a group of words is given in which students are required to arrange the words in a meaningful and logical order.

EXAMPLE 5 Arrange the words in a meaningful/logical order and then select the appropriate sequence from the alternatives given below

    1. Thousand   2. Trillion   3. Billion   4. Hundred

    (a) 4, 3, 2, 1   (b) 4, 1, 3, 2   (c) 3, 2, 4, 1   (d) 2, 3, 1, 4

Think • Observe the given words and try to arrange them from smallest to largest.
    • The given words are related to measure units.

Sol. The words can be arranged in meaningful and logical order as shown below
Hundred → Thousand → Billion → Trillion i.e. 4, 1, 3, 2
Hence, option (b) is correct.

Practice Centre

1. Which of the following words will come first, if all of these are arranged alphabetically as in a dictionary?
   a Wasp b Waste c Wrist d War

2. Which of the following words will come second from right end, if all of them are arranged alphabetically as in a dictionary?
   a Afford b Avoid c Answer d After

Direction (Q. Nos. 3-4) In each of the following questions, a group of letters is given which are numbered 1, 2, 3, 4 and 5. Select from the four alternatives containing the combinations of these numbers, to form a meaningful word.

3. N A E H L D
   1 2 3 4 5 6
   a 2, 6, 4, 3, 5, 1   b 4, 2, 1, 6, 5, 3
   c 4, 3, 6, 5, 2, 1   d 2, 1, 6, 4, 3, 5

4. E H N T O R
   1 2 3 4 5 6
   a 2 5 3 4 1 6   b 4 2 6 5 3 1
   c 2 5 6 3 1 4   d 4 2 5 6 3 1

Direction (Q. Nos. 5-6) Following questions are based on the following alphabet series.
A B C D E F G H I J K L M N O P Q R S T U V W X Y Z

5. If the above alphabets are written in the reverse order, which letter will be twelfth to the left of the sixteenth letter from your left?
   a D b V c W d X

6. Which letter is thirteenth to the right end if the alphabet series is reversed?
   a M b R c P d S

Direction (Q. Nos. 7-8) Study the following number sequence given below and answer the question. 8 9 7 6 3 4 2 8 9 7 6 4 5 9 2 9 7

7. How many 7's are preceded by 9 and followed by 6?
   a 2   b 3
   c 4   d 5

8. How many 9's are there which are preceded by even numbers?
   a 1   b 4   c 2   d 3

9. If in the following numbers, first and last digits are intercphanged, then which one of the given options will be the least numbers?
   319, 409, 418, 719
   a 319 b 409 c 418 d 179

Direction (Q. Nos. 10-11) In each of the following questions, arrange the words in a meaningful and logical order and then select the appropriate sequence from the alternatives provided below.

10. 1. Table 2. Wood 3. Tree 4. Plant 5. Seed
    a 4, 5, 3, 2, 1   b 5, 4, 3, 2, 1
    c 1, 3, 2, 4, 5   d 1, 2, 3, 5, 4

11. 1. Puberty   2. Infancy   3. Adulthood
    4. Childhood 5. Senescence
    a 2, 4, 1, 3, 5   b 5, 4, 3, 2, 1
    c 1, 5, 2, 4, 3   d 2, 4, 3, 1, 5

12. Sohan ranks 7th from the top and 26th from the bottom in a class. How many students are there in the class?
    a 31 b 32 c 34 d 33

13. In a row of ten boys, when Rohit was shifted by two places towards the left, he became seventh from the left end. What was his earlier position from the right end of the row?
    a First b Second c Third d Sixth

14. Rohit obtained more marks than Tarun, but less than Kabir. Raj obtained more than Vansh, but less than Harshit. Kabir obtained less than Vansh. Who obtained the highest marks?
    a Kabir b Harshit c Raj d Vansh

15. Mohit is older than Rajesh and Raman. Namit is older than Rajesh, but younger than Rajeev. Raman is older than Rajeev. Who among them is the oldest?
    a Rajeev   b Rajesh
    c Mohit   d Namit

Chapter 9

Direction Sense Test

There are four main directions i.e. East, West, North and South and four subdirections i.e. North-East, North-West, South-East and South-West.

From the figure given below, we can understand direction sense

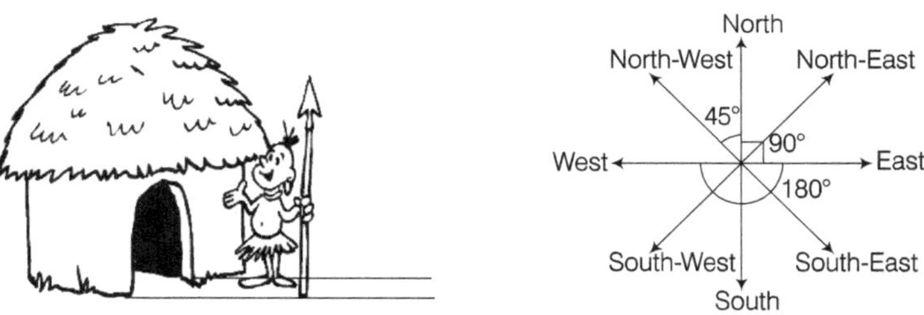

In the above figure, we see that a man comes out from his house and his face is towards South, then his left hand is towards East and his right hand is towards West.

Some important points to solve problems based on direction test

- The direction of moving along clock's hand is called clockwise direction.
- The direction of moving opposite to clock's hand is called anti-clockwise direction.

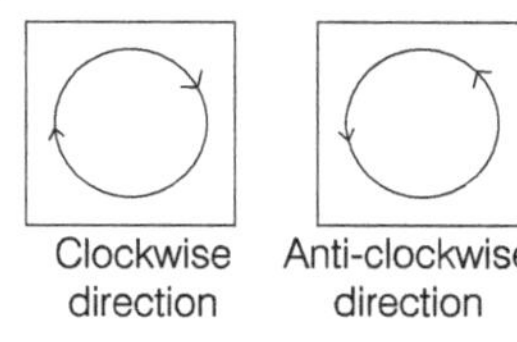

- Angle between two main directions is 90°.
- Angle between two subdirections is 90°.
- Angle between main direction and subdirection is 45°.

In direction sense test, following types of questions are generally asked

EXAMPLE 1 You go North, turn right and then go to left. In which direction are you moving now?

    (a) North   (b) East   (c) South   (d) West

Think Draw a direction graph according to the movements given in question.

Sol. Initially you go North.

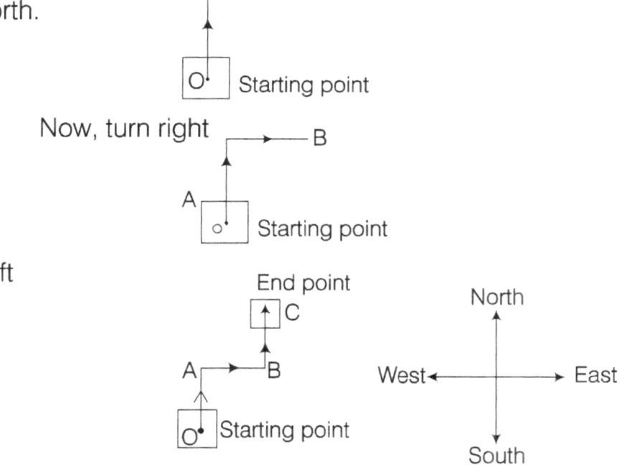

Now, turn right

After this, go to left

Standard direction diagram

When we compare above diagram with standard direction diagram, we see that the final movement is in the direction BC i.e. North.

Hence, option (a) is correct.

EXAMPLE 2 Rahul is facing towards East and turns through 45° clockwise and then turns through 90° anti-clockwise. In which direction is he facing now?

    (a) North-West   (b) North-East   (c) East   (d) South-East

Think Draw a direction graph including subdirection and mark the movement as given in question.

Sol.

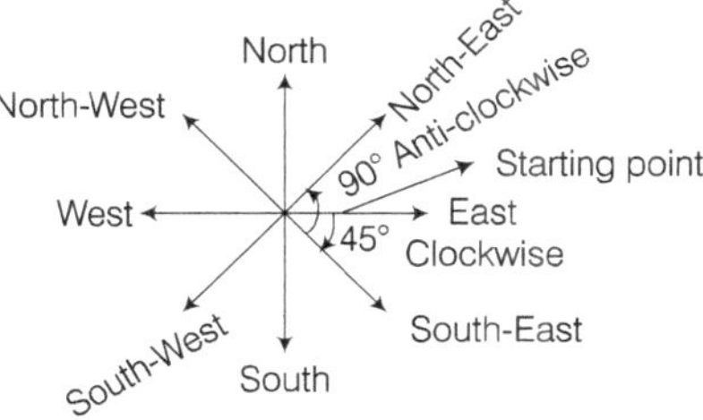

From the above diagram, it is clear that Rahul is facing toward North-East in his final position.

Hence, option (b) is correct.

EXAMPLE 3 Sagar moves 5 km towards East, then turns left, after covering 3 km he turns to left and covers 2 km. Find the total distance covered by Sagar.

    (a) 8 km   (b) 7 km   (c) 10 km   (d) 5 km

Think Draw the direction graph indicating the distances covered by Sagar.

Sol. Initially, Sagar moves 5 km towards East.

Now, he turns left and covers 3 km.

Finally, he turns left and covers 2 km.

From the above direction graph, total distance covered by Sagar $= OA + AB + BC = 5 + 3 + 2 = 10$ km

Hence, option (c) is correct.

Practice Centre

1. Vikas is facing towards West and turns through 90° clockwise, again 45° clockwise and then turns through 180° anti-clockwise. In which direction is he facing now?
   a North-West   b South-West
   c North-East   d South

2. Kamal is facing towards North and turns through 45° anti-clockwise, then 135° clockwise and again 90° clockwise. In which direction is he facing now?
   a East   b West
   c North   d South

3. Seema started walking towards South. She took a right turn after walking 5 m. She again took a left turn after walking 2 m. In which direction is she facing now?
   a South   b East
   c North   d West

4. You go South, turn left, then right again and then go to the right. In which direction are you now?
   a East   b West
   c North   d South

5. If 'South-East' is called 'South', North-West is called 'North', 'South-West' is the called 'West', and so on, what will 'East' be called?
   a East   b North-East
   c South-East   d North

6. If P is in North of S and R is in West of S, in which direction is P with respect to R?
   a North-West
   b North-East
   c South-West
   d South-East

7. A is South-West of B, C is the South-East of B, then C is in which direction of A?
   a West   b East
   c South   d North-East

8. O is in the South of P which is in the East of S. If L is in the West of S, then in which direction of P, is L?
   a East   b West
   c North   d South

9. Kavita was facing bus stop at the beginning. She turned clockwise to face East. What angle did she turn through?

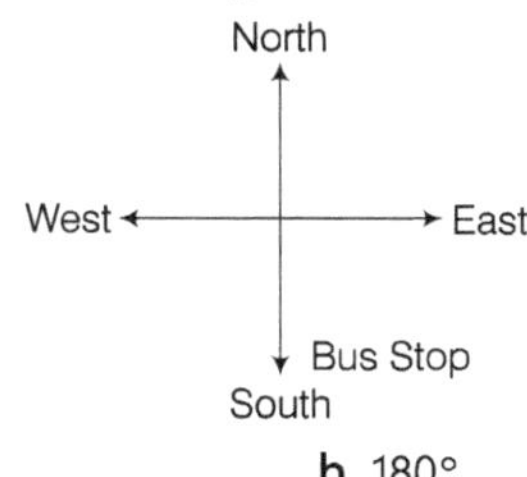

   a 90°   b 180°
   c 270°   d 360°

10. A ship is sailing towards South-East. The captain ordered to turn the ship by angle of 135° in anti-clockwise direction and then 225° in clockwise direction. In which direction is it sailing now?
    a North-West   b South
    c South-West   d East

11. One morning Raju started to walk towards his school. After covering 5 km distance in East, he turned to the left and walk 2 km, then again turns to the right and walk 5 km. He again turns to the left. Now, in which direction is he facing?
    a East   b West
    c North   d South

12. Deepa faced North-East after turning 315° anti-clockwise. Which direction she was facing at the start?

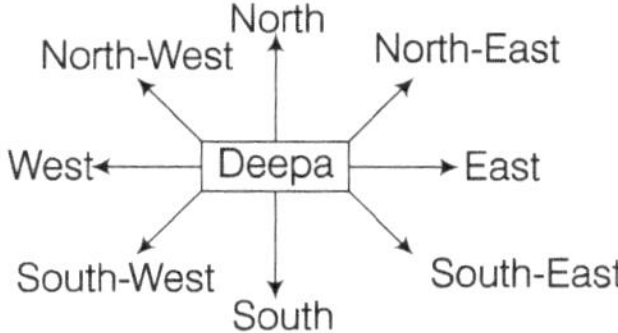

   a East
   b West
   c North
   d South

13. Amar is facing KFC. What will he be facing, if he turns 225° anti-clockwise?

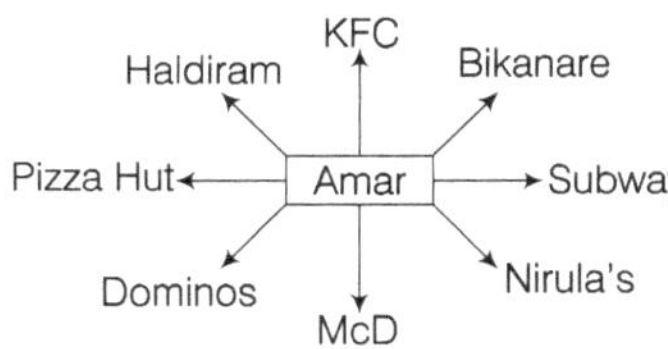

   a McD
   b KFC
   c Subway
   d Nirula's

14. A man walks 1 km towards East and then he turns to South and walks 5 km. Again he turns to East and walks 2 km after this he turns to North and walks 9 km. Now, in which direction he is facing from his starting point?

   a South-West
   b North-East
   c South-East
   d North-West

15. One morning, Ram started to walk towards the Sun. After covering some distance he turned to the left, then again to the right and after covering some distance he again turn to the left. Now, in which direction is he facing?

   a North-East
   b East
   c North
   d West

16. Suhani walked 20 km towards East, took a left turn and walked 10 km. Then, she took right turn and walked 15 km. In which direction is she now from the starting point?

   a North-East   **b** West
   c North   **d** South-East

17. A boy first goes in South direction, then he turns forwards left and travels for some distance. After that he turns right and moves certain distance. At last he turns left and travels again for some distance. Now, in which direction is he moving?

   a South   **b** West
   c East   **d** North

18. Ashwini goes 8 km towards East, then he goes 4 km towards South. In the end, he goes 4 km towards East. Find the total distance covered by Ashwini.

   a 8 km   **b** 16 km
   c 20 km   **d** 10 km

19. Shravan goes Northward 10 m. He turns left and walks 30 m, then he again turns left and walks 50 m, than how much distance Shravan travelled?

   a 60 m   **b** 20 m
   c 10 m   **d** 90 m

20. A man walked 3 km towards North, then 8 km towards South. His position at the end of the walk is

   a 5 km towards East
   b 3 km towards South
   c 8 km towards North
   d 5 km towards South

21. Starting from the point X, Sweta walked 15 m towards West. She turned left and walked 20 m. She then turned left and walked 15 m. After this she turned to her right and walked 12 m. How far and in which direction is now Sweta from point X?

   a 32 m, South   **b** 47 m, East
   c 42 m, North   **d** 27 m, South

Chapter 10

Venn Diagram

A 'Venn Diagram' is used to show relation between two or more objects (group of objects). This relation is shown in a pictorial manner, using circles and (other geometrical shapes) to represent objects.

The region common to the circles helps one to understand the type of relation that exists between the objects. If the given objects have no relation amongst them, then the circles representing them have no common region i.e. they do not intersect.

For example, Which of the following diagrams indicates the best relation amongst teachers, females and girls?

(a) 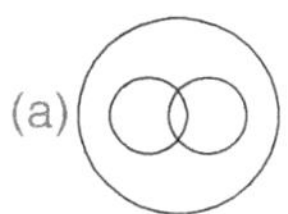   (b) 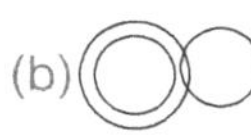   (c) 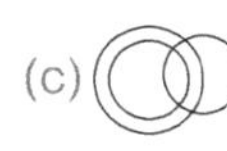   (d) 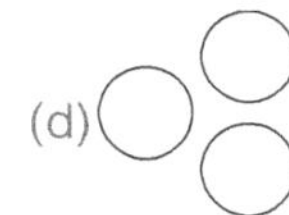

The relation amongst the given objects can be represented as

Hence, option (c) is correct.

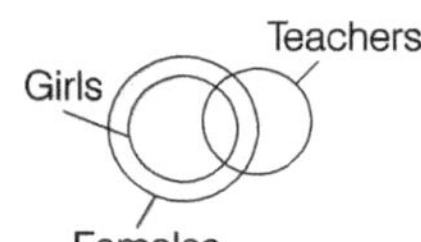

In Venn diagram, following types of questions are generally asked

EXAMPLE 1 In the given figure, the square represents boys, the circle represents disciplined students and the triangle represents intelligent students. Which part of the diagram represents all the three?

    (a) B   (b) A   (c) D   (d) C

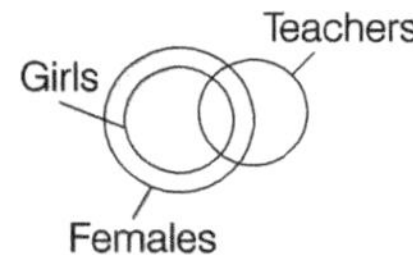

Think • First of all, label the given figure according to the information given in the question.

    • After this, find the common region lying in all the three shapes.

Sol. The given figure can be labelled as

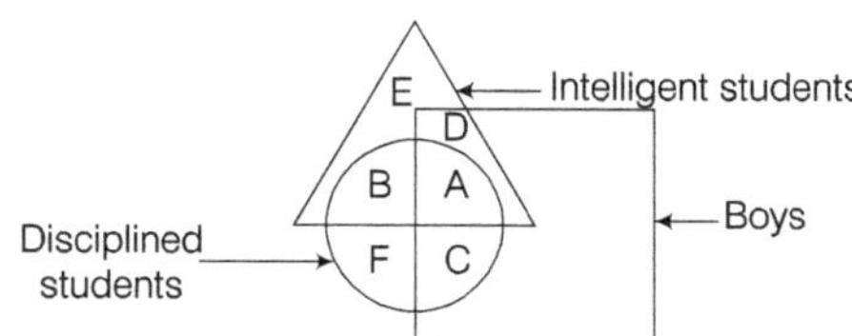

Here, all the three are represented by a region common to the square, triangle and circle and this is represented by 'A'.

Hence, option (b) is correct.

Practice
Centre

1. Which of the following diagrams indicates the best relation amongst aeroplane, ship and train?

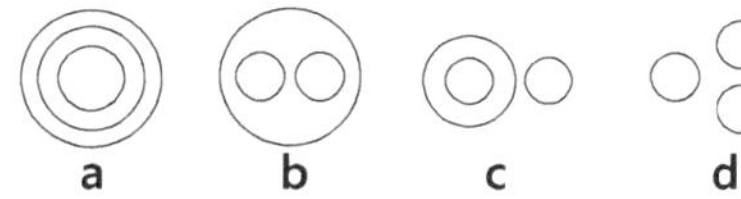

2. Which of the following diagrams indicates the best relation amongst petals, bouquet and flowers?

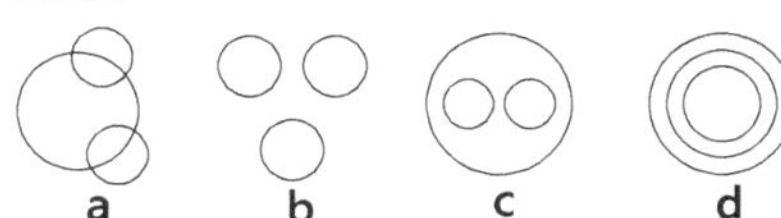

3. Which of the following diagrams indicates the best relation amongst teacher, parents and guardian?

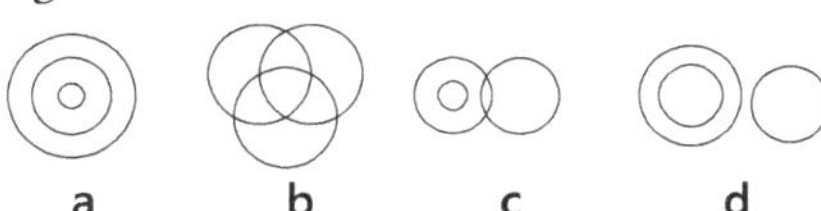

4. Which of the following diagrams indicates the best relation amongst parrot, bird and cat?

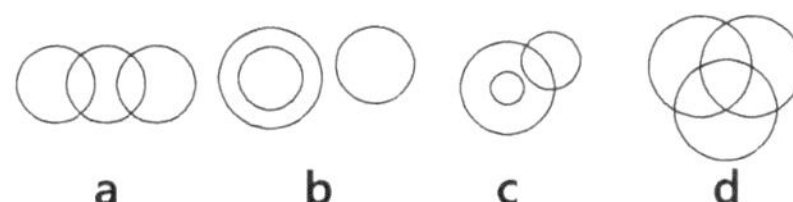

5. Which of the following diagrams indicates the best relation amongst rings, ornaments and diamond rings?

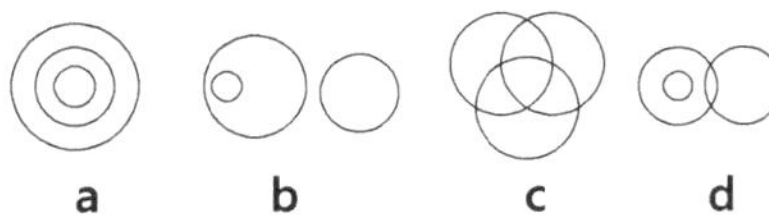

6. Which of the following diagrams indicates the best relation amongst mustard, barley and potato?

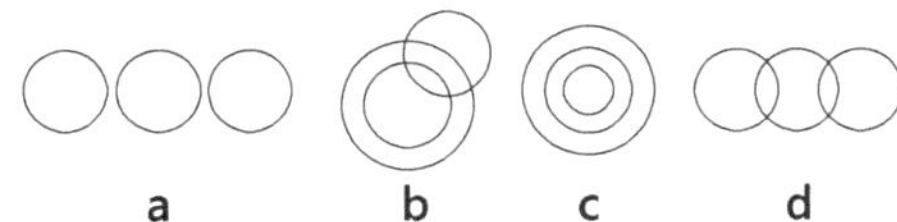

7. Which of the following diagrams indicates the best relation amongst classroom, blackboard and school?

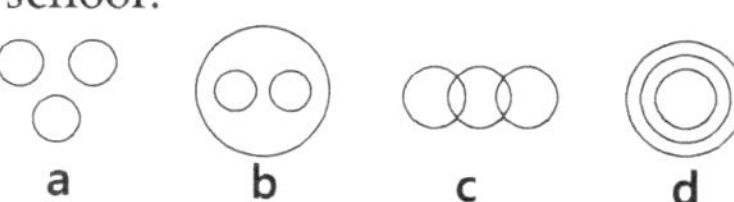

Direction (Q.Nos. 8-13) Choose the Venn diagram which best illustrates the three given classes in each question.

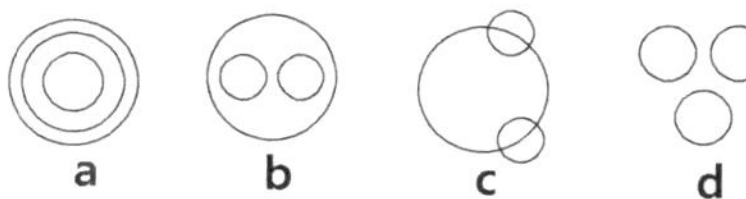

8. House, brick, bridge

9. Stationery, paper, pen

10. Lips, eye, body

11. India, Japan, US

12. Mango, apple, fruits

13. Badminton, carrom, table tennis

14. In the given figure, the triangle represents Hindi speaking people, circle represents English speaking people and rectangle represents French speaking people. Find the area in the figure which represents people, who speak both Hindi and French?

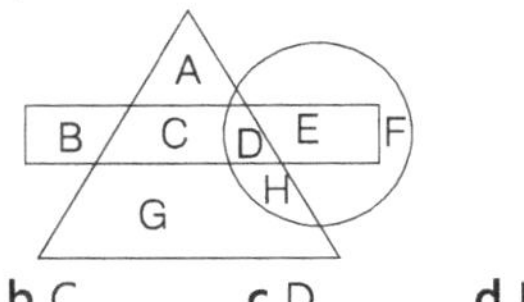

a A   **b** C   **c** D   **d** B

15. If '☐' represents the natural numbers, '▭' represents the whole numbers, '◯' represents the zero, '▷' represents the negative numbers and '▭▷' represents the integers, then which diagram best represents the number system?

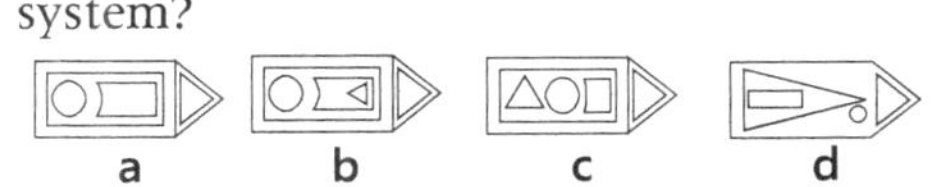

Chapter 11

Blood Relations

'Blood Relations' are logical problems, which deal with hierarchical structure of the family. By the following example students can easily understand how to solve problems based on blood relation.

In the above picture an information is given that Rohan is the son of Pinki's father. Based on this information Rohan asked to Pinki that how is he related to Pinki?

Now, Pinki thinks mentally to follow the given information and gives answer that he is her real brother.

Blood relations may be broadly divided into two main categories
   (i) Relations on mother's side are called **maternal**.
   (ii) Relations on father's side are called **paternal**.

Some blood relations can be summarised as

1. Mother's or Father's father	Grandfather		9. Brother's daughter	Niece
2. Mother's or Father's mother	Grandmother		10. Brother's son	Nephew
3. Mother's or Father's brother	Uncle		11. Husband's or Wife's father	Father-in-law
4. Mother's or Father's sister	Aunt		12. Husband's or Wife's mother	Mother-in-law
5. Grandmother's or Grandfather's son	Father or Uncle		13. Husband's or Wife's sister	Sister-in law
6. Grandmother's or Grandfather's only son	Father		14. Husband's or Wife's brother	Brother-in-law
7. Grandmother's or Grandfather's only daughter-in-law	Mother		15. Son's wife	Daughter-in-law
8. Uncle's or Aunt's son or daughter	Cousin		16. Daughter's husband	Son-in-law
			17. Sister's husband	Brother-in-law
			18. Brother's wife	Sister-in-law

In blood relations, following types of questions are generally asked

EXAMPLE 1 Vimal is the brother of Renu. Renu is the mother of Kunal. How is Kunal related to Vimal?

    (a) Uncle   (b) Father   (c) Nephew   (d) Son

Think • Read each statement carefully and relate one person to other.

        • It is also useful to draw a relation diagram for better understanding.

Sol. Renu is the sister of Vimal and Kunal is the son of Renu. So, Kunal is the son of Vimal's sister i.e. nephew. The relation diagram can be drawn as

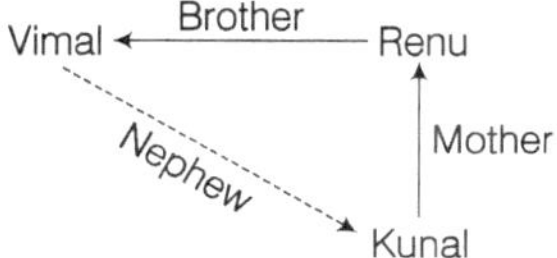

Hence, option (c) is correct.

EXAMPLE 2 Pointing to a lady, I said, "She is the mother of my father's sister". How is that lady related to me?

    (a) Grandmother   (b) Mother   (c) Daughter   (d) Granddaughter

Think Relate each relative to determine the asked relation.

Sol. My father's sister is my aunt and my aunt's mother is also my father's mother. So, she is my grandmother. The relation diagram can be represented as

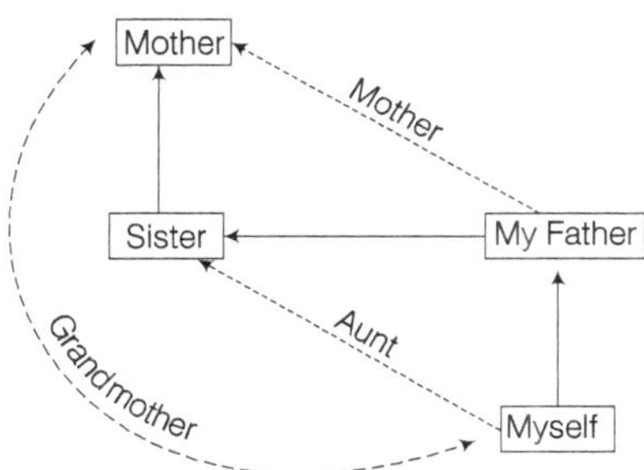

Hence, option (a) is correct.

EXAMPLE 3 P and Q are sisters. A and B are brothers. P's daughter is A's sister. How is Q related to B?

    (a) Aunt   (b) Uncle   (c) Mother   (d) Grandmother

Think Connect one person to other according to the statements.

Sol. P's daughter is A's sister and A and B are brothers. So, P is the mother of A and B. Q is the sister of B's mother, so she is his aunt.

The relation diagram can be drawn as

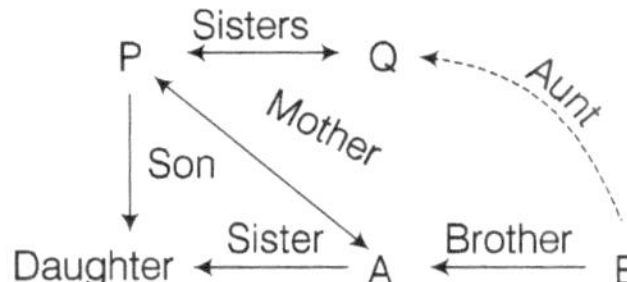

Hence, option (a) is correct.

Practice Centre

1. I am brother of Sunil and Meena, Mr. Rakesh is my father's father. How is Meena related to Mr. Rakesh?
   - **a** Daughter
   - **b** Sister
   - **c** Granddaughter
   - **d** Mother

2. Ramu is my father's real brother. Janvi is my grandmother. How is Ramu related to Janvi?
   - **a** Brother
   - **b** Father
   - **c** Uncle
   - **d** Son

3. Seema is the daughter of Radhika. Mohan is the brother of Radhika. Kirti is the wife of Mohan. How is Kirti related to Seema?
   - **a** Sister
   - **b** Aunt
   - **c** Mother
   - **d** Grandmother

4. If A is the sister of B and B is the brother of C. C is the father of D, then how is A related to D?
   - **a** Mother
   - **b** Sister
   - **c** Sister-in-law
   - **d** Aunt

5. Pointing to a man in photograph, Radhika says, "His father's daughter is my sister". How is Radhika related to that man?
   - **a** Daughter
   - **b** Sister
   - **c** Mother
   - **d** Sister-in-law

6. A boy introduced a woman as the only daughter of the father of his mother. How is boy related to woman?
   - **a** Brother
   - **b** Father
   - **c** Uncle
   - **d** Son

7. Kunal says, "Ayushi's mother is the only daughter of my mother-in-law". How is Ayushi related to Kunal?
   - **a** Wife
   - **b** Mother
   - **c** Aunt
   - **d** Daughter

8. A man said to Vimal, "Your mother's husband is my brother-in-law". How is man related to Vimal?
   - **a** Uncle
   - **b** Father
   - **c** Father-in-law
   - **d** Brother

9. Pointing to a woman, Karan said, "She is the sister of my son's mother". How is woman related to Karan?
   - **a** Sister
   - **b** Mother
   - **c** Sister-in-law
   - **d** Aunt

10. A and B are brothers. C and D are brothers and C's mother is A's wife. How D is related to B?
    - **a** Niece
    - **b** Nephew
    - **c** Uncle
    - **d** Son

11. Aditya is Bhavi's brother. Bharat is Jayant's father. Esha is Bhavi's mother. Aditya and Jayant are brothers. What is Esha's relationship with Bharat?
    - **a** Sister
    - **b** Mother
    - **c** Daughter
    - **d** Wife

12. Ritesh is son of Varun. Sarika, Varun's sister has a son Rahul and a daughter Riya. Sahil is the maternal uncle of Rahul. How is Ritesh related to Rahul?
    - **a** Nephew
    - **b** Cousin
    - **c** Uncle
    - **d** Father

Direction (Q. Nos. 13-16) Study the following information carefully and answer the questions that follow.

Members of a family A, B, C, D, E, F and G are sitting together. A is son of G who is brother of F. F is mother of E and B. E is brother of B and B is sister of C. C is a male. D is a female and child of C.

13. How is B related to A?
    - **a** Cousin
    - **b** Mother
    - **c** Aunt
    - **d** Sister-in-law

14. Which of the following is the pair of female?
    - **a** BA
    - **b** GF
    - **c** FC
    - **d** FB

15. How many male members are there in the family?
    - **a** 1
    - **b** 2
    - **c** 3
    - **d** 4

16. Who is the uncle of C?
    - **a** E
    - **b** A
    - **c** G
    - **d** D

Non-Verbal Reasoning

Chapter 12

Similar Pairs

In 'Similar Pairs', figures or shapes in a pair are related to each other in a certain way and the figures or shapes in another pair are related to each other in the same way as first pair.

'Similar Pairs' are also known as 'Analogy' and two pairs are called analogous pairs.

For example, Consider the following pairs of figures and find out the missing figure.

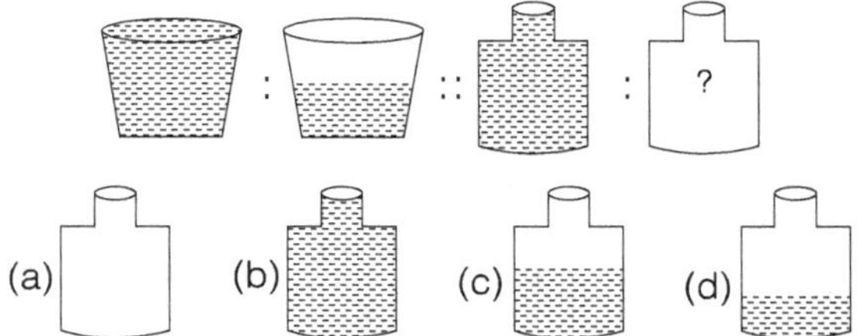

Here, we see that in first pair a glass filled upto the brim becomes half and similarly in second pair bottle filled upto brim will become half. So, option figure (c) will complete the second pair.

Hence, option (c) is correct.

In similar pairs, following types of questions are generally asked

EXAMPLE 1 Which figure will complete the second pair in the similar way as first pair?

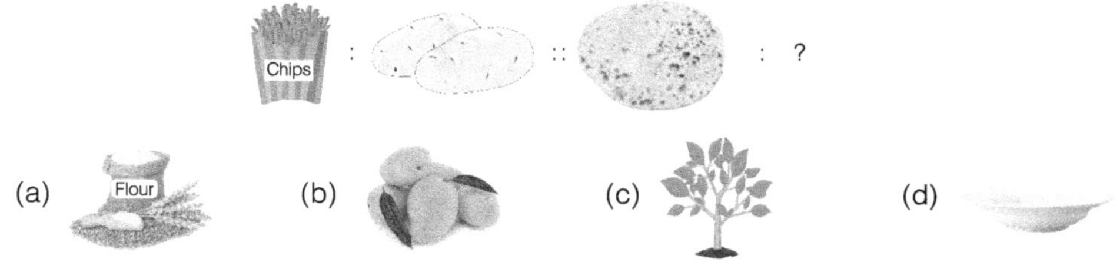

Think • First of all, look at the first pair of figures and try to find out the relation of first figure to second figure.
• After careful observation we find that, second one is the raw material which is used to make the first one.

Sol. As, chips is made from potato in the same way chapati is made from flour.

So, Flour will complete the second pair.

Hence, option (a) is correct.

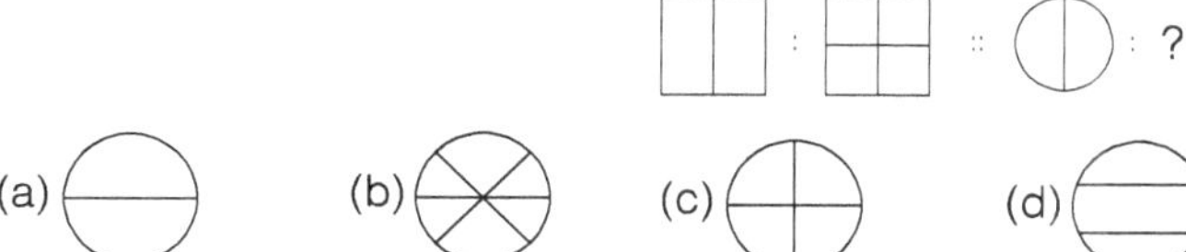

EXAMPLE 2 Which shape/figure will complete the second pair in the same way as first pair?

(a)   (b)   (c)   (d)

Think After careful observation we see that, the main figures are similar in first pair. But the first figure is divided into two parts and second one into four parts.

Sol. In first pair, square is divided into four equal parts from two equal parts. In the same way, circle will be divided into four equal parts from two equal parts as shown below

Hence, option (c) is correct.

EXAMPLE 3 Which shape/figure will complete the second pair in the same way as first pair?

(a)   (b)   (c)   (d)

Think After observing we see that, the figures follow rotation pattern.

Sol. In first pair, triangle with an arrow rotates 90° in clockwise direction as shown below

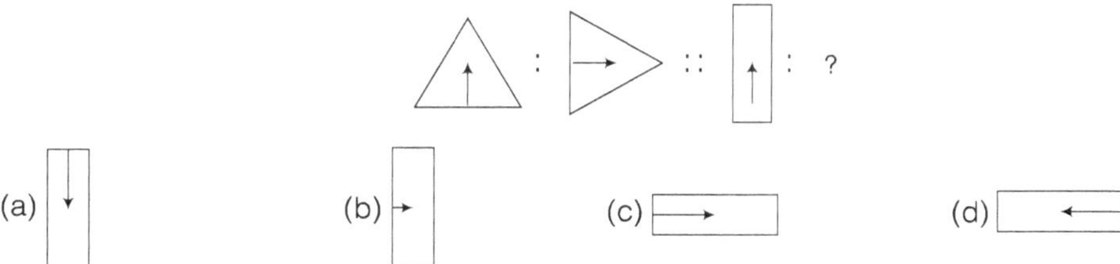

Similarly, the rectangle with an arrow will be rotated 90° in clockwise direction as shown below

Hence, option (c) is correct.

EXAMPLE 4 Which shape/figure will complete the second pair in the same way as first pair?

(a)   (b)   (c)   (d)

Think After careful observation we see that, the number of elements is increasing from first figure to second figure.

Sol. In first pair, the number of rectangles gets double from first figure to second figure. In the same way, in second pair the number of circular shapes will get double from first figure to second figure as shown in adjacent figure

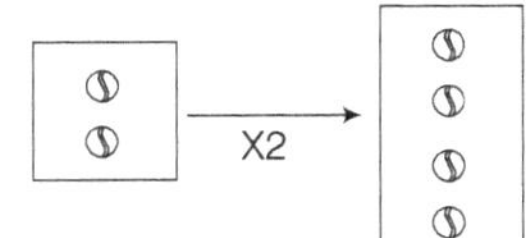

Hence, option (d) is correct.

Practice
Centre

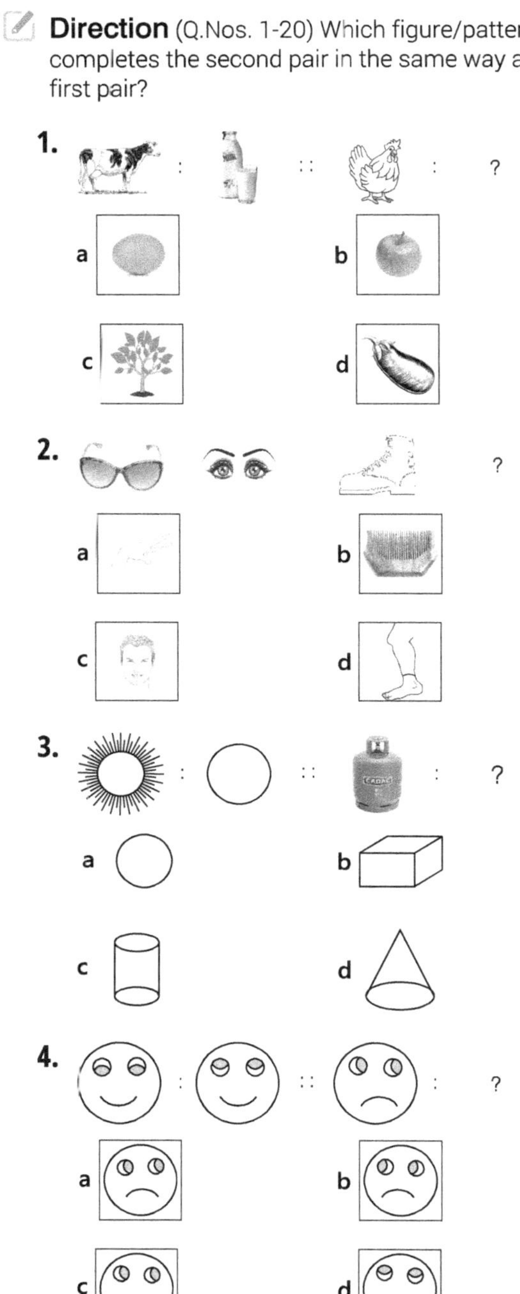

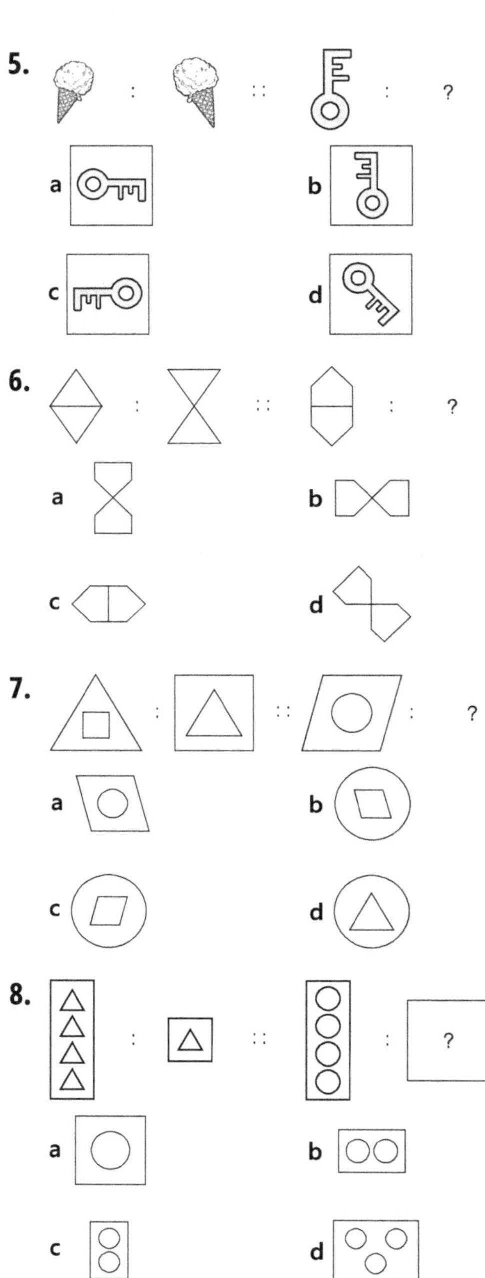

9. 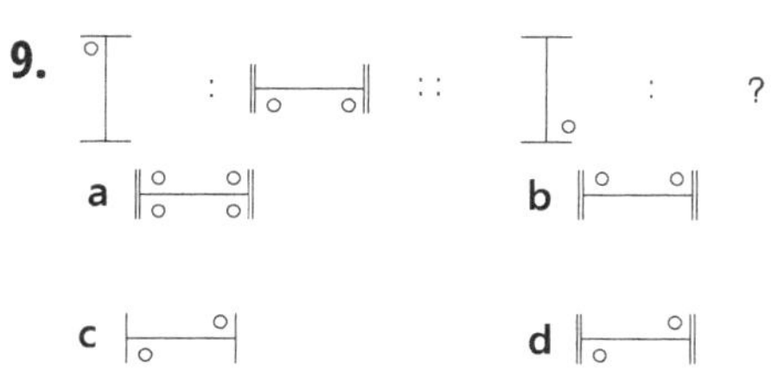

10. 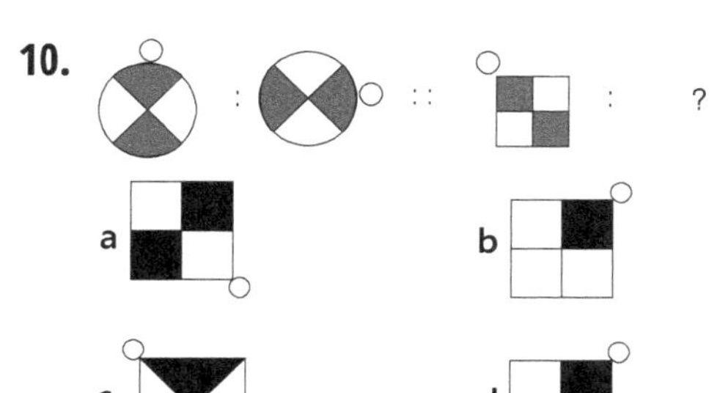

11. 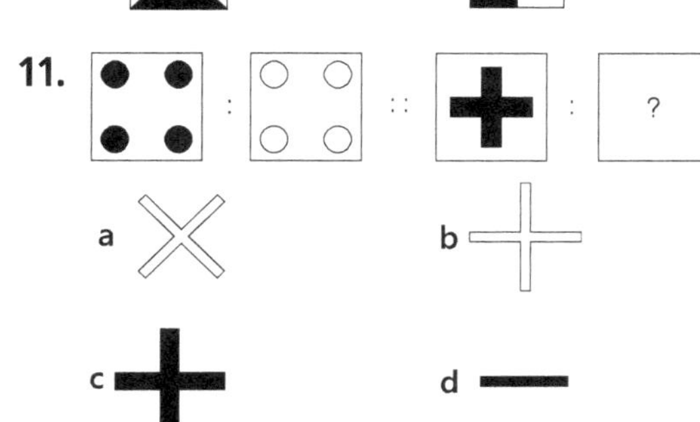

12. 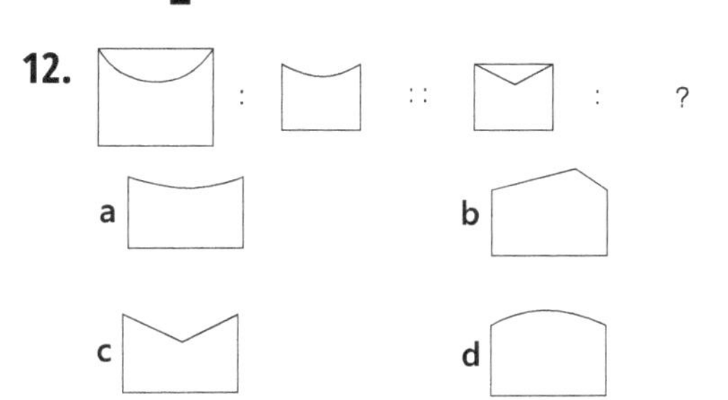

13. 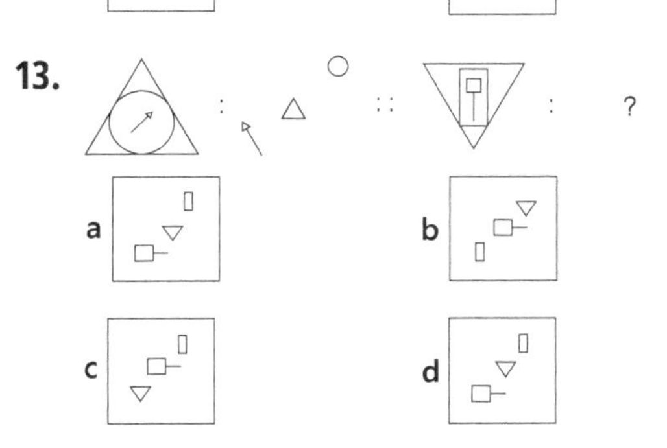

14.

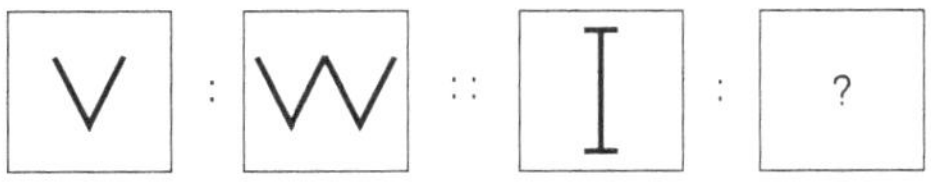

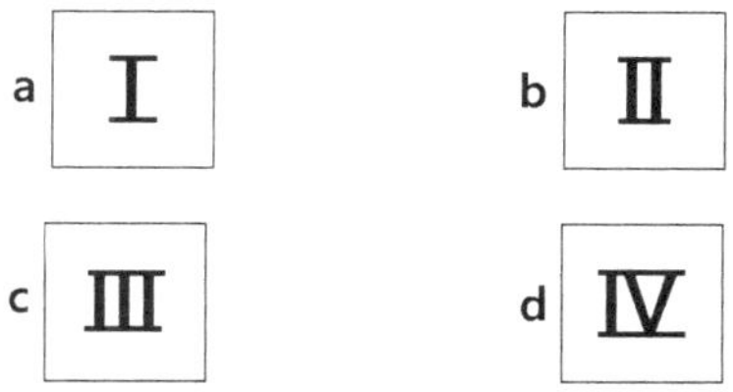

15.

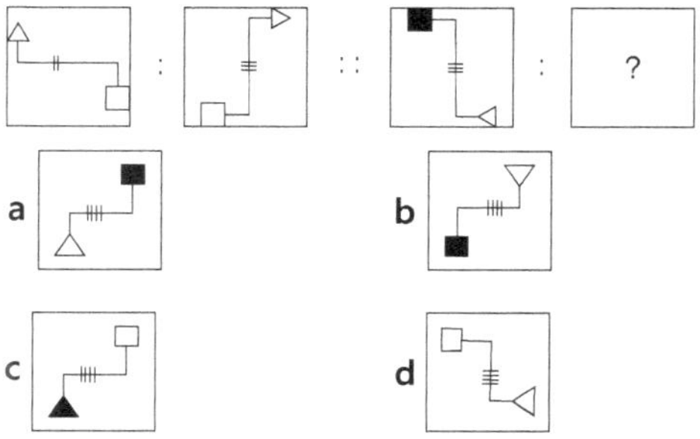

16.

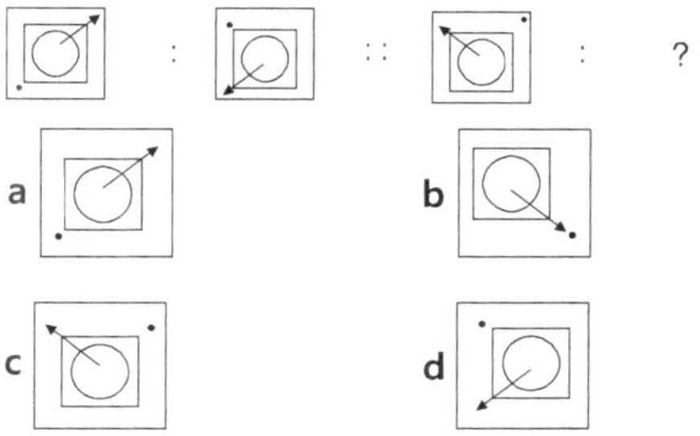

17.

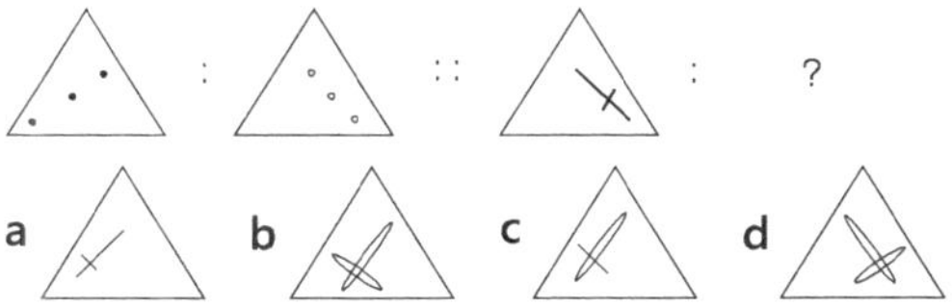

18.

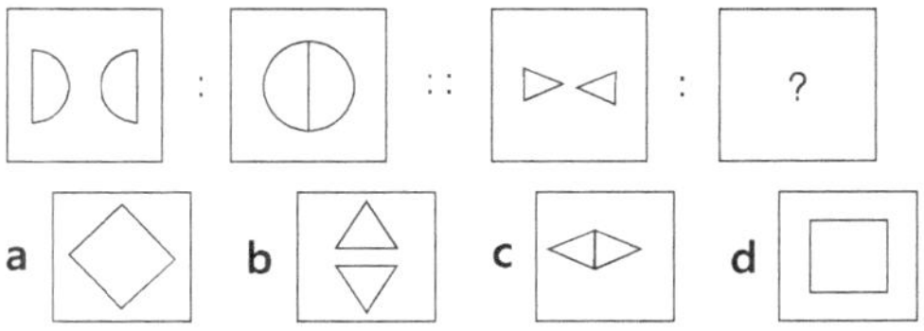

19.

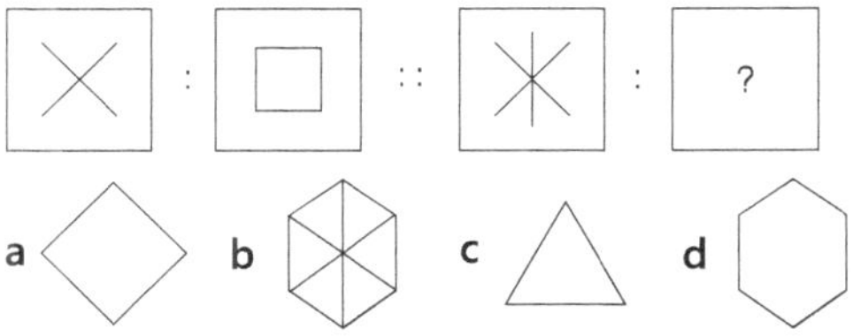

20.

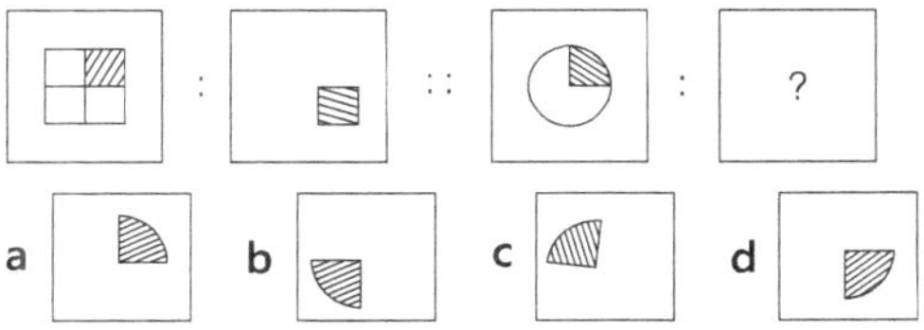

What Comes Next?

In 'What Comes Next?', figures/shapes are arranged in a certain pattern, in which the students are required to identify the next or missing figure/shape that follows the same pattern. 'What Comes Next?' is also known as 'Series'.

You will need your observation and analytical skills to solve these questions types

For example, Consider the following series of figures and find out the next figure

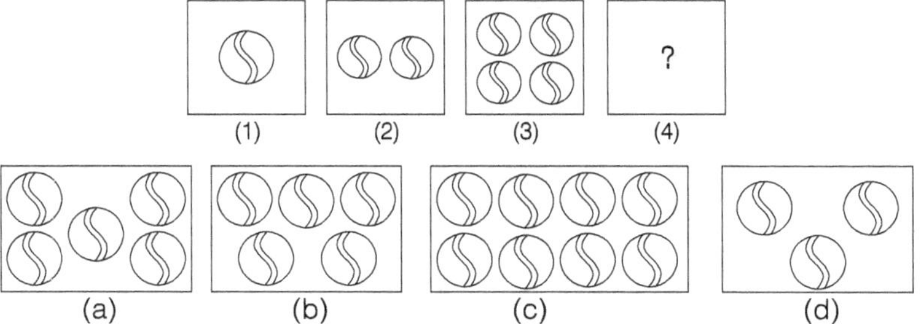

If we carefully observe the above figures we see that, the number of balls is increasing in each step by multiplying the number of balls in the previous step by 2 as shown below

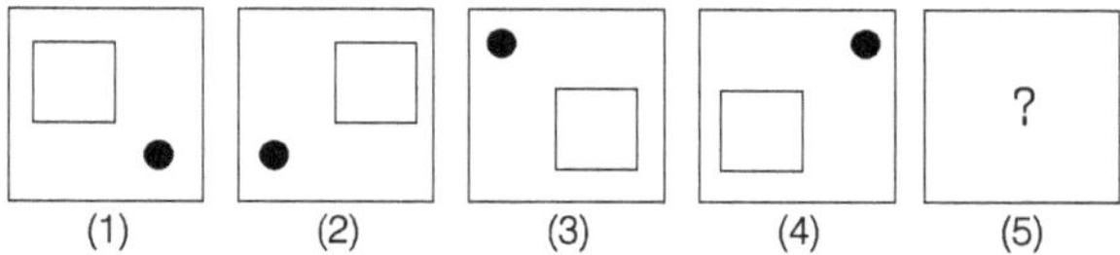

So, it will be $4 \times 2 = 8$ balls in the next step,

Hence, option (c) is correct.

In what comes next, following types of questions are generally asked

(i) Series completion   (ii) Figure matrix

Series Completion

In series completion, figures, shapes or symbols are arranged in a sequence following step-by-step changes. The students are required to observe these steps and find out the next or missing figure or shape following same changes.

In series completion, following types of questions are generally asked

EXAMPLE 1 Find the next term for the series given below.

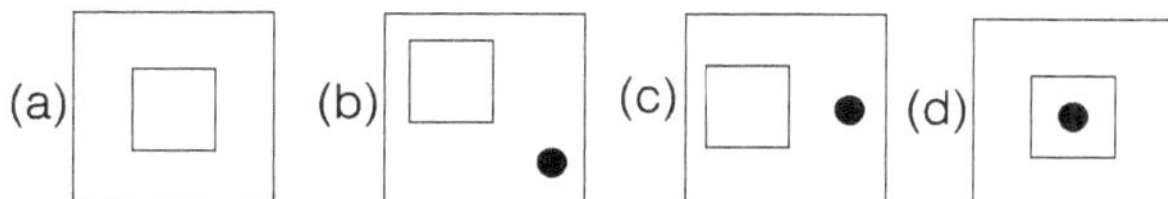

Think • Look at the each figure carefully and analyse the pattern followed by each figure
• Here, we find that in each successive step the dot with square is moving from one corner to another corner in clockwise direction

Sol. The series can be represented as

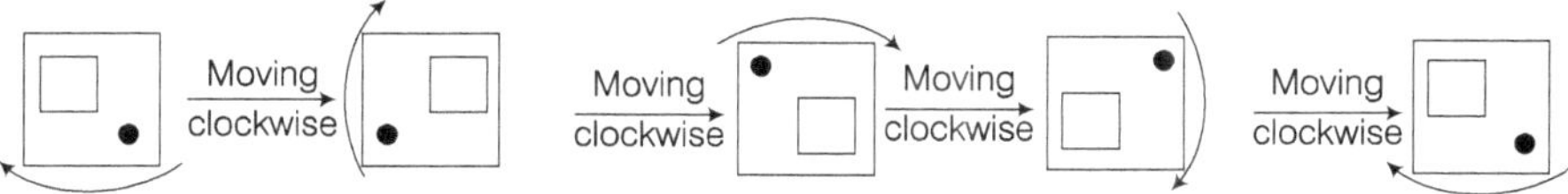

Therefore, option figure (b) will complete the series.

Hence, option (b) is correct.

Figure Matrix

In figure matrix, figures or shapes are arranged in cells of a matrix following a certain pattern. The pattern follows either rowwise or columnwise or both. Students are required to observe the pattern and identify the missing figure or shape following the same pattern. Figure matrix is also known as 'grid completion'.

In figure matrix, following types of questions are generally aske

EXAMPLE 2 Select the figure from the options that will complete the following grid.

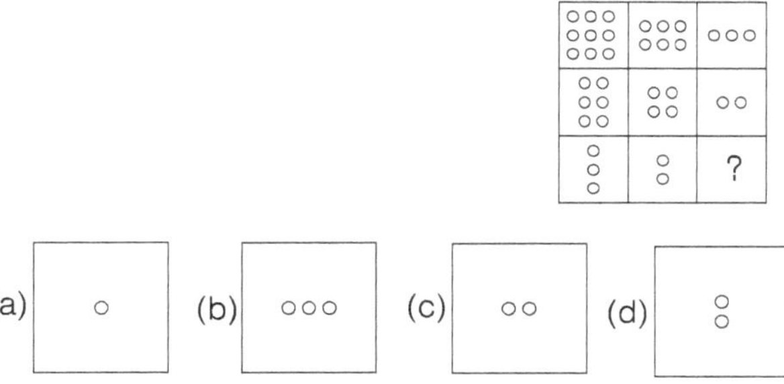

Think Look at the figure matrix carefully and analyse the pattern of matrix.

Sol. Here, we find that, the pattern of both rows and columns are followed by the matrix.

After observing, the grid we see that, horizontal line of circles is removed columnwise i.e. from column (i) to (ii) and column (ii) to (iii). And vertical line of circles is removed rowwise i.e. from row (i) to (ii) and row (ii) to (iii).

On following the above pattern, option figure (a) will complete the grid.

Hence, option (a) is correct.

Practice
Centre

Series Completion

1.

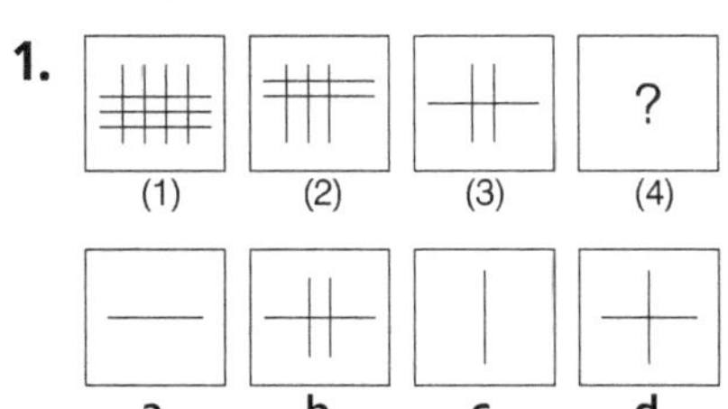

2.

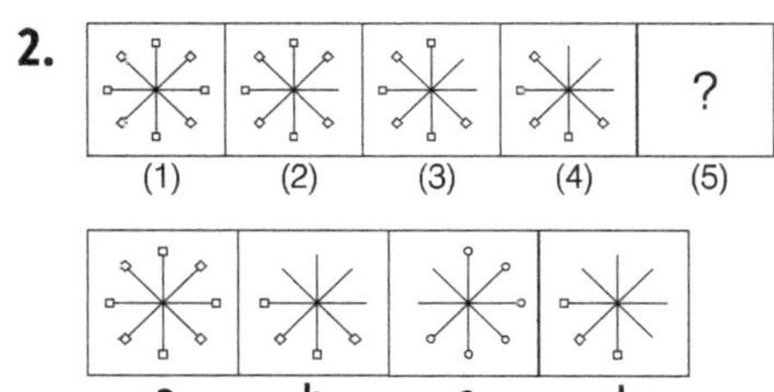

3.

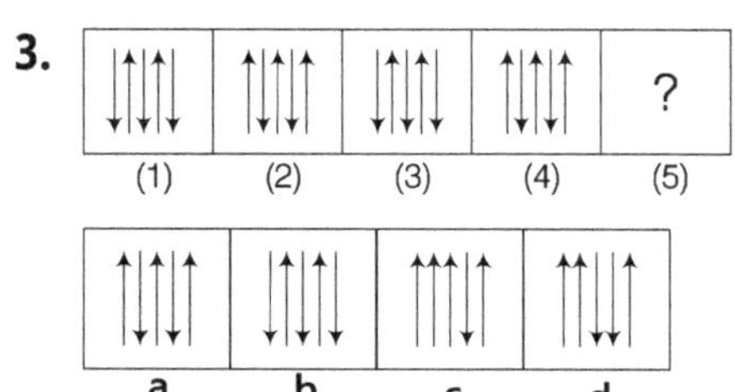

4.

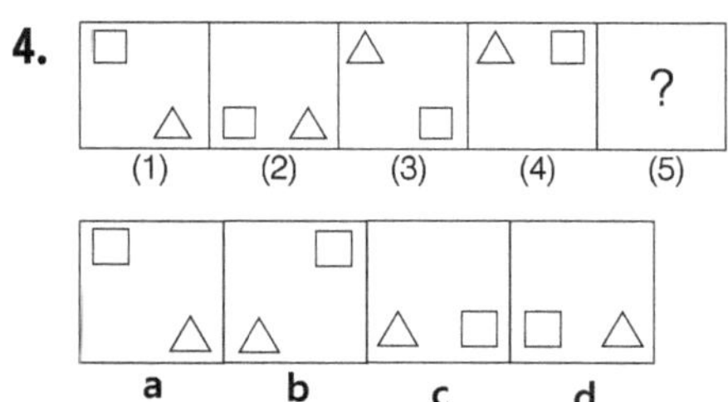

5.

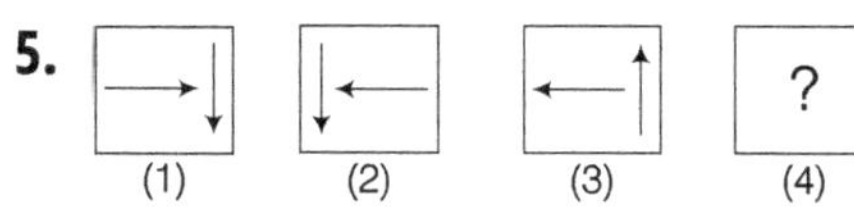

6.

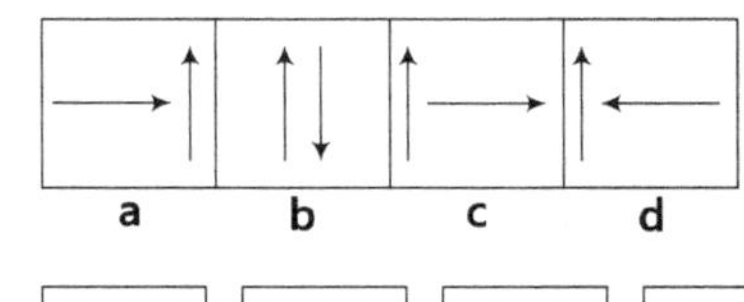

7.

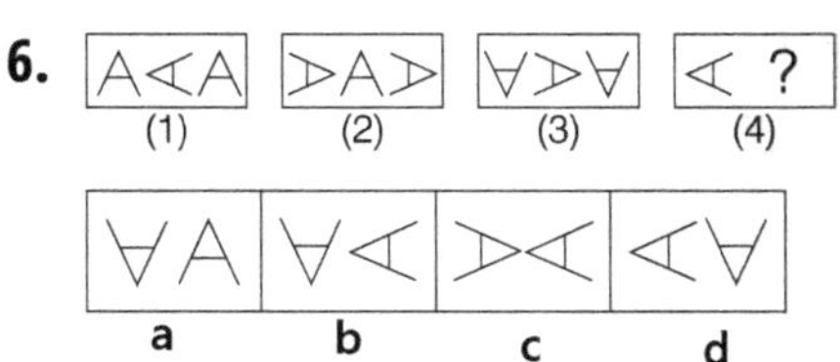

8.

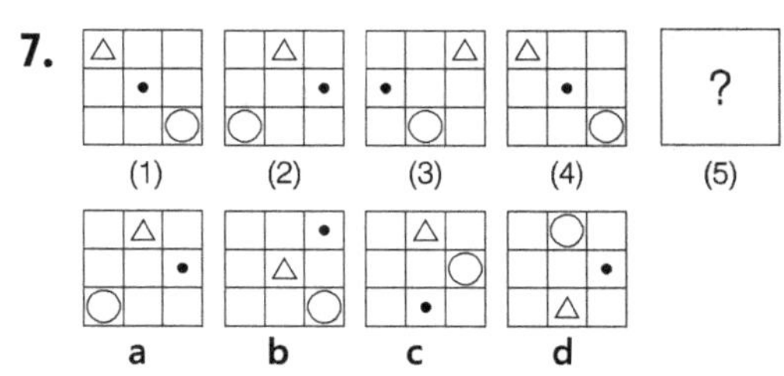

9.

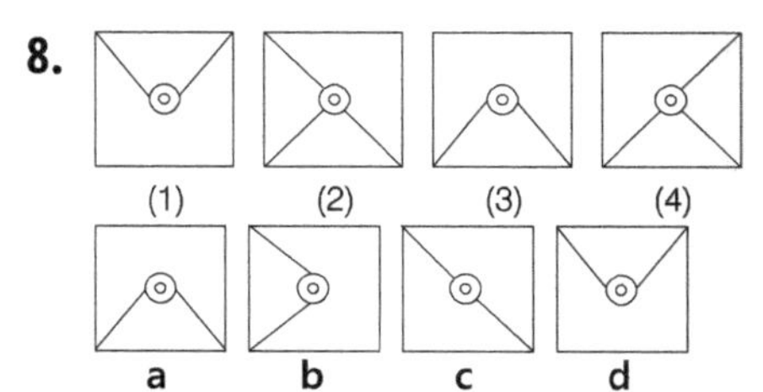

10.

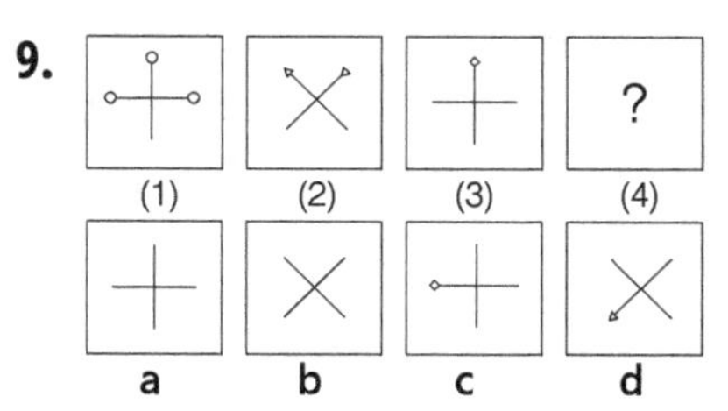

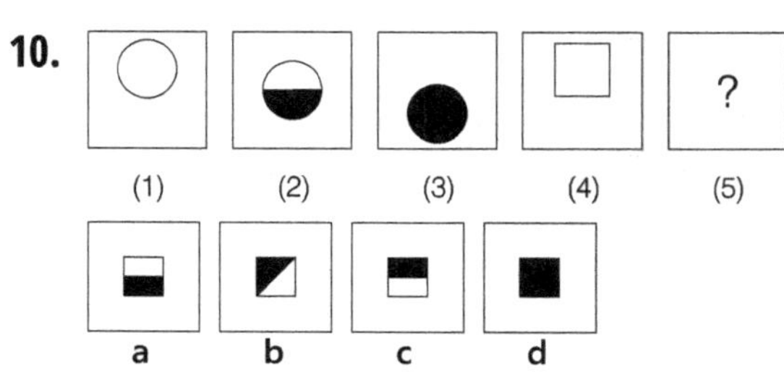

11. 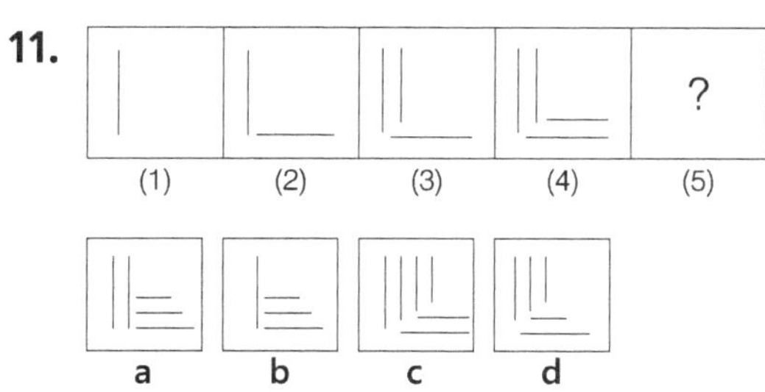

12. 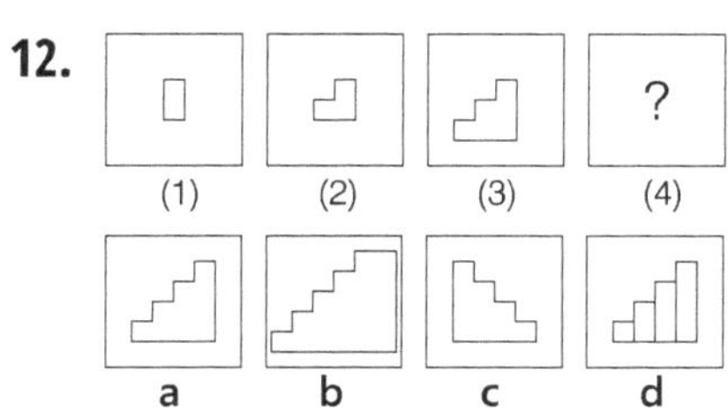

13. 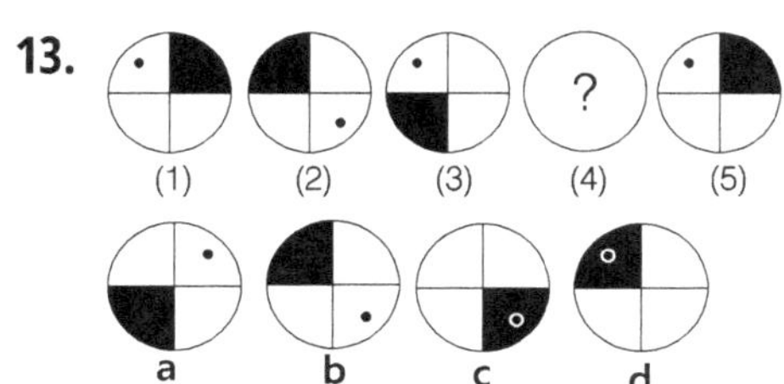

14. 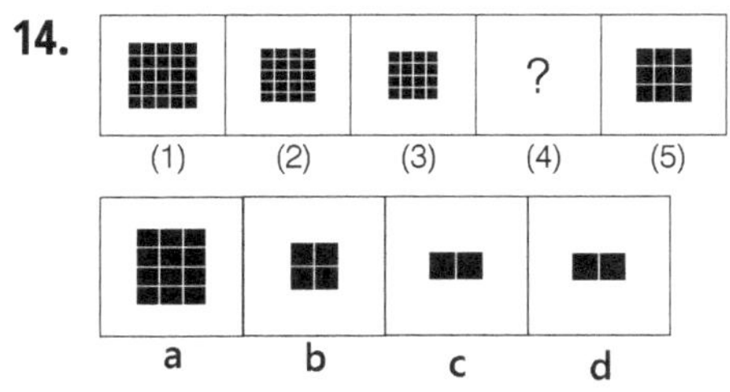

15. 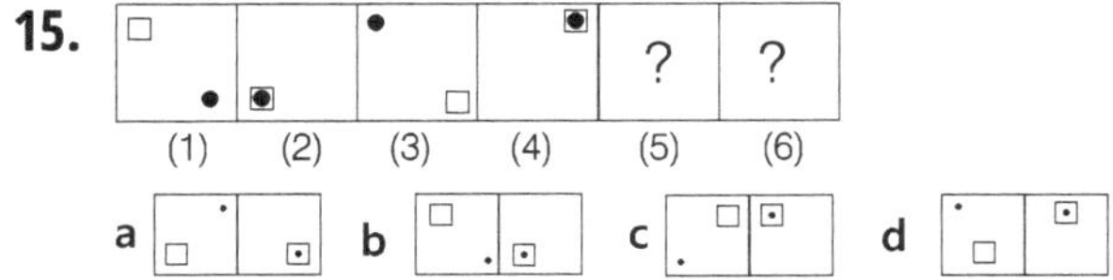

Figure Matrix

Direction (Q. Nos. 16-20) Identify and choose the correct pattern or figure that will complete the large square.

16. 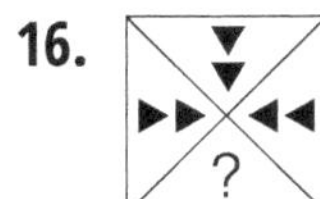 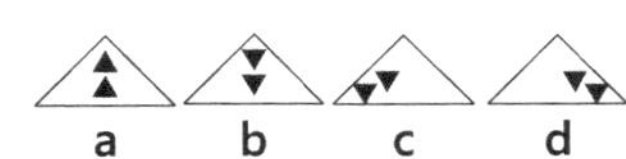

17. 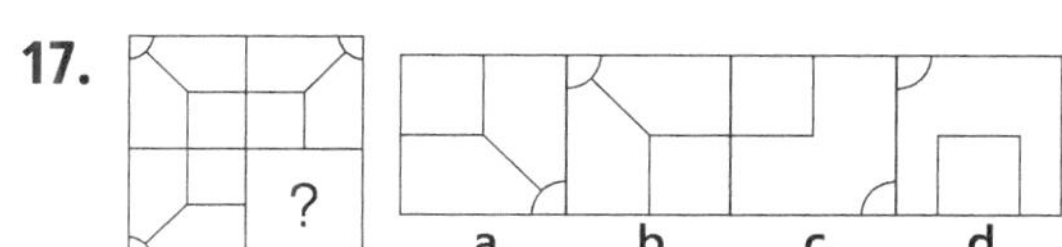

18. 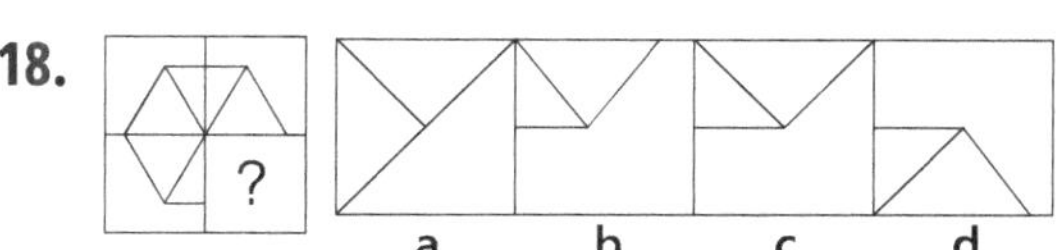

19. 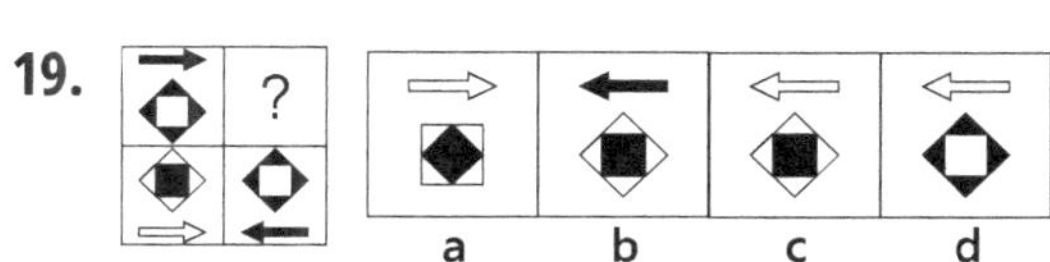

20. 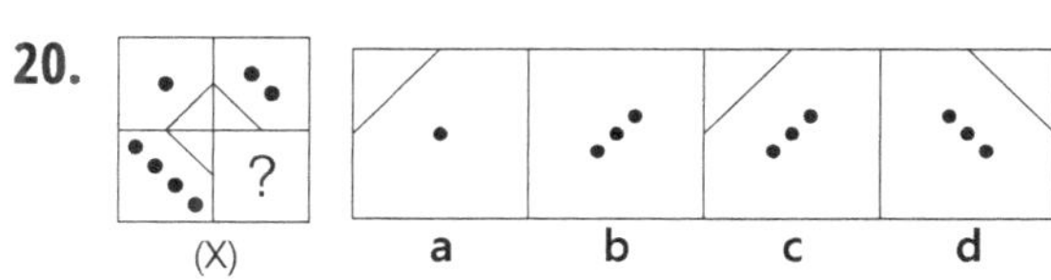

Direction (Q. Nos. 21-24) Identify and choose the correct pattern or figure that will complete the grid.

21. 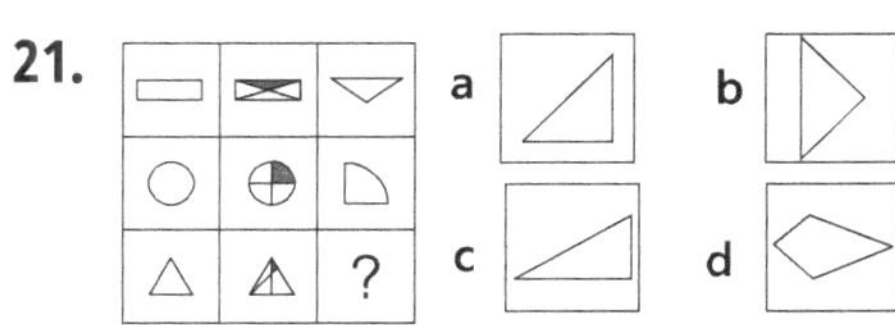

22. 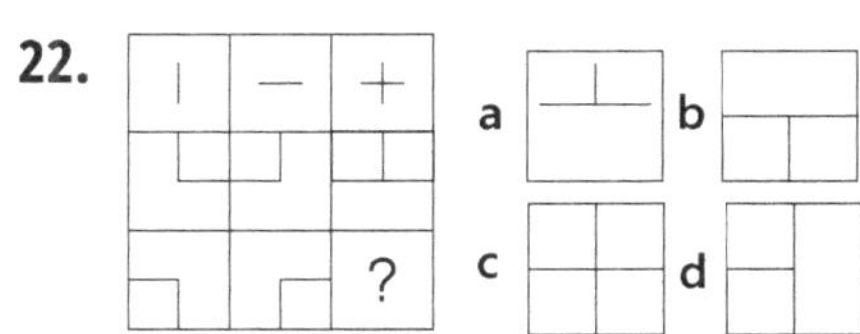

23. 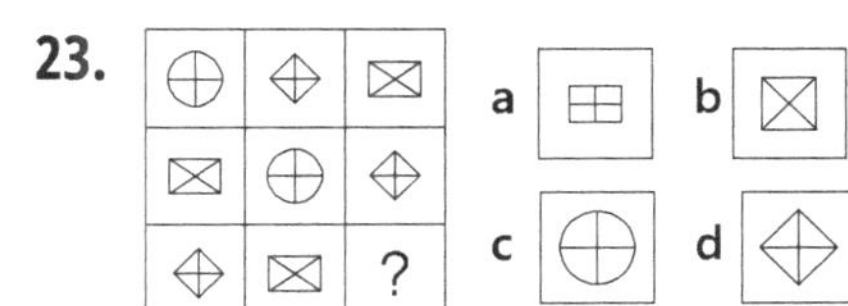

24. 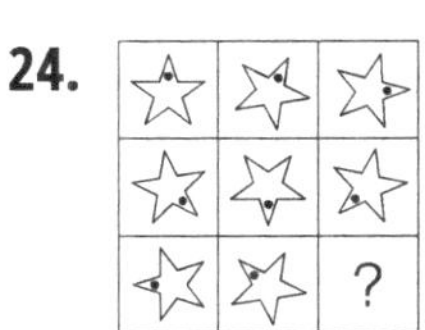

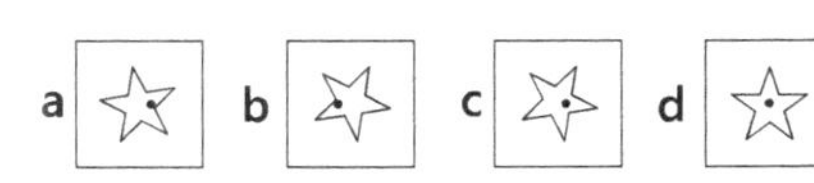

Chapter 14

Odd One Out

In odd one out, a set of figures are given such that all except one have common features/characteristics. One of the figure does not have common features as others and the students are required to select that figure, which does not belong to the group.

For example, Choose the figure which is odd one?

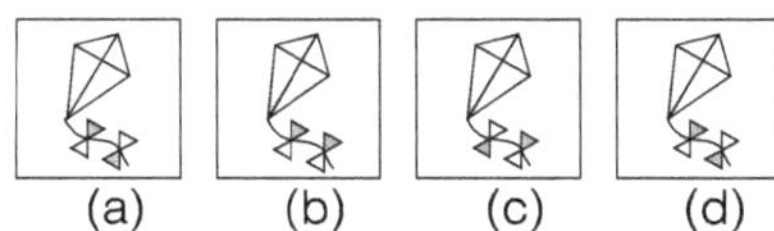

Here, in all the figures, except figure (b) one upper and one lower triangles are shaded at the tail of the kite but in figure (b), both the upper triangles are shaded.

So, figure (b) is odd one.

Hence, option (b) is correct.

In odd one out, following types of questions are generally asked

EXAMPLE 1 Find the odd one out.

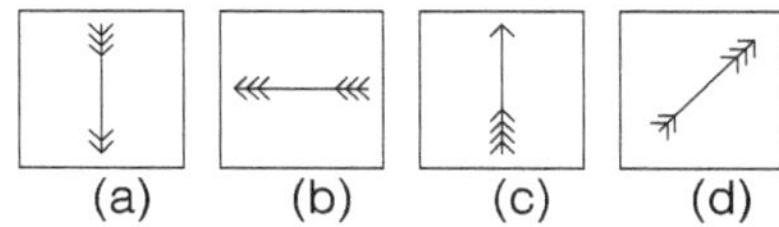

Think • After observing the figures carefully we see that, all figures have certain number of arrow heads.

  • Count the number of arrow heads of each figure.

Sol. Here, except figure (b), all others have five number of arrow heads each, but figure (b) has six arrow heads.

So, figure (b) is odd one.

Hence, option (b) is correct.

EXAMPLE 2 Choose the odd one out.

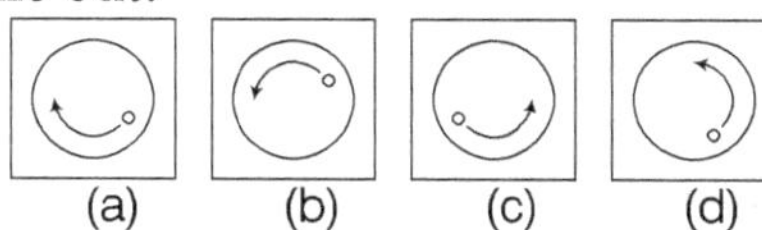

Think • After observing the figures, we see that, the arrows inside the circles are pointing in certain direction.

Sol. In all the figures, except figure (a) the arrow inside the circle is in anti-clockwise direction ⟳, but in figure (a) arrow is pointing in clockwise direction ⟲.

So, figure (a) is odd one.

Hence, option (a) is correct.

Practice
Centre

✏ **Direction** (Q. Nos. 1 - 20) In each of the following figures choose the odd one out.

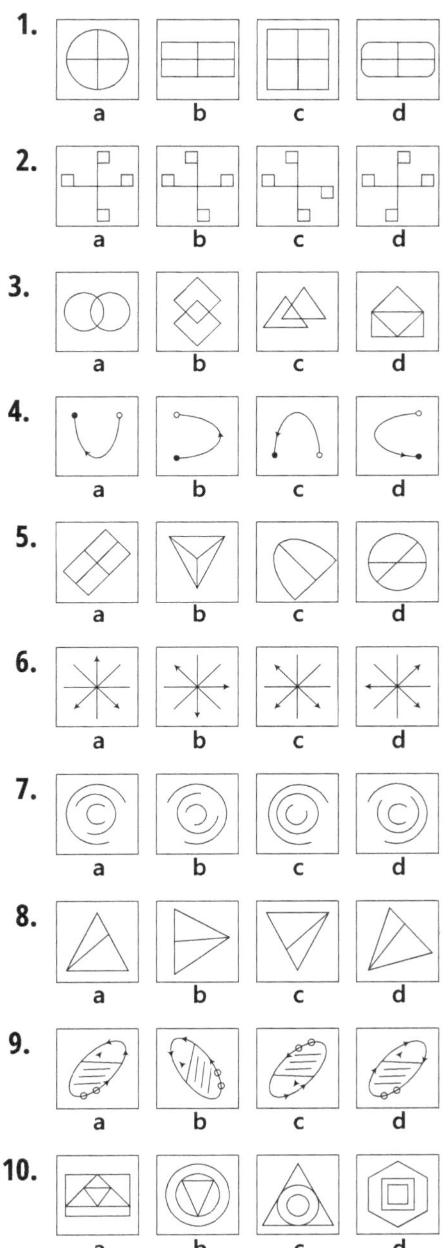

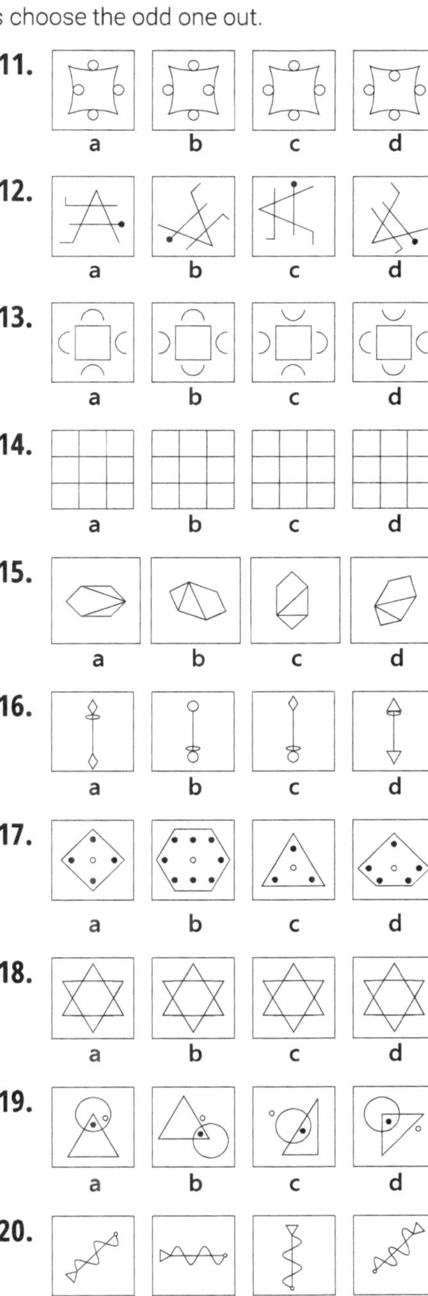

Chapter 15

Mirror and Water Images

Mirror Images

The image of an object as seen in a plane mirror is known as mirror image or mirror reflection. In mirror image, the right side of the object appears on the left side and the left side of the object appears on the right side.

For example, Identify the mirror image of the figure (x) given below.

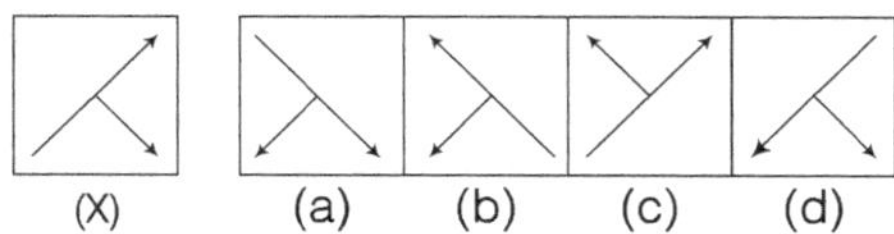

(X)   (a)   (b)   (c)   (d)

Note *If not mentioned, the mirror is assumed to be placed to vertically right of the object.*

Here, the arrow pointing towards the top right corner will point toward the to left corner and arrow pointing towards bottom right corner will point bottom left corner in mirror image as shown below.

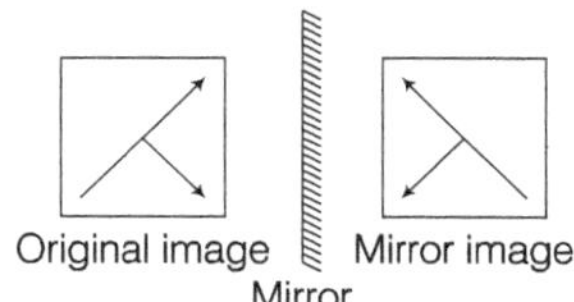

Original image   Mirror image
Mirror

Hence, option (b) is correct.

Let us observe the mirror image of capital letters and numbers.

Mirror image of capital letters and numbers

Letters	Mirror image	Letters	Mirror image	Letters	Mirror image	Numbers	Mirror image
A	A	J	L	S	Ƨ	1	ꓲ
B	ꓭ	K	ꓘ	T	T	2	Ƨ
C	Ɔ	L	ꓶ	U	U	3	Ɛ
D	ꓷ	M	M	V	V	4	Ꙅ
E	Ǝ	N	И	W	W	5	ꙅ
F	ꓞ	O	O	X	X	6	ꓭ
G	ꓚ	P	ꟼ	Y	Y	7	⊦
H	H	Q	Ϙ	Z	Ƨ	8	8
I	I	R	ꓤ			9	e

In mirror images, following types of questions are generally asked

EXAMPLE 1 Choose the correct mirror image of the figure (X) given below.

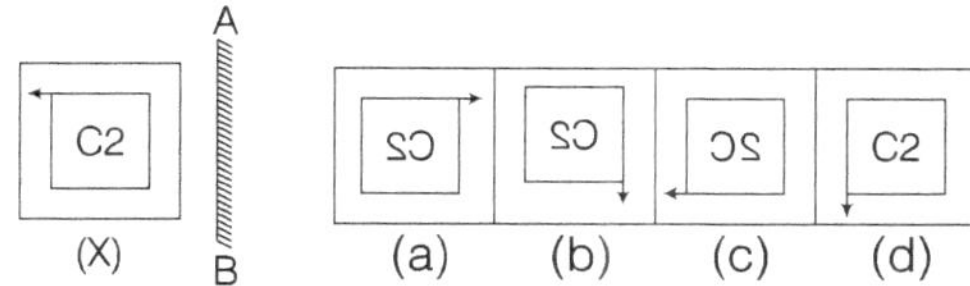

Think · Look at the figure carefully and use your visualisation power to reverse the object.
· The line with arrow will identically reflect to the right side of the box in mirror image.

Sol. The mirror image of the given object is shown as

Hence, option (a) is correct.

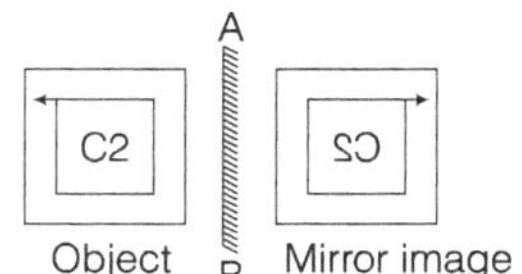

Water Images

The reflection of an object as seen in water is known as water image. It is obtained by inverting an object vertically i.e. the upper part of the object will become the lower part and *vice-versa*.

For example, Consider the following figure (x) and find out its water image.

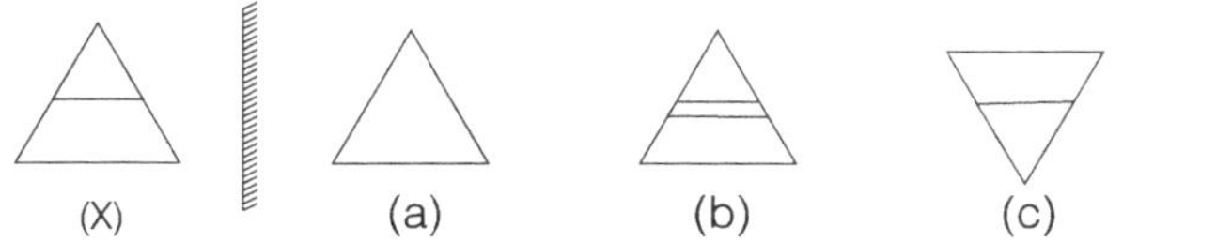

Here, the triangle pointing upward will point downward and the upper shaded part will become lower as shown in adjacent figure.

Hence, option (c) is correct.

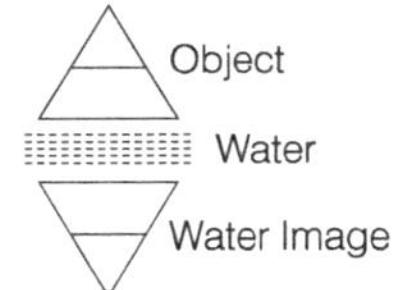

Let us observe the water image of digits and capital letters.

(i) **Water images of the digits**

Digits	0	1	2	3	4	5	6	7	8	9
Water images	0	⌐	S	3	⩜	ට	ට	⅂	8	ට

(ii) **Water images of the capital letters**

Digits	A	B	C	D	E	F	G	H	I	J	K	L	M	N	O	P	Q	R	S	T	U	V	W	X	Y	Z
Water images	∀	B	C	D	E	Ⱶ	G	H	I	ʔ	K	Ⲅ	W	И	O	Ь	Ơ	Я	Ƨ	⊥	∩	∧	W	X	⅄	Ƨ

In water images, following types of questions are generally asked

EXAMPLE 2 Choose the correct water image of the given figure (X).

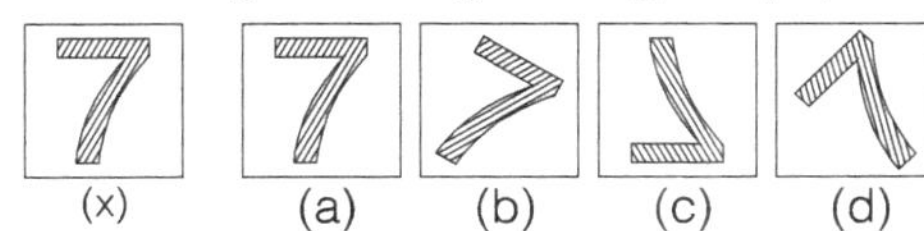

Think Carefully invert the number vertically.

Sol. The water image can be obtained as

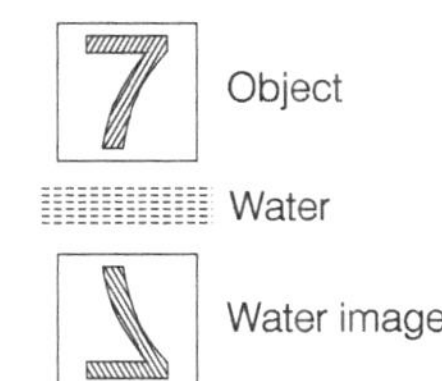

Hence, option (c) is correct.

Practice
Centre

1. DL4C

   a CI4Ɔ   **b** ᗡⱢ4Ɔ   **c** ƆⱯ⅃ᗡ   **d** ᗡ⅃4Ɔ

2. TRAIN

   a ИIАЯT   **b** ТЯАIИ   **c** ИIАЯТ   **d** ТЯⱯIИ

3. 3681

   a 3ට81   **b** 188ට   **c** 186ට   **d** 308ꓕ

4.

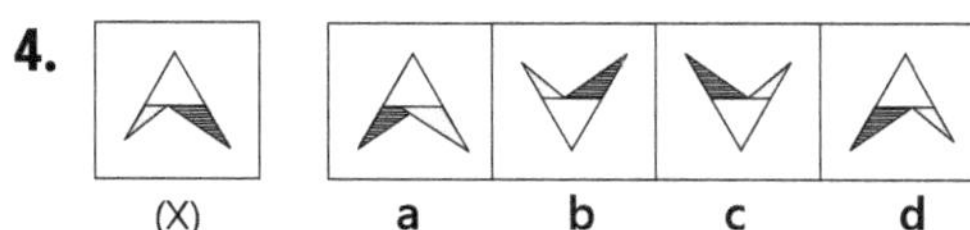

(X)   a   b   c   d

5.

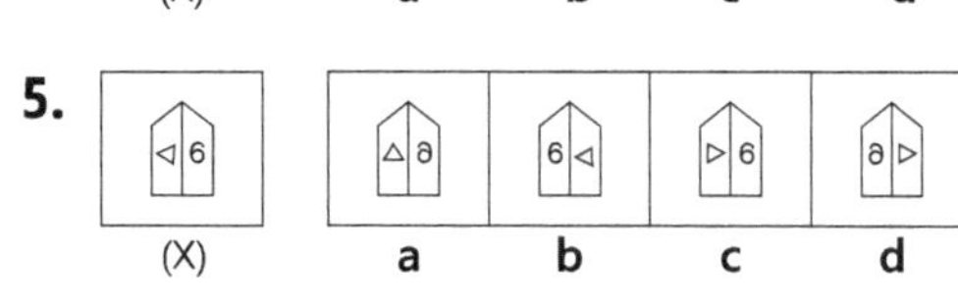

(X)   a   b   c   d

6.

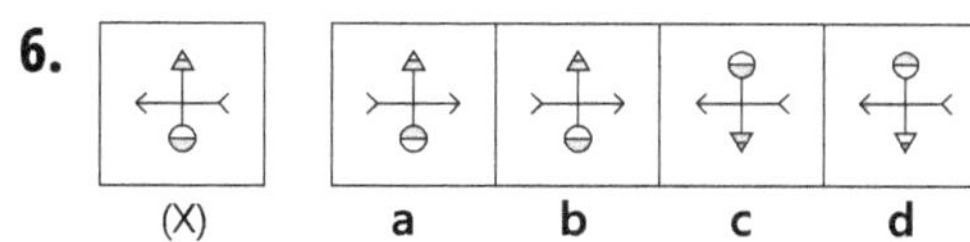

(X)   a   b   c   d

7.

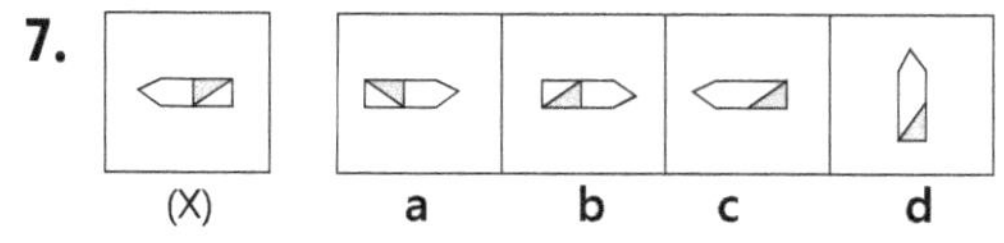

(X)   a   b   c   d

8.

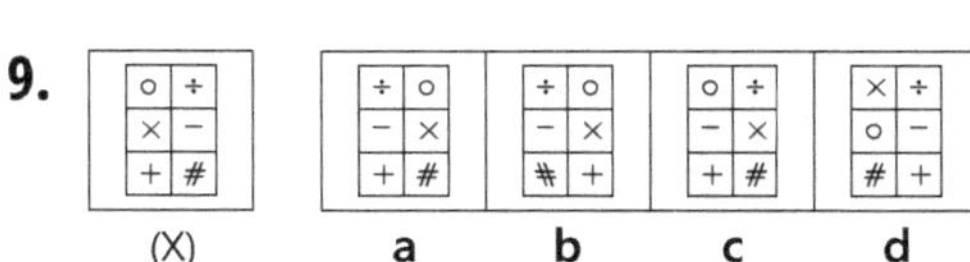

(X)   a   b   c   d

9.

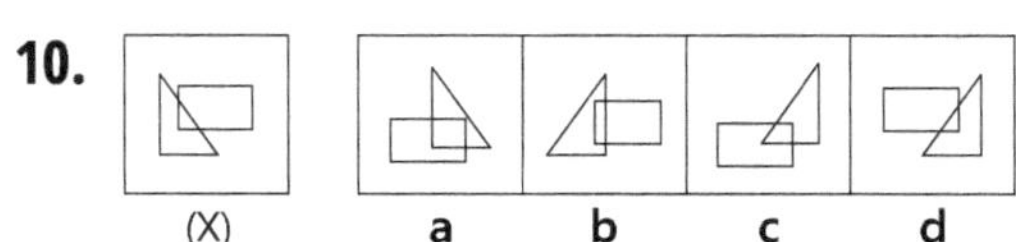

(X)   a   b   c   d

10.

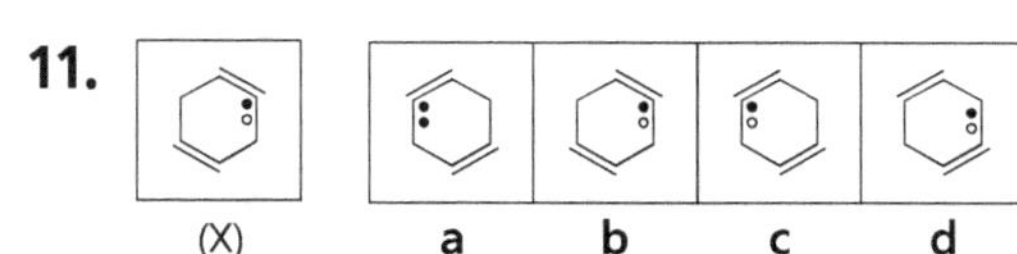

(X)   a   b   c   d

11.

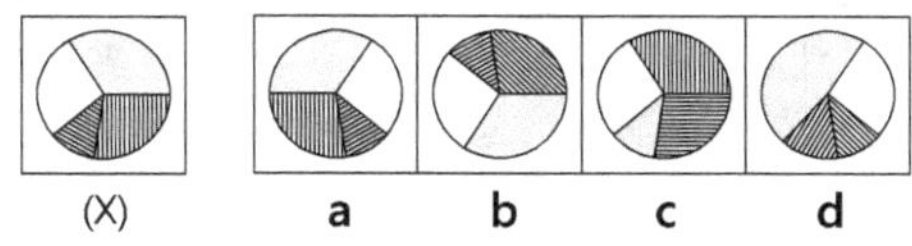

(X)   a   b   c   d

12. Identify the mirror image of the figure given below.

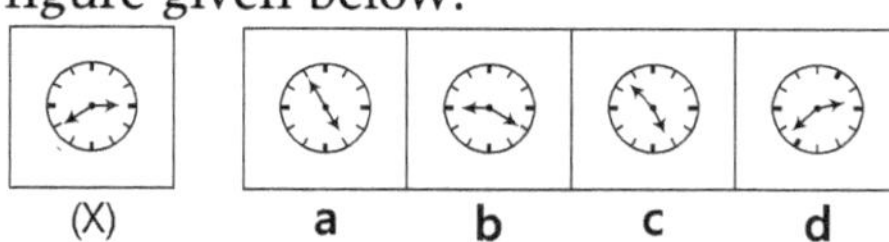

(X)   a   b   c   d

13. Choose the correct mirror image of the figure given below.

(X)   a   b   c   d

14. CODE

   a CODE   **b** EDOC   **c** ƆOᗡE   **d** ƆOᗡƎ

15. TAMNCZ

   a ⊥ⱯWNƆƧ   **b** TⱯMИCZ   **c** ⊥ⱯWИƆƧ   **d** TAMNCZ

16. 43867

   a 43867   **b** 43867

   c 43834   **d** 43867

Direction (Q. Nos. 17-25) In each of the following questions, find out the correct water image of the given object (X).

17.

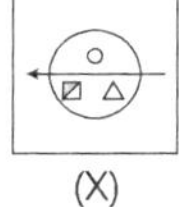

(X)

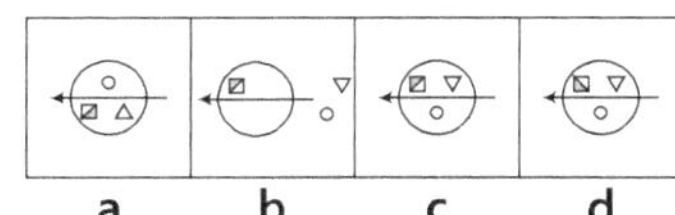

   a   **b**   **c**   **d**

18.

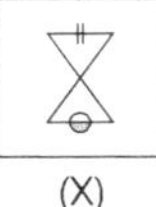

(X)

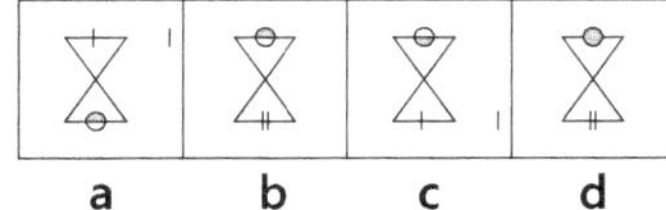

   a   **b**   **c**   **d**

19.

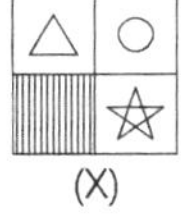

(X)

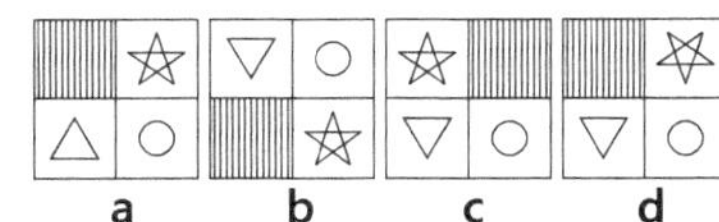

   a   **b**   **c**   **d**

20.

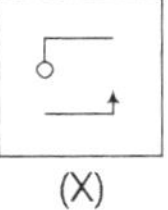

(X)

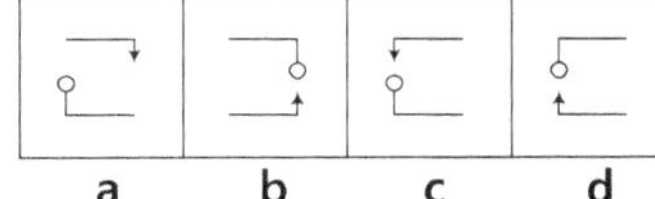

   a   **b**   **c**   **d**

21.

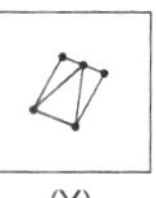

(X)

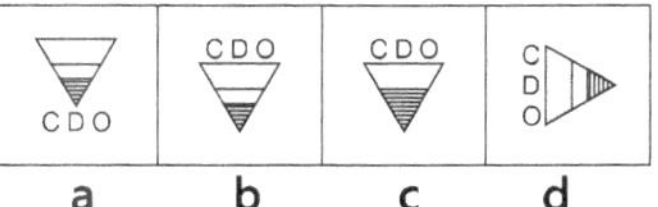

   a   **b**   **c**   **d**

22.

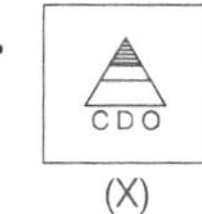

(X)

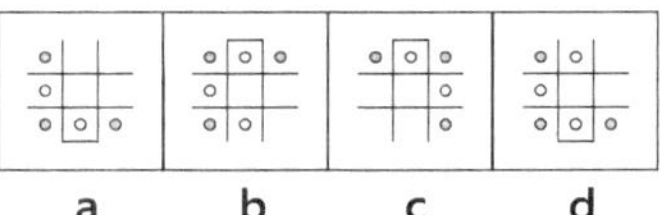

   a   **b**   **c**   **d**

23.

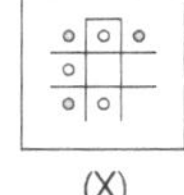

(X)

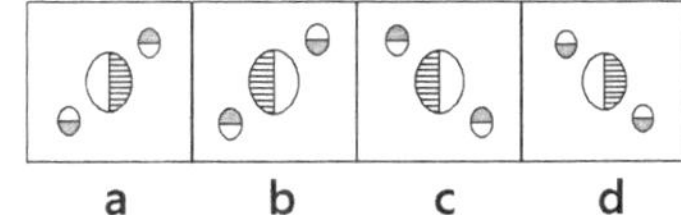

   a   **b**   **c**   **d**

24.

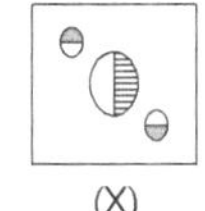

(X)

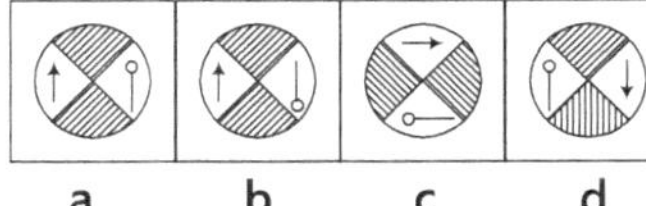

   a   **b**   **c**   **d**

25.

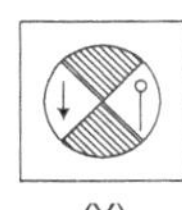

(X)

   a   **b**   **c**   **d**

Chapter 16

Paper Folding and Paper Cutting

'Paper Folding and Paper Cutting' problems are based on a sheet of paper which is folded along a dotted line or cut (punched) in a particular manner.

Paper Folding

Paper folding involves selection of a figure which would most closely resemble the pattern that would be formed when a transparent sheet carrying certain designs on either sides of a dotted line, is folded along the line.

For example, Consider a transparent sheet as shown below and choose a figure from the options which represents the sheet (X) after folding along the dotted line.

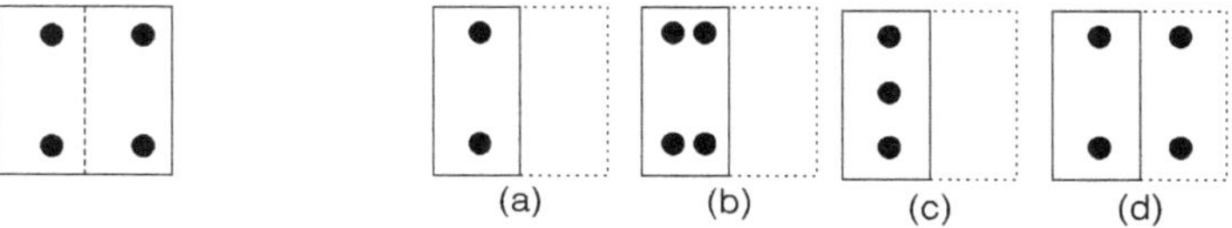

Here, we see that there are four black dots on the above transparent sheet (X).

Now, when the sheet is folded along the dotted line it will appear as adjacent figure.

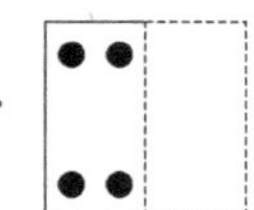

Hence, option (b) is correct.

In paper folding, following types of questions are generally asked

Direction (Example 1) In the following question, a transparent sheet having certain design on either sides of dotted line is given. The figure is followed by four answer figures and one out of these is obtained by folding the transparent sheet along the dotted line. Choose the correct option.

EXAMPLE 1 Transparent Sheet   Answer Sheet

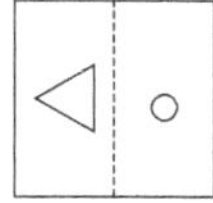

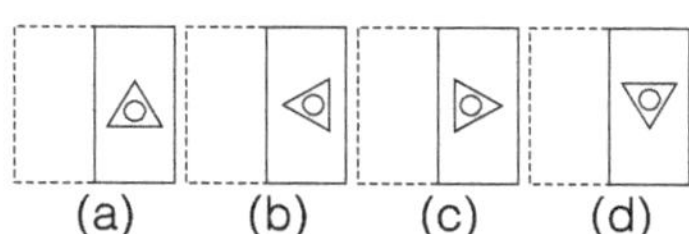

Think After observing, we see that, the left half of the transparent sheet is folded along the dotted line and placed on the right half to form a design.

Sol. The folded transparent sheet will appear as adjacent figure

Hence, option (c) is correct.

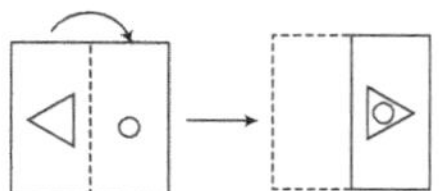

Paper Cutting

In paper cutting a piece of paper is folded twice or thrice in certain directions indicated by the arrows and then cuts are made into it. Students are required to determine the pattern which will be formed when the sheet is unfolded.

For example, A sheet has been folded and cut is made as shown below. Then, find the sheet that will be obtained when sheet (Z) will be unfolded.

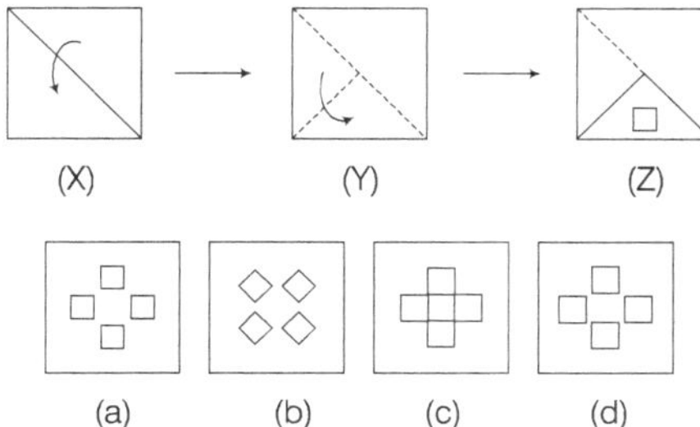

Here, we see that, the paper is folded along the dotted line as indicated by the arrows and then a cut is made in rectangular shape as shown in figure (Z).

Now, the unfolded pattern of the sheet will appear as

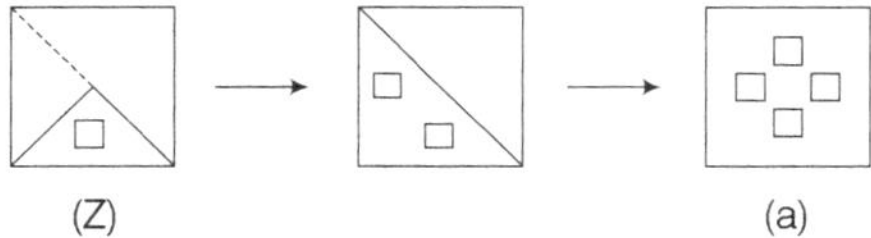

In paper cutting, following types of questions are generally asked

Direction (Example 2) In the following question, a set of three figures showing a sequence in which a paper is folded and cut in a particular manner. You have to select the answer figure. Showing the design which the paper actually acquires when it is unfolded.

EXAMPLE 2 Transparent Sheets   Answer Sheets

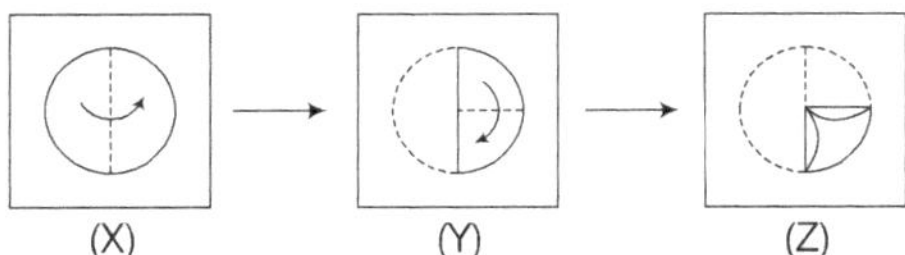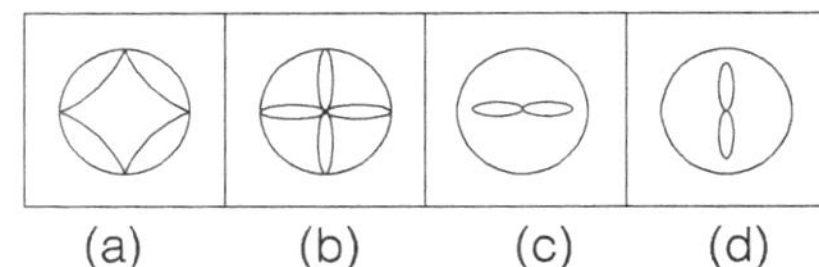

Think After observing, we see that, the circle is folded quarterly and then cuts are made.

Sol. When the first fold is opened the paper will look like as

Now, when the paper is unfolded completely it will look like as

Hence, option (b) is correct.

Practice
Centre

Direction (Q. Nos. 1-7) In each of the following questions, a transparent sheet having certain design on either sides of dotted line is given. One out of these four alternatives is obtained by folding the transparent sheet along the dotted line. Choose the correct option.

answer figure, showing the design which the paper actually acquires when it is unfolded.

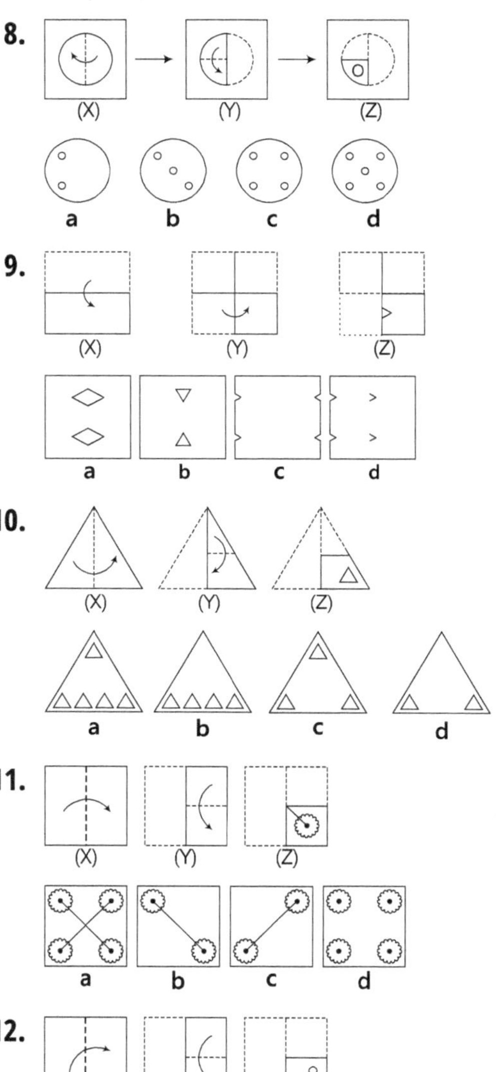

Direction (Q. Nos. 8-12) In each of the following questions, a set of three figures is given, showing a sequence in which a paper is folded and finally cut in a particular manner. Now, you have to select the

Chapter 17

Cubes and Dice

Cube

A cube is a three-dimensional solid, which is shaped like a box and has six square faces. It has 8 corners, 6 faces and 12 edges.

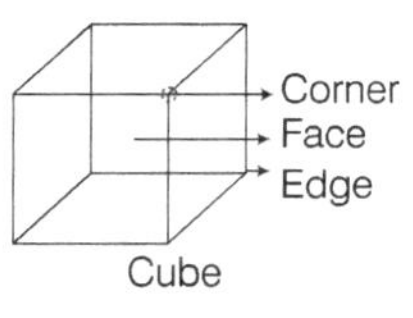

Dice

A dice is a small cube having one to six dots on its faces.

In this section, three types of questions are asked

 (i) Counting the number of small cubes

 (ii) Construction of cubes (dice) from unfolded dice (net)

 (iii) Finding the digit/dot/letter/symbol on the face opposite to a particular face

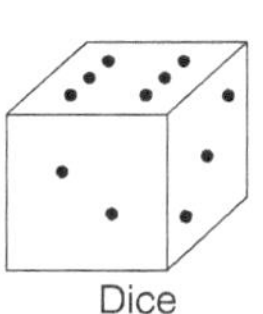

 (i) **Counting of Number of Small Cubes**

In this topic, a stack of cubes is given and students are required to count the number of small cubes in the given stack of cubes.

In cubes and dice, following types of questions are generally asked

EXAMPLE 1 Count the number of small cubes in the given figure.

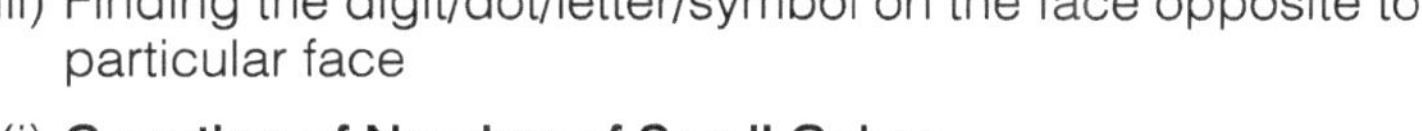

 (a) 10   (b) 9   (c) 18   (d) 12

Think Make the number on each cube and count the cubes carefully to avoid the repetition.

Sol.

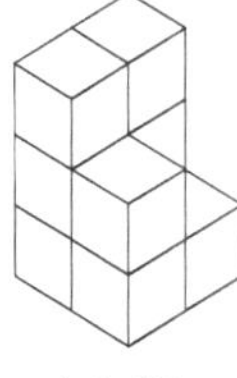

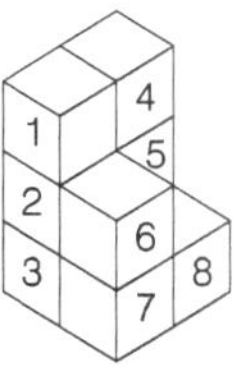

Here, we see that, there are 8 visible cubes and 1 hidden cube below the cube number 5.

∴ Total number of cubes = 8 + 1 = 9

Hence, option (b) is correct.

(ii) **Construction of Cubes** (dice) **from Unfolded Cube** (dice)

In this section, a figure of unfolded dice (net) with different elements on it is given and students are required to find out the cube or dice which can be formed by folding the given net.

Various formats of unfolded dice (net) can be obtained by unfolding a dice in different ways. Four such nets are as shown below

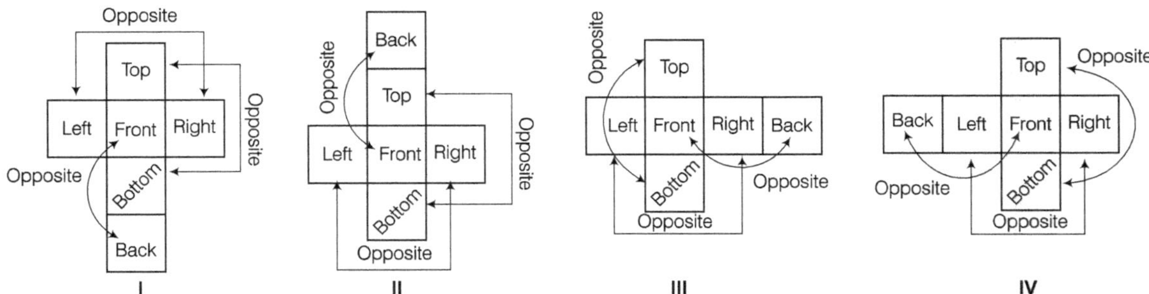

As seen in the above figures, the top face is opposite to the bottom face, the left face is opposite to the right face and the front face is opposite to the back face.

EXAMPLE 2 A sheet of paper shown in fig. (X), is folded to form a box. Choose a box from the options, that is similar to the box given in fig. (X).

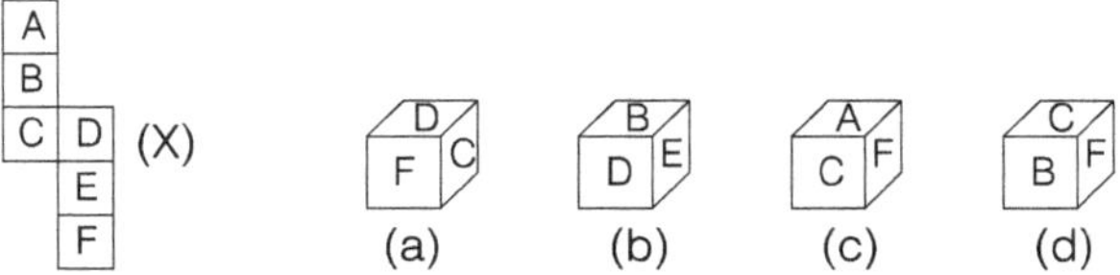

Think • First of all, find out the opposite faces from the given net.
• Now analyse each alternative cube to see that no opposite faces are shown adjacent to each other.

Sol. The opposite faces can be obtained as

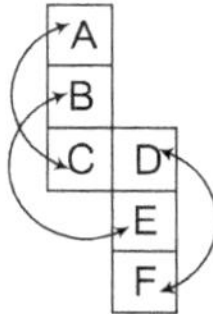

A is opposite to C, B is opposite to E and D is opposite to F.

Now, in cube (a) D and F are shown on adjacent faces, in cube (b), B and E are shown on adjacent faces and in cube (c) A and C are shown on adjacent faces, so these cubes cannot be formed. Only cube (d) can be formed because in this cube B, C and F are shown on adjacent faces and this can be possible.

Hence, option (d) is correct.

(iii) **Finding the Digit/Dot/Letter/Symbol on Face Opposite to a Particular Face**

In this topic, two or more positions of a dice having numbers/letters/ symbols are given and we have to find out the number/letter/symbol on face opposite to a particular face.

EXAMPLE 3 In the following question, the two positions of a single die are given which have letters A to F on it. Find the letter on the face which is opposite to the letter A.

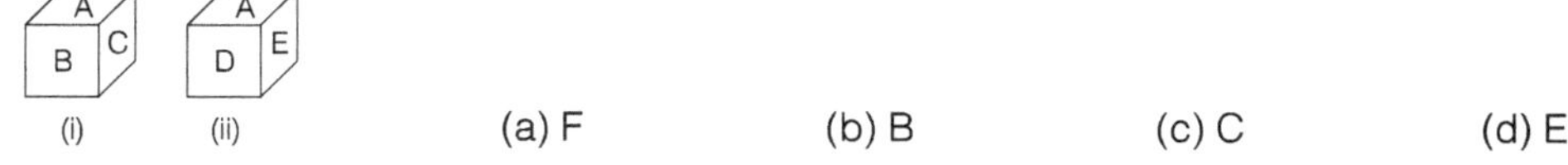

(a) F   (b) B   (c) C   (d) E

Think • First of all, analyse the figures and find out the common element in two positions.
• After this consider both positions and write down the adjacent faces of the common element from both the positions to find out the remaining face.

Sol. Here, we see that letter 'A' is common in both the positions. Now, adjacent faces of 'A' are B, C, D and E. So, the remaining face having letter 'F' will be opposite to the face having letter 'A'.

Hence, option (a) is correct.

Practice
Centre

Direction (Q. Nos. 1-5) Count the number of small cubes in the following figures.

1.

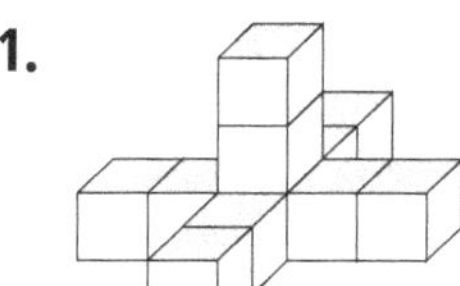

  a 12   **b** 10
  c 11   **d** 13

2.

  a 11   **b** 12
  c 15   **d** 15

3.

  a 10   **b** 7
  c 8   **d** 9

4.

  a 16   **b** 20
  c 21   **d** 22

5.

  a 36   **b** 32
  c 30   **d** 28

6. Which number will appear on the face opposite to 2?

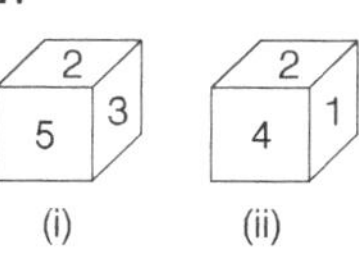

(i)   (ii)

  a 6   **b** 5
  c 4   **d** 3

7. Two positions of a dice are given below, when 1 is at the top, which number will be at the bottom?

(i)   (ii)

  a 1   **b** 2
  c 3   **d** 6

8. Two positions of a dice, whose faces are marked as A, B, C, D, E and F are given below. Find the letter opposite A.

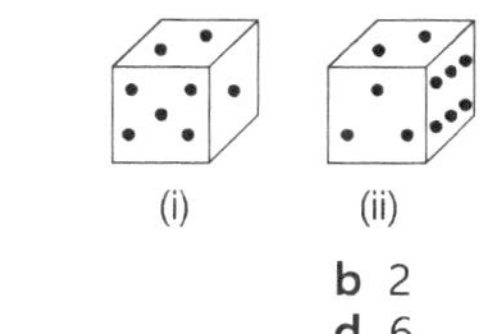

(i)   (ii)

  a B   **b** E
  c C   **d** D

9. What will be the number at the bottom, if 6 is at the top?

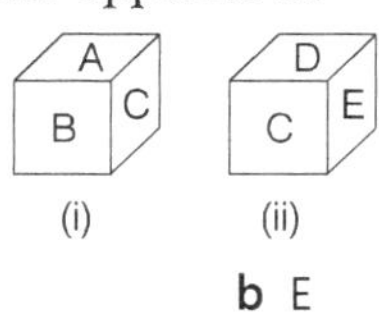

(i)   (ii)

  a 2   **b** 3
  c 5   **d** 5

10.

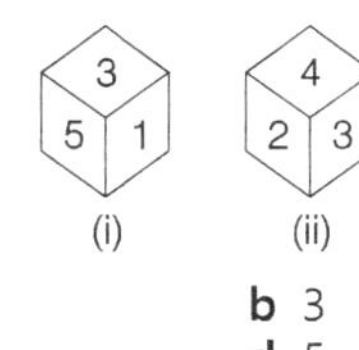

(i)   (ii)   (iii)

How many dots lie opposite 2 dots?

  a 3   **b** 6
  c 5   **d** 1

11. Six sides of a block are coloured with 1, 2, 3, 4, 5 and 6 in the following manner.

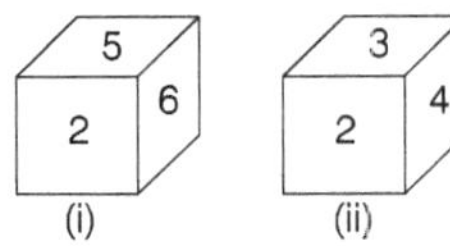

(i)   (ii)

Which number will be on the face opposite to face having 2?

a 4
b 1
c 5
d 4

 (Q. Nos. 12-15) In each of the following questions, an unfolded dice is given with the four options in the form of complete dice. Select the correct answer choice which is formed by unfolded dice.

12.

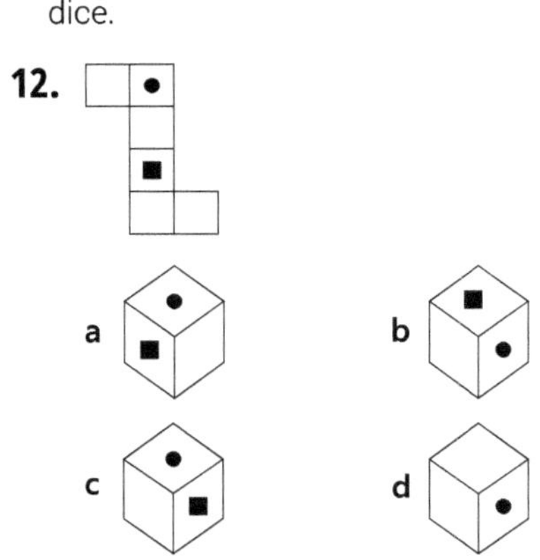

a   b

c   d

13.

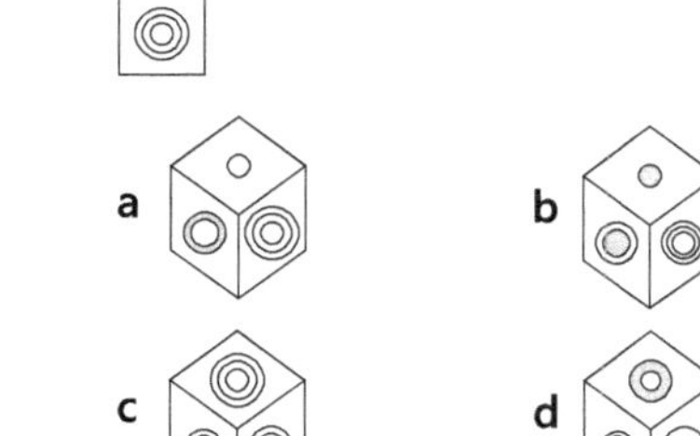

a   b

c   d

14.

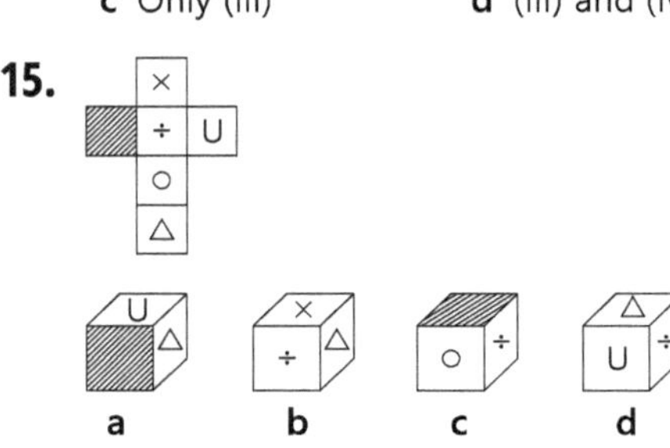

(i)   (ii)   (iii)   (iv)

a Only (i)   b (i) and (ii)
c Only (iii)   d (iii) and (iv)

15.

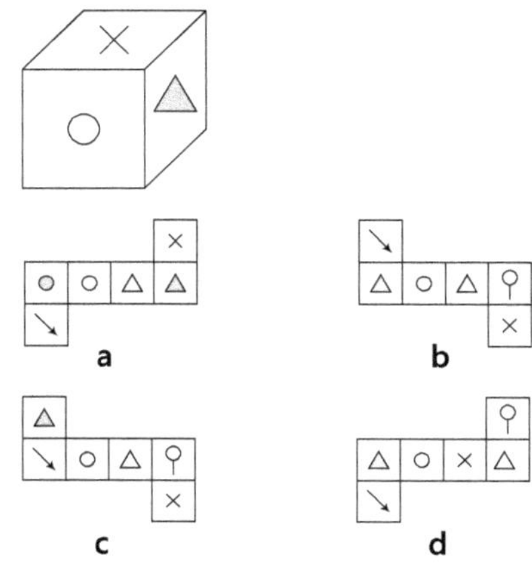

a   b   c   d

16. Which of the following net can be used to form a dice given below?

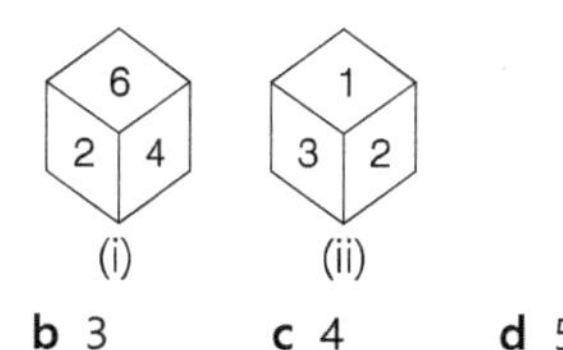

a   b

c   d

17. A dice is thrown two times and its different positions are shown below. What number is opposite to face shown 2?

(i)   (ii)

a 6   b 3   c 4   d 5

Embedded Figures, Figure Formation and Analysis

Embedded Figures

Embedded figure refers to a simple geometrical figure which is present in other large or complex figure. Here, a figure is said to be embedded in another figure when the second figure completely contains the first figure.

For example, Consider the given fig. (X) and choose the figure from the given options in which the given fig. (X) is exactly embedded.

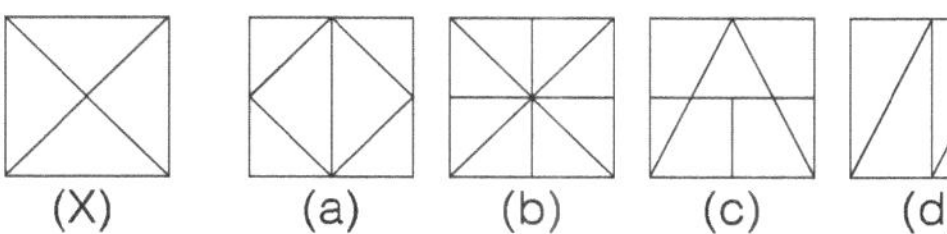

The given fig. (X) can be traced out in figure (b) as shown below

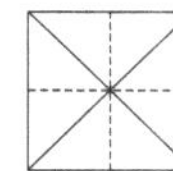

Hence, option (b) is correct.

In embedded figures, following types of questions are generally asked

EXAMPLE 1 Find out the alternative figure which contains fig. (X) as its part.

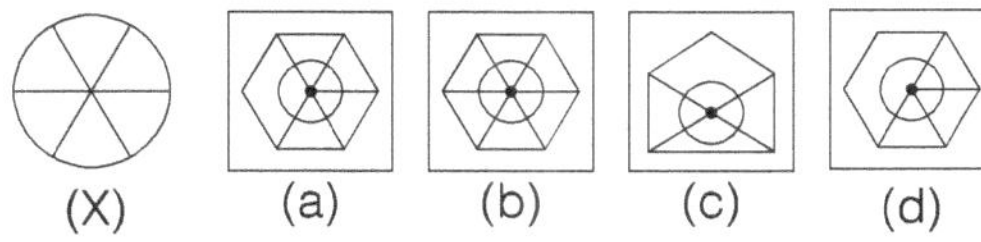

Think • Look at the fig. (X) carefully and analyse the pattern.
• After analysing we see that, the circle is divided into six equal parts.

Sol. After close observation, we find that fig. (X) is exactly embedded in figure (b) as shown below

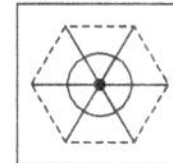

Hence, option (b) is correct.

Figure Formation and Analysis

In figure formation and analysis, we form figures such as squares or other format by joining two or more than two components and we also identify identical figures or components of the given figure from a given set of figures.

For example, Consider the following set of pieces and choose a figure from the given options which can be formed from these pieces.

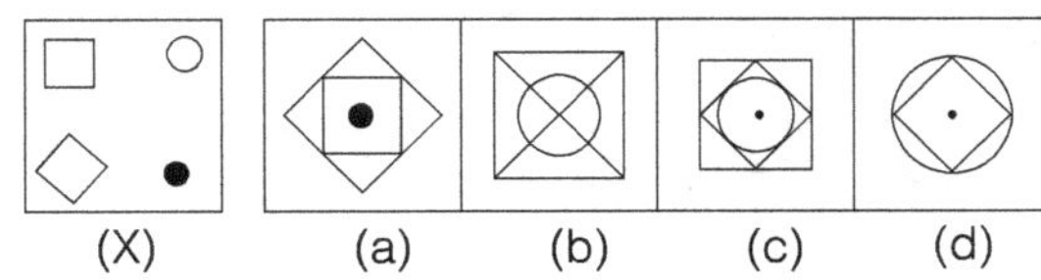

(X)   (a)   (b)   (c)   (d)

If we carefully observe the option figures we see that, figure (c) has all the pieces given in fig. (X). So, only the figure (c) can be formed.

Hence, option (c) is correct

In figure formation and analysis, following types of questions are generally asked

EXAMPLE 2 Which of the following shapes, when fitted to the piece in fig. (X) will form a perfect square?

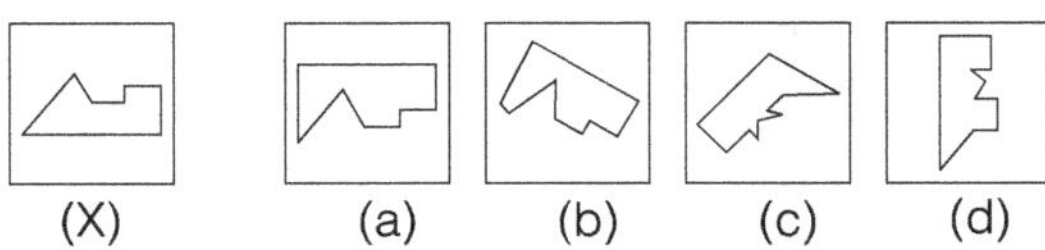

(X)   (a)   (b)   (c)   (d)

Think First of all, observe the pattern of fig. (X) and then observe the pattern of option figure to find out that which piece will fit into the fig (X).

Sol. It is clear from the given options that figure (a) will form the square when join with fig. (X) as shown below

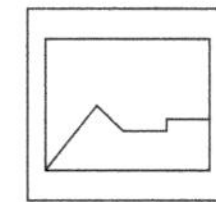

Hence, option (a) is correct.

EXAMPLE 3 Group the following figures into three classes on the basis of identical properties.

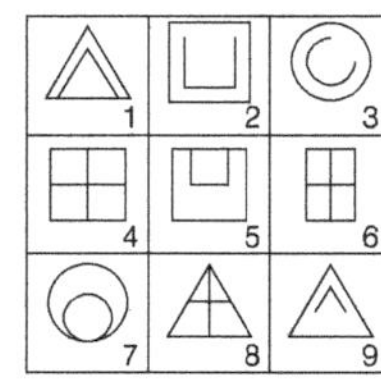

(a) 1, 5, 7; 2, 3, 9; 4, 6, 8   (b) 1, 3, 9; 2, 4, 6; 5, 7, 8
(c) 2, 4, 5; 9, 1, 3; 7, 8, 6   (d) 3, 2, 1; 4, 6, 5; 9, 7, 8

Think • Observe the figures carefully to identify the identical properties.
• After this, group the figures on the basis of their identical properties.

Sol. From the above figures, it is clear that figures (1), (5) and (7) follow same property with two similar shapes. In figures (2), (3) and (9), the object has incomplete figure inside it. And in figures (4), (6) and (8) each figure is divided into four parts.

Thus, the given nine figures may be divided into three groups as (1, 5, 7); (2, 3, 9); (4, 6 8).

Hence, option (a) is correct.

Practice Centre

Direction (Q. Nos. 1-3) In the following questions, a question fig. (X) and a set of four answer figures (a), (b), (c) and (d) are given. Find out answer figure in which the question fig. (X) is embedded.

1.
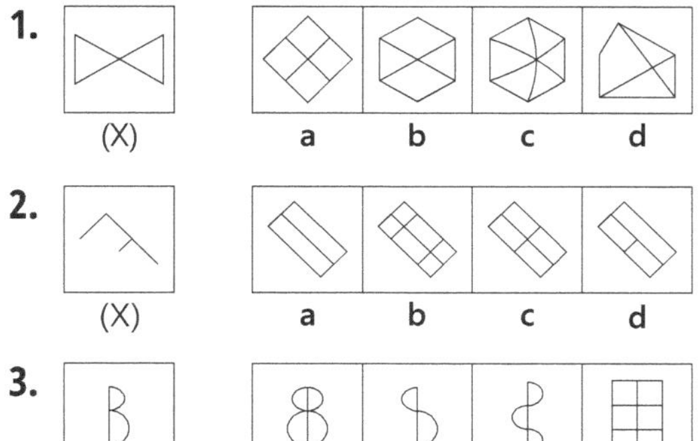

2.

3.

Direction (Q. Nos. 4-5) In each of the following questions find out the figure from the answer figures, that can be formed by joining the pieces given in the question figure.

4.
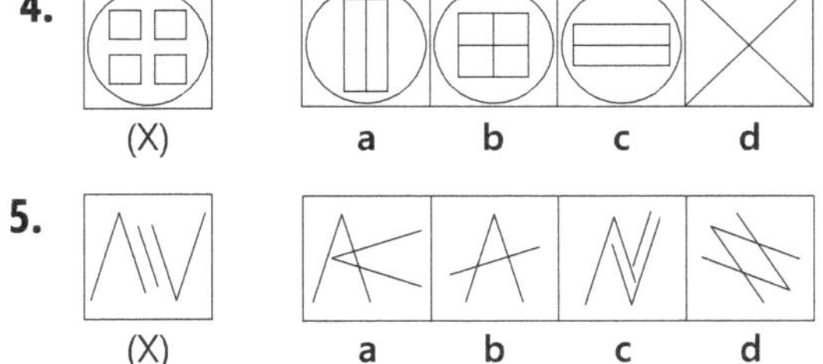

5.

Direction (Q. Nos. 6-7) In each of the following questions, select the option in which all the components of the question fig. (X) are available.

6.
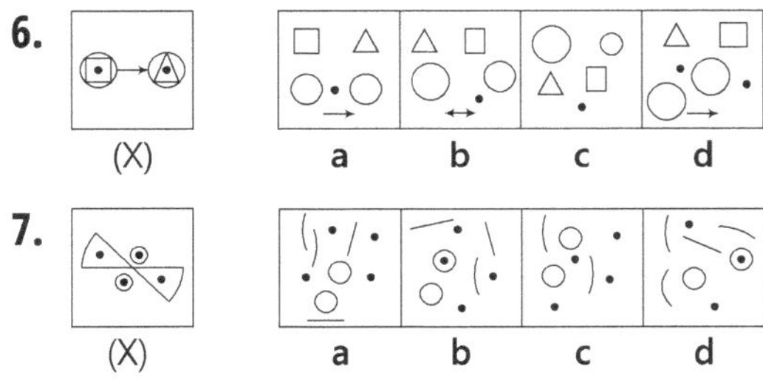

7.

Direction (Q. Nos. 8-9) In each of the following questions, question fig. (X) is given followed by other four alternative figures. It is required to select one figure from the alternatives, which exactly fits into fig. (X), to form a perfect square.

8.
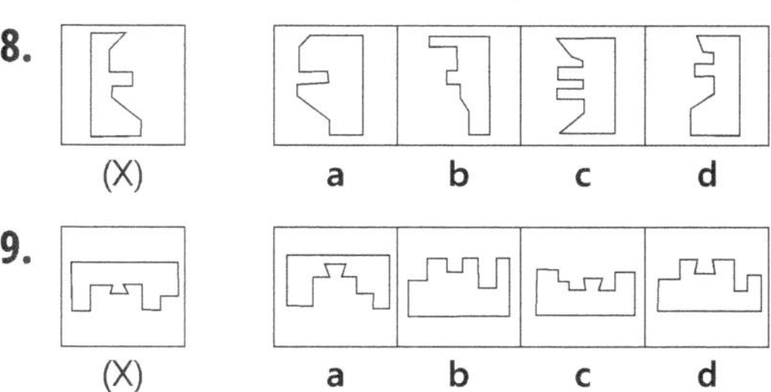

9.

Direction (Q. Nos. 10-11) In each of the following questions, group the given figures into three classes using each figure only once.

10.
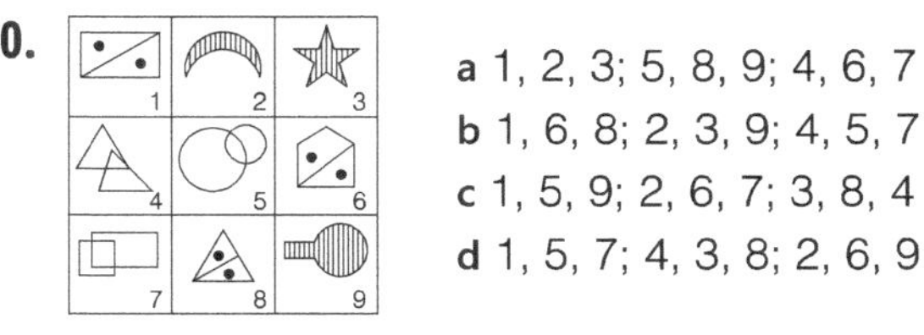

a 1, 2, 3; 5, 8, 9; 4, 6, 7
b 1, 6, 8; 2, 3, 9; 4, 5, 7
c 1, 5, 9; 2, 6, 7; 3, 8, 4
d 1, 5, 7; 4, 3, 8; 2, 6, 9

11.
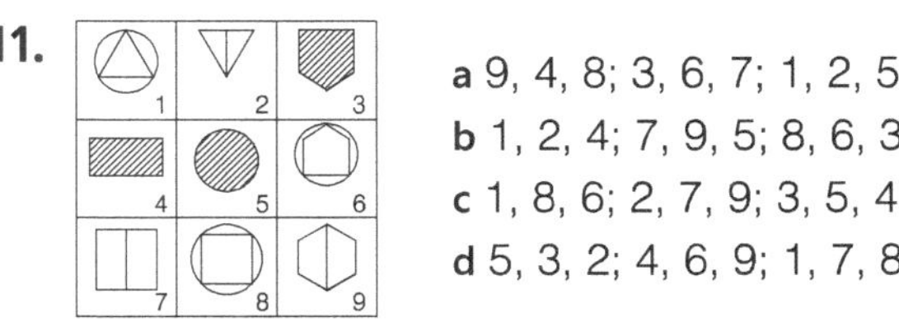

a 9, 4, 8; 3, 6, 7; 1, 2, 5
b 1, 2, 4; 7, 9, 5; 8, 6, 3
c 1, 8, 6; 2, 7, 9; 3, 5, 4
d 5, 3, 2; 4, 6, 9; 1, 7, 8

Direction (Q. Nos. 12-13) Identify and choose the correct figure that will complete the pattern.

12.
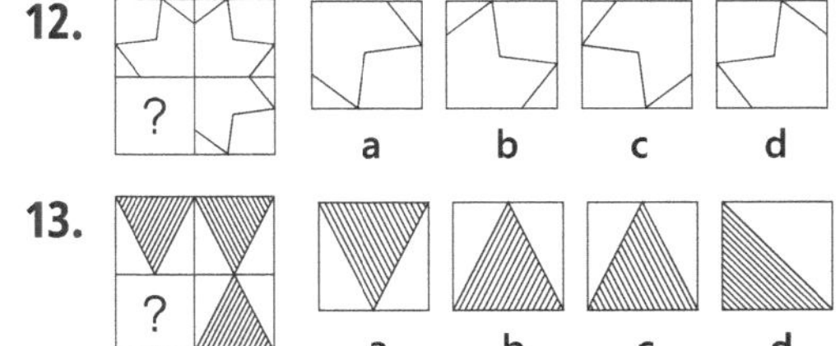

13.

Counting of Figures

'Counting of Figures' means counting the number of geometrical shapes like straight lines, circles, squares, rectangles, triangles etc., that make up a given complex figure.

For example, Consider the following figure.

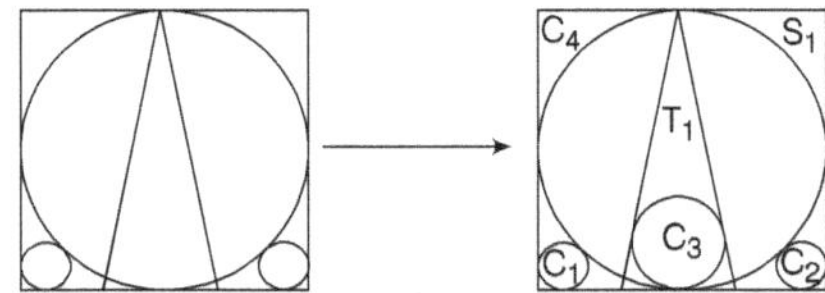

In the above figure, there are four circles, one triangle and one square.

Note

- **To count the straight lines** Add all the numbers of vertical ($|$), horizontal ($-$) and slanting ($/$) lines.
- **To count the triangles/squares/rectangles** Add all the number of triangles/squares/rectangles formed by 1 component, 2 components, 3 components and so on.
- **To count the circles** Count all the centres of circles.

In counting of figures, following types of questions are generally asked

EXAMPLE 1 How many straight lines are there in the figure given below?

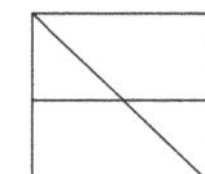

(a) 5 　　　　(b) 6 　　　　(c) 7 　　　　(d) 8

Think · First of all observe the figure carefully and try to find out the different forms of the figure (which is asked). In this case lines can be divided in three different forms (i) horizontal lines (ii) vertical lines and (iii) slanting lines.

· Now, label the figure and draw a table containing the number of lines of different forms.

Sol. The given figure may be labelled as

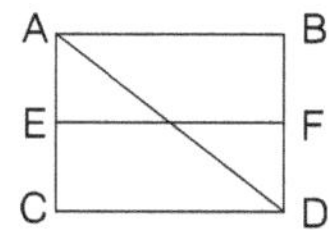

The number of lines of different forms are shown in below table

Type of line	Name of the lines	Number of lines
Horizontal	AB, EF and CD	3
Vertical	AC and BD	2
Slanting	AD	1
Total		6

Therefore, the number of straight lines are 6. Hence, option (b) is correct.

EXAMPLE 2 How many triangles are there in the given figure?

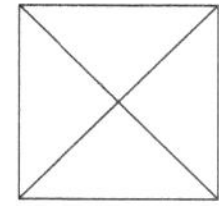

(a) 8   (b) 6   (c) 10   (d) 12

Think • After observing the given figure, we find the two different forms of triangle (i) single triangle and (ii) triangle made from two triangles.
• Now, we label the given figure and draw a table containing these two forms of triangles.

Sol. The figure may be labelled as

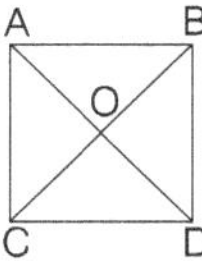

Now, the number of triangles of different forms are shown in below table

Type of triangle	Name of triangles	Number of triangles
Formed by one component	AOB, BOD, DOC and COA	4
Formed by two components	ABC, CDB, ACD and ABD	4
Total		8

Therefore, total number of triangle = 8

Hence, option (a) is correct.

EXAMPLE 3 How many rectangles are there in the figure given below?

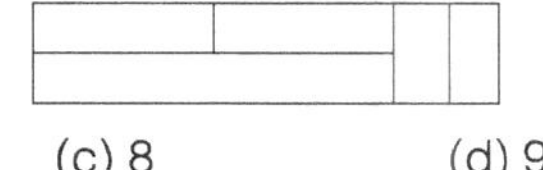

(a) 10   (b) 6   (c) 8   (d) 9

Think • After observing the given figure we find the five different forms of rectangle i.e. single rectangle, rectangle formed from two, three, four and five rectangles.
• Now, we label the given figure and draw a table containing these five different forms of rectangles.

Sol. The figure may be labelled as

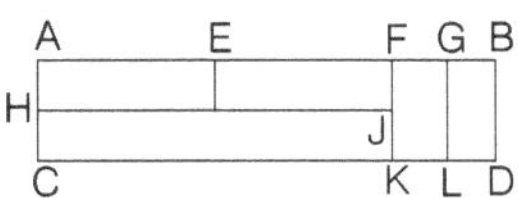

Now, the number of rectangles of different forms are shown in below table

Type of rectangle	Name of rectangles	Number of rectangles
Formed by one component	AEIH, EFJI, HJKC, FGLK and GBDL	5
Formed by two components	AFJH and FBDK	2
Formed by three components	AFKC	1
Formed by four components	AGLC	1
Formed by five components	ABDC	1
Total		10

Therefore, total number of rectangles = 10

Hence, option (a) is correct.

Practice
Centre

Direction (Q.Nos.1-3) In each of the following questions find the number of straight lines used information of the given figure.

1. 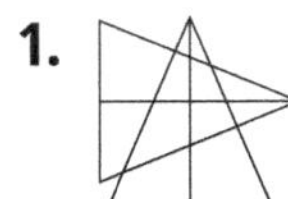

a 10   b 9
c 8   d 7

2. 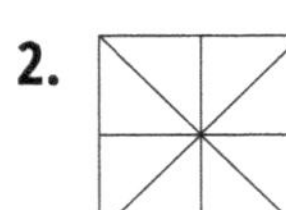

a 10   b 11
c 9   d 8

3. 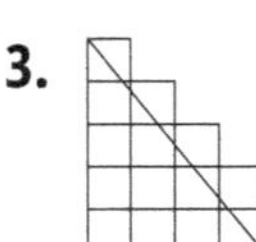

a 13   b 12
c 15   d 14

4. How many triangles are there in the figure given below?

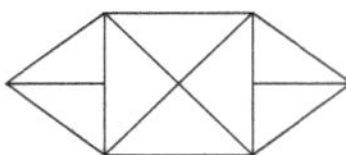

a 11   b 10
c 15   d 14

5. How many squares are there in the figure given below?

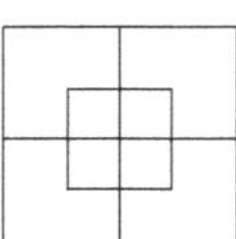

a 8   b 9
c 10   d 11

6. How many triangles are there in the given figure?

a 8   b 9
c 10   d 11

7. How many triangles are there in the given figure?

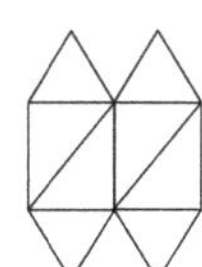

a 10   b 9
c 8   d 11

8. How many rectangles are there in the figure given below?

a 14   b 10
c 11   d 9

9. How many squares are there in the figure given below?

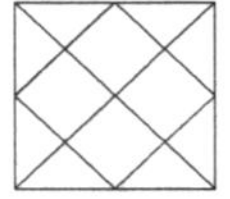

a 8   b 6
c 4   d 10

10. How many square are there in the figure given below?

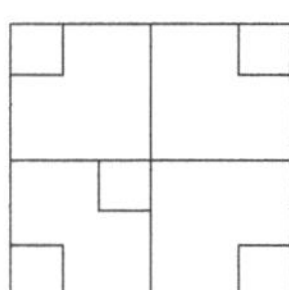

a 10   b 12
c 8   d 14

11. How many rectangles are there in the figure given below?

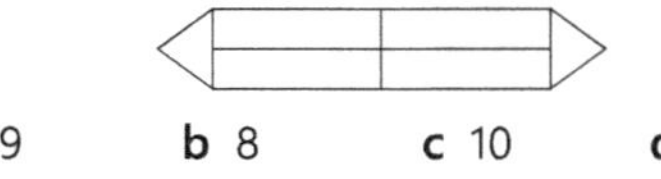

a 9   b 8   c 10   d 7

12. How many triangles are there in the given figure below?

a 15   b 13
c 16   d 18

13. How many circles are there in the figure given below?

a 9   b 10
c 11   d 12

Practice
Sets

Practice Set ①

A Whole Content Based Test for Class 6th Reasoning Olympiad

1. Find the next term in the series ⑦⑪⑰㉕㉟? .
 a 45 b 47 c 49 d 51

2. HJL is related to JMP, in the same way as OQS is related to
 a PSV b MHJ c QTW d RUX

3. The letter of the words given in each of the four options have been jumbled up. Identify the word in the option for the clue given below.
 'A week day'
 a ACMRH b AOTDY c OMDANY d LOHIYAD

4. Which number will replace the question mark?
 ⑧—③—④, ⑩—⑤—⑩, ⑮—?—⑨
 a 6 b 4 c 8 d 42

5. Which of the following diagram indicates the best relation amongst mango, vegetable and fruits?
 a   b   c   d

6. Select the correct mirror image of the following NAME25
 a ИAMƎ2 b 2ƎMAИ c 2ƎMAИ d 2ƎMAИ

7. If '×' means '÷', '+' means '×', '−' means '+' and '÷' means '×', then 125 × 25 + 20 − 80 = ?
 a 180 b 90 c 200 d 20

8. If 'X' is the wife of 'Y', 'Y' is the brother of 'Z' and 'P' is the father of 'Z', then how is 'P' related to 'X'?
 a Aunt b Brother
 c Father-in-law d Sister

9. Which figure completes the second pair in the same way as first pair?
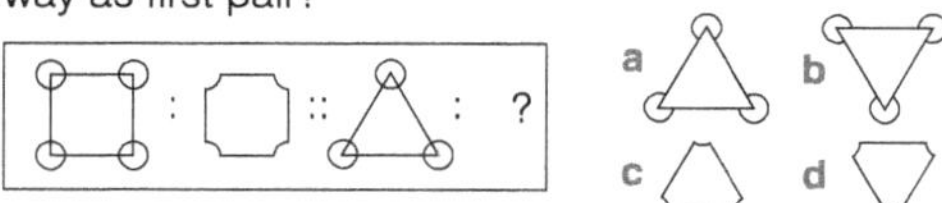

10. Choose the figure which is different from others.

11. Five children are sitting on a bench. P is to the left of Q and to the right of R. S is to the right of Q. T is between Q and S. Then, whose position is fourth from the right?
 a R b Q
 c S d P

12. Find the one which does not belong to the group.
 a Tail b Hale
 c Nail d Sail

13. Find the next figure in the series given below.

14. If the following transparent sheet with a certain design is folded along the dotted line, then how will it appear

 (X) a b c d

15. Count the number of straight lines in the figure given below.
 a 12
 b 16
 c 17
 d 20

16. Consider the figures (X) and (Y) showing a sheet of paper folded and punched in Fig. (Z). Select the figure, which will most closely resemble the unfolded form of figure?

 (X) (Y) (Z) a b c d

17. In which of the following options, Fig. (X) is embedded as its part?

 (X) a b c d

18. Ram is facing East. He turn 135° in clockwise direction and then 180° in anti-clockwise direction. Which direction he is facing now?
 a East b North
 c North-East d South-West

19. If in a certain code, HAPPY is coded as YPPAH, how is TEACH coded in that code?
 a HCAET b AETHC
 c EACTH d HCEAT
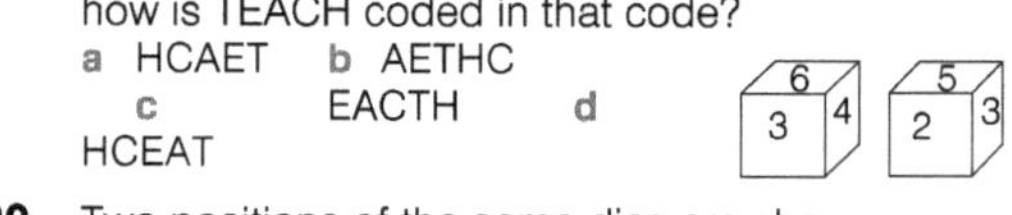

20. Two positions of the same dice are shown. Which digit will appear on the face opposite to the face having number 3?
 a 2 b 5 c 4 d 1

Practice Set 2

A Whole Content Based Test for Class 6th Reasoning Olympiad

1. 'Chapter' is related to 'Book', in the same way as Brick is related to
  a Clay b Mud
  c Building d Mason

2. Find the odd one out.
  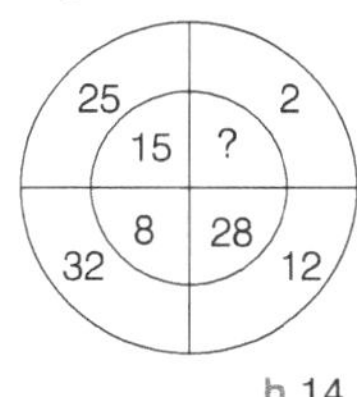
  a T W U b G K I
  c O S Q d H L J

3. What comes next in the series given below?

  L N Q U ?
  a T b W
  c Y d Z

4. If SLOW is coded as 1598 and TAKE is coded as 2437, then LATE is coded as
  a 9 2 4 7 b 5 4 2 7
  c 5 8 3 4 d 7 5 9 4

5. Find the missing number in the following figure.
  25 2
  15 ?
  8 28
  32 12
  a 38 b 14
  c 28 d 30

6. The letters of the words given in each of the four options have been jumbled up. Identify the word in the options for the clue given below.
  Synonym of 'Heal'.
  a CUQIK b AEBRK
  c GMDAAE d UCER

7. If 7 * 8 = 56, 6 * 9 = 54 and 4 * 6 = 24, then find the value of 11 * 5.
  a 55 b 40 c 50 d 44

8. Which of the following diagram indicates the best relation amongst chair, pages and book?
  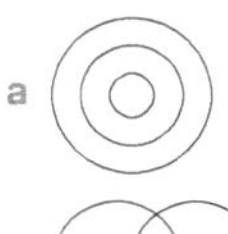 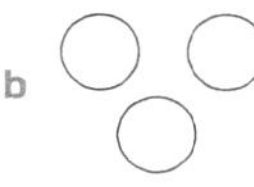 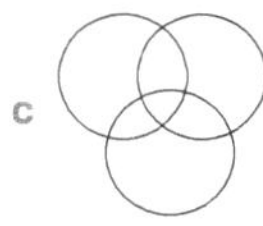
  a b
  c d

9. Akanksha moves 8 km towards West, then 2 km towards South and then 6 km towards East. Find the total distance covered by Akanksha.
  a 18 km b 16 km
  c 4 km d 6 km

10. Ashwini said pointing towards Sachin, ''He is my sister's only brother's Son''. How is Sachin related to Ashwini?
  a Father b Brother
  c Son d Uncle

11. Arrange the following words according to English dictionary.
  1. Hepatitis 2. Cholera
  3. Peptidoglycan 4. Chitin
  a 2, 3, 1, 4 b 4, 2, 1, 3
  c 4, 1, 3, 2 d 3, 1, 4, 2

12. Read the following information carefully and answer the question given below.

  Raghu and Gyan are good players in cricket and hockey. Sohan and Gyan are good players in hockey and chess. Raghu and Govind are good players in swimming and cricket.

  Who is good in cricket, hockey and chess?
  a Raghu b Gyan
  c Sohan d Govind

13. Choose the figure which is different from others.
  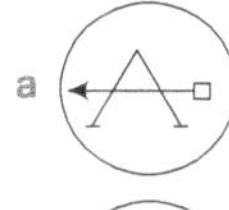 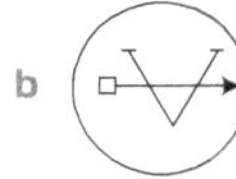 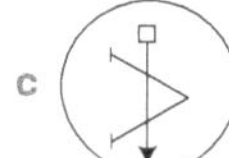
  a b
  c d

14. Find the next figure in the series given below.

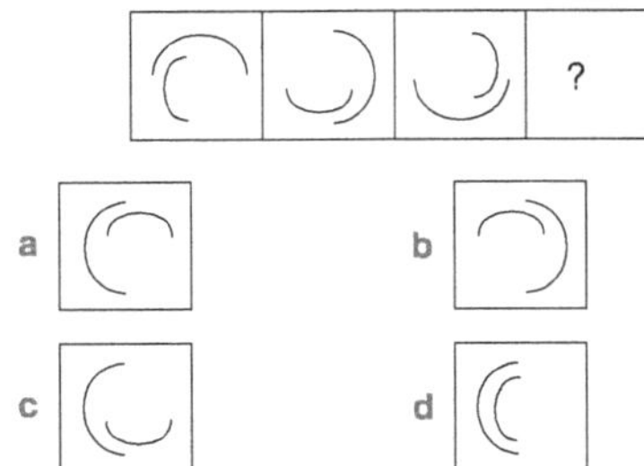

a b

c d

15. Complete the second pair in the same way as first pair.

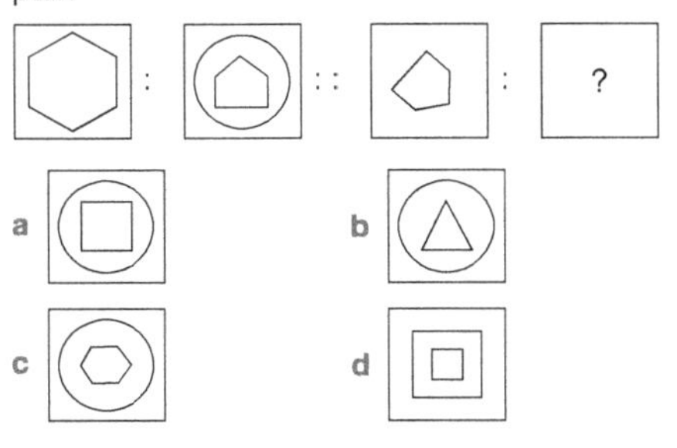

a b

c d

16. Count the number of squares in the following figure.

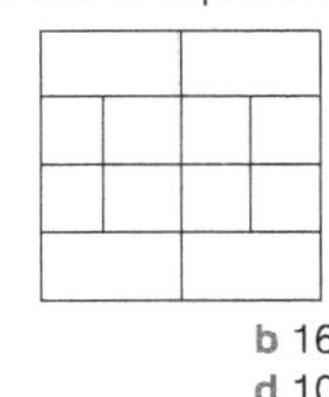

a 18   b 16
c 20   d 10

17. In the following question, a problem figure is given followed by four answer figures. You have to choose that answer figure which on joining will make a complete square with the problem figure.

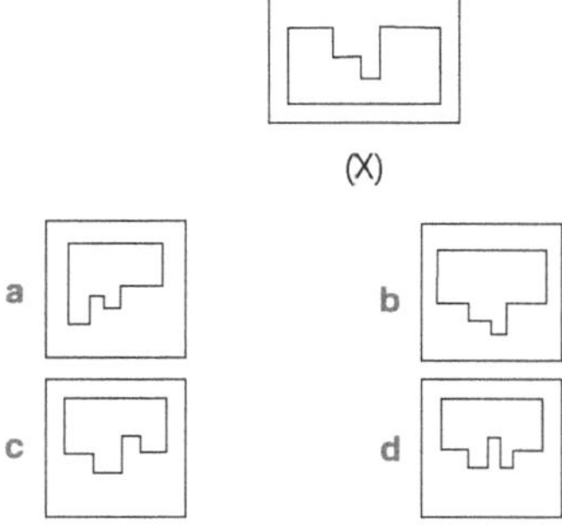

(X)

a b

c d

18. Find the pattern which will appear on the transparent sheet after it is folded along the dotted line.

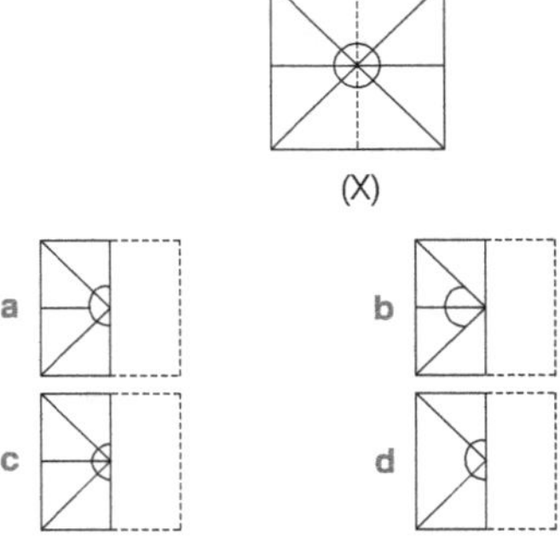

(X)

a b

c d

19. Select the correct mirror image of the figure given below.

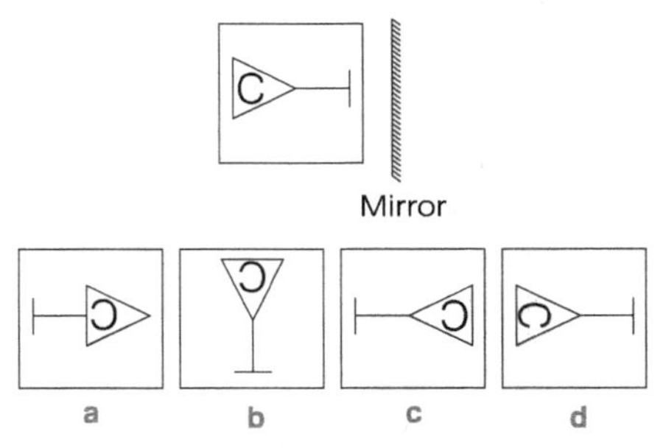

Mirror

a b c d

20. In the following question, an unfolded dice followed by four answer choices is given. Select the correct answer choice which can be formed by folding the unfolded dice.

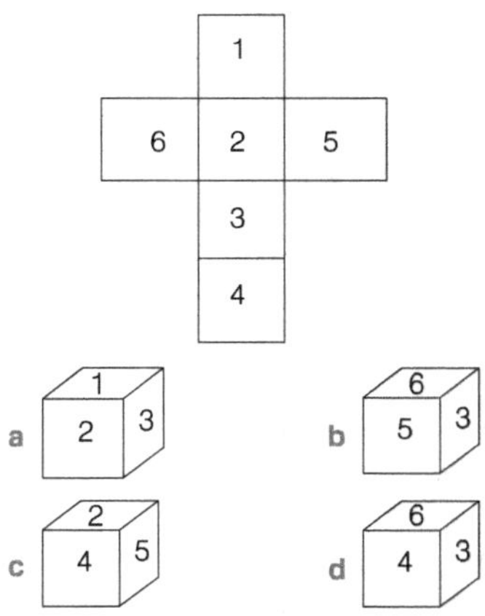

a b

c d

Practice Set 2

Answer & Explanations

Answer Sheet

Chapter_1 Similar Pairs

1.(a)	**2.**(c)	**3.**(d)	**4.**(b)	**5.**(a)	**6.**(c)	**7.**(c)	**8.**(b)	**9.**(b)	**10.**(a)
11.(b)	**12.**(c)	**13.**(b)	**14.**(d)	**15.**(a)	**16.**(b)	**17.**(c)	**18.**(d)	**19.**(b)	**20.**(a)
21.(a)	**22.**(b)	**23.**(b)	**24.**(c)	**25.**(d)	**26.**(a)	**27.**(c)	**28.**(b)	**29.**(d)	**30.**(c)
31.(b)									

Chapter_2 What Comes Next?

1.(c)	**2.**(d)	**3.**(b)	**4.**(d)	**5.**(b)	**6.**(c)	**7.**(c)	**8.**(b)	**9.**(c)	**10.**(d)
11.(c)	**12.**(a)	**13.**(d)	**14.**(a)	**15.**(c)	**16.**(d)	**17.**(b)	**18.**(c)	**19.**(c)	**20.**(a)
21.(c)	**22.**(c)	**23.**(b)	**24.**(d)	**25.**(d)	**26.**(b)	**27.**(a)	**28.**(b)	**29.**(a)	**30.**(b)
31.(a)	**32.**(d)	**33.**(d)	**34.**(b)	**35.**(a)					

Chapter_3 Odd One Out

1.(c)	**2.**(c)	**3.**(b)	**4.**(b)	**5.**(d)	**6.**(c)	**7.**(a)	**8.**(b)	**9.**(c)	**10.**(d)
11.(c)	**12.**(c)	**13.**(c)	**14.**(d)	**15.**(b)	**16.**(d)	**17.**(d)	**18.**(a)	**19.**(a)	**20.**(c)
21.(b)	**22.**(c)	**23.**(c)	**24.**(a)	**25.**(b)	**26.**(b)	**27.**(a)	**28.**(b)	**29.**(c)	**30.**(b)
31.(d)	**32.**(c)	**33.**(a)							

Chapter_4 Coding-Decoding

1.(d)	**2.**(d)	**3.**(a)	**4.**(d)	**5.**(b)	**6.**(b)	**7.**(b)	**8.**(c)	**9.**(c)	**10.**(a)
11.(d)	**12.**(a)	**13.**(c)	**14.**(d)	**15.**(d)	**16.**(c)	**17.**(c)	**18.**(b)	**19.**(a)	**20.**(c)

Chapter_5 Jumbled Words

1.(d)	**2.**(b)	**3.**(b)	**4.**(a)	**5.**(c)	**6.**(d)	**7.**(b)	**8.**(a)	**9.**(c)	**10.**(c)
11.(b)	**12.**(c)	**13.**(d)	**14.**(c)	**15.**(a)	**16.**(b)	**17.**(b)	**18.**(c)	**19.**(d)	**20.**(b)

Chapter_6 Mathematical Reasoning

1.(a)	**2.**(b)	**3.**(b)	**4.**(d)	**5.**(c)	**6.**(d)	**7.**(a)	**8.**(b)	**9.**(a)	**10.**(d)
11.(b)	**12.**(b)	**13.**(c)	**14.**(b)	**15.**(b)	**16.**(b)	**17.**(c)	**18.**(d)	**19.**(c)	**20.**(b)
21.(a)	**22.**(b)	**23.**(d)	**24.**(c)	**25.**(b)	**26.**(a)	**27.**(b)	**28.**(a)	**29.**(c)	

Chapter_7 Puzzle Test

1.(c)	**2.**(b)	**3.**(b)	**4.**(d)	**5.**(c)	**6.**(b)	**7.**(d)	**8.**(c)	**9.**(b)	**10.**(c)

Chapter_8 Number, Ranking and Alphabet Test

1.(d)	**2.**(c)	**3.**(b)	**4.**(b)	**5.**(c)	**6.**(a)	**7.**(a)	**8.**(d)	**9.**(c)	**10.**(b)
11.(a)	**12.**(b)	**13.**(b)	**14.**(b)	**15.**(c)					

Chapter_9 Direction Sense Test

1.(b)	**2.**(d)	**3.**(a)	**4.**(b)	**5.**(c)	**6.**(b)	**7.**(b)	**8.**(b)	**9.**(c)	**10.**(c)
11.(c)	**12.**(c)	**13.**(d)	**14.**(b)	**15.**(c)	**16.**(a)	**17.**(c)	**18.**(b)	**19.**(d)	**20.**(d)
21.(a)									

Chapter_10 Venn Diagram

1.(d)	**2.**(d)	**3.**(b)	**4.**(b)	**5.**(a)	**6.**(a)	**7.**(d)	**8.**(c)	**9.**(b)	**10.**(b)
11.(d)	**12.**(b)	**13.**(d)	**14.**(b)	**15.**(a)					

Chapter_11 Blood Relation

1.(c)	2.(d)	3.(b)	4.(d)	5.(b)	6.(d)	7.(d)	8.(a)	9.(c)	10.(b)
11.(d)	12.(b)	13.(a)	14.(d)	15.(d)	16.(c)				

Chapter_12 Similar Pairs

1.(a)	2.(d)	3.(c)	4.(b)	5.(b)	6.(a)	7.(c)	8.(a)	9.(b)	10.(d)
11.(b)	12.(c)	13.(d)	14.(b)	15.(a)	16.(b)	17.(b)	18.(c)	19.(d)	20.(d)

Chapter_13 What Comes Next

1.(c)	2.(b)	3.(b)	4.(a)	5.(a)	6.(c)	7.(b)	8.(d)	9.(b)	10.(a)
11.(d)	12.(a)	13.(c)	14.(a)	15.(b)	16.(a)	17.(a)	18.(b)	19.(c)	20.(c)
21.(b)	22.(b)	23.(c)	24.(d)						

Chapter_14 Odd One Out

1.(a)	2.(c)	3.(d)	4.(b)	5.(d)	6.(c)	7.(c)	8.(b)	9.(d)	10.(b)
11.(c)	12.(d)	13.(c)	14.(b)	15.(a)	16.(c)	17.(b)	18.(c)	19.(a)	20.(d)

Chapter_15 Mirror and Water Images

1.(c)	2.(a)	3.(b)	4.(d)	5.(d)	6.(b)	7.(a)	8.(c)	9.(b)	10.(d)
11.(c)	12.(a)	13.(b)	14.(a)	15.(c)	16.(d)	17.(d)	18.(b)	19.(d)	20.(a)
21.(c)	22.(b)	23.(d)	24.(a)	25.(b)					

Chapter_16 Paper Folding and Paper Cutting

1.(c)	2.(b)	3.(c)	4.(a)	5.(c)	6.(a)	7.(b)	8.(c)	9.(a)	10.(d)
11.(a)	12.(c)								

Chapter_17 Cubes and Dice

1.(c)	2.(a)	3.(b)	4.(c)	5.(a)	6.(a)	7.(d)	8.(b)	9.(b)	10.(c)
11.(b)	12.(d)	13.(a)	14.(a)	15.(c)	16.(b)	17.(d)			

Chapter_18 Embedded Figures, Figure Formation and Analysis

1. (b)	2. (c)	3. (a)	4. (b)	5. (c)	6. (d)	7. (d)	8. (a)	9. (d)	10. (b)
11. (c)	12. (c)	13. (c)							

Chapter_19 Counting of Figures

1.(c)	2.(d)	3.(b)	4.(d)	5.(c)	6.(a)	7.(a)	8.(c)	9.(b)	10.(a)
11.(a)	12.(b)	13.(a)							

Practice Set_01

1.(b)	2.(c)	3.(c)	4.(a)	5.(d)	6.(c)	7.(a)	8.(c)	9.(c)	10.(b)
11.(d)	12.(b)	13.(b)	14.(c)	15.(b)	16.(d)	17.(d)	18.(c)	19.(a)	20.(d)

Practice Set_02

1.(c)	2.(a)	3.(d)	4.(b)	5.(a)	6.(d)	7.(a)	8.(d)	9.(b)	10.(c)
11.(b)	12.(b)	13.(c)	14.(a)	15.(a)	16.(b)	17.(b)	18.(c)	19.(c)	20.(d)

1. As, $17 + 15 = 32$
Similarly, $11 + 15 = 26$
Hence, option (a) is correct.

2. As, $4 \times 2 = 8$ and $8 + 1 = 9$
Similarly, $7 \times 2 = 14$
and $14 + 1 = 15$
Hence, option (c) is correct.

3. As, $(14)^2 = 196$,
Similarly, $(16)^2 = 256$
Hence, option (d) is correct.

4. As, $15 \times 5 = 75$
Similarly, $12 \times 5 = 60$
Hence, option (b) is correct.

5. Here, in each pair first two digits of the given number is taken forward to obtain the second number.
So, 77 will complete the second pair.
Hence, option (a) is correct.

6. As, $6248 / 2 = 3124$
Similarly, $4024 / 2 = 2012$
Hence, option (c) is correct.

7. The digits of the first number are multiplied to get the second number.
As, $4 \times 9 = 36$
Similarly $6 \times 4 = 24$
Hence, option (c) is correct.

8. Here, $24 / 2 = 12$
and $12 + 2 = 14$
Similarly, $32 / 2 = 16$
and $16 + 2 = 18$
Hence, option (b) is correct.

9. As, $423539 - 1000 = 422539$
Similarly,
$253682 - 1000 = 252682$
Hence, option (b) is correct.

10. In each pair, the second number is the square of first number.
As, $5^2 = 25$ and $6^2 = 36$
Similarly, $7^2 = 49$
Hence, option (a) is correct.

11. In each pair, digits of the first number are reversed to obtain the second number. Upon reversing the digits of 929, we get 929.
Hence, option (b) is correct.

12. As, $X \xrightarrow{+2} Z$, $W \xrightarrow{+2} Y$
Similarly, $D \xrightarrow{+2} \boxed{F}$, $J \xrightarrow{+2} \boxed{L}$
Hence, option (c) is correct.

13. As, $R \xrightarrow{-3} O$ Similarly, $K \xrightarrow{-3} \boxed{H}$
$Q \xrightarrow{-3} N$ $J \xrightarrow{-3} \boxed{G}$
$P \xrightarrow{-3} M$ $I \xrightarrow{-3} \boxed{F}$
Hence, option (b) is correct.

14. As, $B \xrightarrow{-1} A$, $A \xrightarrow{-1} B$, $D \xrightarrow{-1} C$
Similarly, $C \xrightarrow{-1} B$, $A \xrightarrow{-1} B$,
$T \xrightarrow{-1} S$
Hence, option (d) is correct.

15. As, $A \xrightarrow{+1} B$
$B \xrightarrow{+2} D$
$C \xrightarrow{+3} F$
Similarly, $\boxed{L} \xrightarrow{+1} M$
$\boxed{M} \xrightarrow{+2} O$
$\boxed{J} \xrightarrow{+3} M$
Hence, option (a) is correct.

16. As, $A \xrightarrow{+2} C$,
$B \xrightarrow{+2} D$
$C \xrightarrow{+2} E$
Similarly, $P \xrightarrow{+2} \boxed{R}$
$D \xrightarrow{+2} \boxed{F}$
$F \xrightarrow{+2} \boxed{H}$
Hence, option (b) is correct.

17. As, $C \xrightarrow{+5} H$, $A \xrightarrow{+5} F$,
$R \xrightarrow{+5} W$, $E \xrightarrow{+5} J$
Similarly, $G \xrightarrow{+5} L$, $O \xrightarrow{+5} T$,
$A \xrightarrow{+5} F$, $L \xrightarrow{+5} Q$
Hence, option (c) is correct.

18. The positional values of 'G' and 'M' in the English alphabetical order are 7 and 13, respectively. Thus, the given pair has been formed using these positional values. The only pair amongst the four given alternatives, which shows a similar relationship is (P*T, 16*20).
Hence, option (d) is correct.

19. 'A' is the first letter from the start of the English alphabet and 'Z' is the first letter from the end. Likewise, the letters 'C' and 'X' are present at the same position (i.e. 3rd) from the start and end, respectively. The third pair has the first letter as 'E', whose position is 5th from the start of the English alphabet. The missing letter is thus 'V', because its position is also 5th, but from the end.
Hence, option (b) is correct.

20. In each pair, the positional values of the letters are summed upto give the number.
As, $A = 1$, $B = 2$ and $1 + 2 = 3$
and $C = 3$, $D = 4$ and $3 + 4 = 7$
Similarly, $E = 5$, $F = 6$
and $5 + 6 = 11$
Hence, option (a) is correct.

21. Here in first pair, the letters in first group are reversed to obtain the second group of letters.
Similarly, reversing the letters HIJ, we get JIH.
Hence, option (a) is correct.

22. Here, the positional values of the letters in English alphabets are added to obtain the number.
As, $B = 2$, $D = 4$ and $2 + 4 = 6$
Similarly,
$L = 12$, $K = 11$ and $12 + 11 = 23$
Hence, option (b) is correct.

23. As, a helicopter is a type of an aircraft. Similarly, an almond is a type of a nut.
Hence, option (b) is correct.

24. Peacock is the national bird of India. In the same way, kangaroo is the national animal of Australia.
Hence, option (c) is correct.

25. Just as an engine is a part of a car, in the same way as lens is a part of a microscope.
Hence, option (d) is correct.

26. Pessimist is the opposite of optimist. Likewise, clean is the opposite of filthy.
Hence, option (a) is correct.

27. A car is a type of an automobile. Similarly, a cat is a type of an animal.
Hence, option (c) is correct.

28. As, a mother is a parent, in the same way a sister is a sibling.
Hence, option (b) is correct.

29. Someone who is a fool lacks wisdom. Likewise, someone who is a liar lacks honesty.
Hence, option (d) is correct.

30. As, potato is a kind of vegetable, similarly banana is a kind of fruit.
Hence, option (c) is correct.

31. Mind is used for thinking. Likewise, teeth are used for chewing.
Hence, option (b) is correct.

2 *What Comes Next?*

Letter Series

1. The pattern is as follows

$$C \xrightarrow{+4} G \xrightarrow{+4} K \xrightarrow{+4} O \xrightarrow{+4} \boxed{S}$$

Therefore, the next letter will be S.
Hence, option (c) is correct.

2. The pattern is as follows

Therefore, next letter will be H.
Hence, option (d) is correct.

3. The pattern is as follows

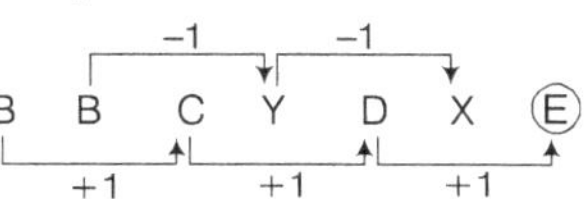

Therefore, next letter will be E.
Hence, option (b) is correct.

4. The pattern is as follows

$$A \xrightarrow{+2} C \xrightarrow{+3} F \xrightarrow{+4} J \xrightarrow{+5} \boxed{O}$$
$$B \xrightarrow{+3} E \xrightarrow{+4} I \xrightarrow{+5} N \xrightarrow{+6} \boxed{T}$$

Therefore, next term will be OT.
Hence, option (d) is correct.

5. The pattern is as follows

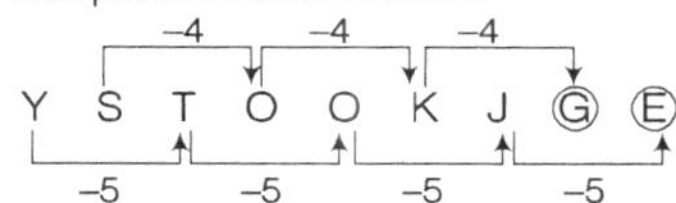

Therefore, next term will be MO.
Hence, option (b) is correct.

6. Here, the consecutive letters starting from B are given. The terms in the series have capital and small letters, alternately
So, the next two letters will be capital letters.
Therefore, the next term will be JK.
Hence, option (c) is correct.

7. The pattern is as follows

$$A \xrightarrow{+1} B \xrightarrow{+1} C \xrightarrow{+1} D \xrightarrow{+1} \boxed{E}$$
$$B \xrightarrow{+2} D \xrightarrow{+2} F \xrightarrow{+2} H \xrightarrow{+2} \boxed{J}$$
$$Z \xrightarrow{+1} A \xrightarrow{+1} B \xrightarrow{+1} C \xrightarrow{+1} \boxed{D}$$

Therefore, the next term will be EJD.
Hence, option (c) is correct.

8. The pattern is as follows

Therefore, the next two letters are G and E.
Hence, option (b) is correct.

9. The pattern is as follows

$$B \xrightarrow{+0} B \xrightarrow{+1} C \xrightarrow{+2} E \xrightarrow{+3} H \xrightarrow{+4} \boxed{L} \xrightarrow{+5} \boxed{Q}$$
$$A \xrightarrow{+0} A \xrightarrow{+1} B \xrightarrow{+2} D \xrightarrow{+3} G \xrightarrow{+4} \boxed{K} \xrightarrow{+5} \boxed{P}$$

Therefore, the missing terms will be LK and QP.
Hence, option (c) is correct.

10. The pattern is as follows

$$A \xrightarrow{+4} E \xrightarrow{+4} I \xrightarrow{+4} M \xrightarrow{+4} Q \xrightarrow{+4} \boxed{U} \xrightarrow{+4} \boxed{Y}$$
$$B \xrightarrow{+4} F \xrightarrow{+4} J \xrightarrow{+4} N \xrightarrow{+4} R \xrightarrow{+4} \boxed{V} \xrightarrow{+4} \boxed{Z}$$
$$D \xrightarrow{+4} H \xrightarrow{+4} L \xrightarrow{+4} P \xrightarrow{+4} T \xrightarrow{+4} \boxed{X} \xrightarrow{+4} \boxed{B}$$

Therefore, the missing terms will be UVX and YZB.
Hence, option (d) is correct.

11. The pattern of the series is follows

$$Y \xrightarrow{-1} X \xrightarrow{-1} W \xrightarrow{-1} V \xrightarrow{-1} \boxed{U} \xrightarrow{-1} \boxed{T}$$
$$B \xrightarrow{+2} D \xrightarrow{+2} F \xrightarrow{+2} H \xrightarrow{+2} \boxed{J} \xrightarrow{+2} \boxed{L}$$
$$I \xrightarrow{-1} H \xrightarrow{-1} G \xrightarrow{-1} F \xrightarrow{-1} \boxed{E} \xrightarrow{-1} \boxed{D}$$

So, the missing terms will be $\boxed{UJE}$ and $\boxed{TLD}$.
Hence, option (c) is correct.

Number Series

12. The pattern is as follows

$$9 \xrightarrow{+4} 13 \xrightarrow{+4} 17 \xrightarrow{+4} 21 \xrightarrow{+4} \boxed{25}$$

Therefore, the next number will be 25.
Hence, option (a) is correct.

13. The pattern is as follows

$$98 \xrightarrow{-8} 90 \xrightarrow{-8} 82 \xrightarrow{-8}$$
$$74 \xrightarrow{-8} \boxed{66}$$

Therefore, the next number will be 66.
Hence, option (d) is correct.

14. The pattern is as follows

$$400 \xrightarrow{\div 2} 200 \xrightarrow{\div 2} 100 \xrightarrow{\div 2} 50 \xrightarrow{\div 2} 25$$

Therefore, the next number will be 25.
Hence, option (a) is correct.

15. The pattern is as follows

$$2 \xrightarrow{\times 2} 4 \xrightarrow{\times 3} 12 \xrightarrow{\times 4} 48 \xrightarrow{\times 5} 240 \xrightarrow{\times 6} \boxed{1440}$$

Therefore, the next number will be 1440.
Hence, option (c) is correct.

16. Here, the consecutive prime numbers are given.
Therefore, the next prime number will be 17.
Hence, option (d) is correct.

17. The pattern is as follows

15 45 20 42 25 39 $\boxed{30}$

with -3 and $+5$ steps.

Therefore, the next number will be 30.
Hence, option (b) is correct.

18. The pattern is as follows

100 98 94 86 70 $\boxed{38}$

with $\times 2$ and $-2, -4, -8, -16, -32$ steps.

Therefore, the next number will be 38.
Hence, option (c) is correct.

19. The pattern is as follows

$$5 \xrightarrow{\times 5} 25 \xrightarrow{\times 5} 125 \xrightarrow{\times 5} 625 \xrightarrow{\times 5} \boxed{3125}$$

Therefore, the next number will be 3125.
Hence, option (c) is correct.

20. The pattern is as follows
$1 + 0 = 1, 1 + 1 = 2, 2 + 1 = 3,$
$3 + 2 = 5, 5 + 3 = 8, 8 + 5 = 13$
$13 + 8 = \boxed{21}$
Therefore, next term will be 21.
Hence, option (a) is correct.

21. The pattern is as follows

$$68 \xrightarrow{-12} 56 \xrightarrow{-10} 46 \xrightarrow{-8} 38 \xrightarrow{-6} 32 \xrightarrow{-4} \boxed{28}$$

So, 28 will be the next term.
Hence, option (c) is correct.

22. The series can be represented as

$$3 \xrightarrow{+6} 9 \xrightarrow{+12} 21 \xrightarrow{+24} 45 \xrightarrow{+48} \boxed{93}$$

with $\times 2$ steps.

So, 93 will be the next term.
Hence, option (c) is correct.

23. The pattern is as follows

4 16 36 $\boxed{64}$ 100

$(2)^2$ $(4)^2$ $(6)^2$ $(8)^2$ $(10)^2$

Hence, option (b) is correct.

24. The pattern is as follows

8 64 216 512 $\boxed{1000}$ 1728

$(2)^3$ $(4)^3$ $(6)^3$ $(8)^3$ $(10)^3$ $(12)^3$

Therefore, missing number will be 1000.
Hence, option (d) is correct.

25. The pattern is as follows

$$2004 \xrightarrow{+5} 2009 \xrightarrow{+7} 2016 \xrightarrow{+9}$$
$$2025 \xrightarrow{+11} 2036 \xrightarrow{+13} 2049$$
$$\xrightarrow{+15} 2064$$

Hence, option (d) is correct.

26. The pattern is as follows

$$8 \xrightarrow{-1} 7 \xrightarrow{-1} 6 \xrightarrow{-1} 5 \xrightarrow{-1} \boxed{4}$$
$$1 \xrightarrow{+1} 2 \xrightarrow{+1} 3 \xrightarrow{+1} 4 \xrightarrow{+1} \boxed{5}$$
$$9 \xrightarrow{-1} 8 \xrightarrow{-1} 7 \xrightarrow{-1} 6 \xrightarrow{-1} \boxed{5}$$
$$2 \xrightarrow{+1} 3 \xrightarrow{+1} 4 \xrightarrow{+1} 5 \xrightarrow{+1} \boxed{6}$$

Therefore, the next term will be 4556.
Hence, option (b) is correct.

27. Here, in each successive term a '0' is replaced with '8'.
Therefore, the next term will be 88888.
Hence, option (a) is correct.

28. The series can be represented as

$$6 \xrightarrow{+8} 14 \xrightarrow{+10} 24 \xrightarrow{+12} 36 \xrightarrow{+14} \boxed{50} \xrightarrow{+16} 66$$

So, 50 will be the missing term.
Hence, option (b) is correct.

29. The series can be represented as

$$1024 \xrightarrow{\div 4} 256 \xrightarrow{\div 4} 64 \xrightarrow{\div 4} 16 \xrightarrow{\div 4} 4$$

So, 16 will be the missing term.
Hence, option (a) is correct.

Alpha-Numeric Series

30. In the given series, addition of numbers in each term gives the place value of letter.
The pattern is as

$0 + 1 \longrightarrow 1$, place value of A

$1 + 1 \longrightarrow 2$, place value of B

$2 + 1 \longrightarrow 3$, place value of C

$2 + 2 \longrightarrow 4$, place value of D

$2 + 3 \longrightarrow 5$, place value of E

$3 + 3 \longrightarrow 6$, place value of F

$3 + 4 \longrightarrow 7$, place value of G

In each term, the letter is the next letter of previous one.
So, letter in next term will be G and place value of G is 7.
Hence, option (b) is correct.

31. The pattern is as follows

$$A \xrightarrow{+3} D \xrightarrow{+3} G \xrightarrow{+3} J \xrightarrow{+3} M \xrightarrow{+3} \boxed{P}$$
$$2 \xrightarrow{+3} 5 \xrightarrow{+3} 8 \xrightarrow{+3} 11 \xrightarrow{+3} 14 \xrightarrow{+3} \boxed{17}$$
$$C \xrightarrow{+3} F \xrightarrow{+3} I \xrightarrow{+3} L \xrightarrow{+3} O \xrightarrow{+3} \boxed{R}$$

Therefore, the next term will be P17R.
Hence, option (a) is correct.

32. The pattern is as follows

$$A \longrightarrow A \longrightarrow A \longrightarrow A \longrightarrow A \longrightarrow \boxed{A}$$
$$B \xrightarrow{+1} C \xrightarrow{+1} D \xrightarrow{+1} E \xrightarrow{+1} F \xrightarrow{+1} \boxed{G}$$

9 16 25 36 49 $\boxed{64}$

3^2 4^2 5^2 6^2 7^2 8^2

Therefore, the next term will be AG64.
Hence, option (d) is correct.

33. The pattern is as follows

$$A \xrightarrow{+1} B \xrightarrow{+2} D \xrightarrow{+3} G \xrightarrow{+4} K$$

$$100 \xrightarrow{+100} 200 \xrightarrow{+200} 400$$

$$\xrightarrow{+300} 700 \xrightarrow{+400} 1100$$

Therefore, the next term will be K1100.

Hence, option (d) is correct.

34. The pattern is as follows

$$B \xrightarrow{+2} D \xrightarrow{+2} F \xrightarrow{+2} \boxed{H} \xrightarrow{+2} J \xrightarrow{+2} \boxed{L}$$
$$5 \xrightarrow{+4} 9 \xrightarrow{+4} 13 \xrightarrow{+4} 17 \xrightarrow{+4} 21 \xrightarrow{+4} 25$$
$$C \xrightarrow{+2} E \xrightarrow{+2} G \xrightarrow{+2} \boxed{I} \xrightarrow{+2} K \xrightarrow{+2} M$$

Therefore, the missing terms will be H17I and L25 M.

Hence, option (b) is correct.

35. The pattern is as follows

$$D \xrightarrow{+2} F \xrightarrow{+2} H \xrightarrow{+2} J \xrightarrow{+2} \boxed{L}$$
$$E \xrightarrow{+2} G \xrightarrow{+2} I \xrightarrow{+2} K \xrightarrow{+2} M$$
$$9 \xrightarrow{+4} 13 \xrightarrow{+4} 17 \xrightarrow{+4} 21 \xrightarrow{+4} 25$$

Therefore, the next term will be LM 25.

Hence, option (a) is correct.

3 Odd One Out

Numbers Classification

1. Except 99, all others are perfect squares.

So, 99 is odd one.

Hence, option (c) is correct.

2. All other except 58, are divisible by 5.

So, 58 is odd one.

Hence, option (c) is correct.

3. 19, 13 and 31 are the prime numbers but 91 is not a prime number.

So, 91 is odd one.

Hence, option (b) is correct.

4. If there had been 14 in place of 15, then each number had been twice of its previous number as shown

$14 = 7 \times 2$; $28 = 14 \times 2$

and $56 = 28 \times 2$

So, 15 does not belong to the given set of numbers.

Hence, option (b) is correct.

5. Except 1346, in all the other numbers, each successive digit is greater than its preceding digit by 2. In 2468, we have

$4 = 2 + 2$; $6 = 4 + 2$ and $8 = 6 + 2$.

Similar pattern holds for 1357 and 3579, but not for 1346.

So, 1346 is odd one.

Hence, option (d) is correct.

6. 34<u>5</u>, 365, 380, 30<u>5</u>

Here, every number has 5 at its unit's place.

Hence, option (c) is correct.

7. Except 221, the sum of digits of all the other numbers give a perfect square.

$169 : 1 + 6 + 9 = 16 = 4^2$;

As, $961 : 9 + 6 + 1 = 16 = 4^2$

and $400 : 4 + 0 + 0 = 4 = 2^2$

But $221 : 2 + 2 + 1 = 5$,

which is not a perfect square.

Hence, option (a) is correct.

8. Here, in all options, except option (b) the sum of digits is 10.

As, $7 + 3 = 10$,

$6 + 4 = 10$ and $5 + 5 = 10$

But $8 + 1 = 9 \neq 10$

So, 81 is odd one.

Hence, option (b) is correct.

9. All the given numbers are perfect cubes, but 63 is the only number which is not a perfect cube.

So, 63 is odd one.

Hence, option (c) is correct.

10. Here, all the numbers have odd sum except option (d)

$3002 = 3 + 0 + 0 + 2 = 5$

$4003 = 4 + 0 + 0 + 3 = 7$

$5004 = 5 + 0 + 0 + 4 = 9$

But $6006 = 6 + 0 + 0 + 6 = 12$

So, 6006 is odd one.

Hence, option (d) is correct

Letters Classification

11. Except DCB, all other letter's groups contain one vowel and two consonants. In DCB, all the three letters are consonants.

So, the letters' group DCB is odd one.

Hence, option (c) is correct.

12. In each letter group except DG, one letter is skipped in between the two letters.

So, the letters' group DG is odd one.

Hence, option (c) is correct.

13. Except in DDD, each letter is repeated as many times as its position in the English alphabet.

So, DDD is odd one.

Hence, option (c) is correct.

14. In each letters' group except DON, the letters when read from backward (i.e. the right end) form a group of three consecutive letters.

Hence, option (d) is correct.

15. Except MY, in each letters' group, the second letter is present at the same position as that of the first letter, but from the end of the English alphabet.

HS : H = 8th, S = 19th

(8th from the end)

LO : L = 12th, O = 15th

(12th from the end)

VE : V = 22nd, E = 5th

(22nd from the end)

But MY : M = 13th

and Y = 25th (2nd from the end)

Hence, option (b) is correct.

16. The pattern is as follows

$$M \overset{-1}{\underset{}{\longrightarrow}} L \quad T \overset{-1}{\underset{}{\longrightarrow}} S \quad J \overset{-1}{\underset{}{\longrightarrow}} I$$

But

$$B \overset{+1}{\underset{}{\longrightarrow}} C$$

So, the letters' group BC is odd one.

Hence, option (d) is correct.

17. In each pair except 23G, the sum of the digits gives the positional value of the letter written alongside.

2 + 1 = 3 (C); 1 + 3 = 4 (D);
3 + 3 = 6 (F)
But 2 + 3 = 5, which represents E and not G.
So, 23G is odd one.
Hence, option (d) is correct.

18. All the letters' group, except CDWX, have atleast one vowel, while group CDWX does not have any vowel.

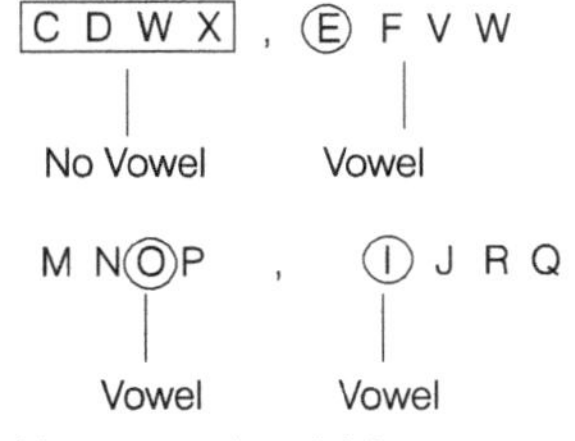

Hence, option (a) is correct.

19. In each group, except option (a), the product of numbers gives a letter at its corresponding position in the English alphabets.
$3 \times 2 = 6$ (F), $5 \times 3 = 15$ (O)
$7 \times 1 = 7$ (G), but $2 \times 2 = 4$ (D)
Hence, option (a) is correct.

20. The pattern is as follows

F K   P H   M R   L   P U
  +5   +5   +5   +5   +4   +5

and

D I   N
  +5   +5

It is clear that, all the letters' group except LPU, follow similar pattern. But LPU follow different pattern. So, LPU is odd one.
Hence, option (c) is correct.

21. Except PUT, in all other groups the first letter is the vowel.
Hence, option (b) is correct.

Words Classification

22. Except colour, all others are types of colour.
Hence, option (c) is correct.

23. Except Umbrella, all others are garments.
Hence, option (c) is correct.

24. Except June, all other months have 31 days.
Hence, option (a) is correct.

25. Except Rule, all other words end with 'ool'.
Hence, option (b) is correct.

26. Except Today, all others are week days.
Hence, option (b) is correct.

27. All except Turnip are fruits. Turnip is a vegetable.
Hence, option (a) is correct.

28. All except 'FAN' are appliances used for getting light.
Hence, option (b) is correct.

29. Plate is an item of crockery, whereas all others are cutlery items.
Hence, option (c) is correct.

30. Except Lungs, all the others are external body parts.
Hence, option (b) is correct.

31. All except Beijing are countries. Beijing is the capital of People's Republic of China.
Hence, option (d) is correct.

32. A bicycle is moved by pedals while all others are motorised vehicles.
Hence, option (c) is correct.

33. All except Rabbit are carnivores (flesh eating animals), whereas rabbit is a herbivore.
Hence, option (a) is correct.

4 Coding-Decoding

1. As,

1 2 3 4   3 1 4 2
B E A N ⟹ A B N E

and
1 2 3 4   3 1 4 2
S A L F ⟹ L S E A

1 2 3 4
Similarly, N E W S ⟹

3 1 4 2
W N S E

Hence, option (d) is correct.

2. As,
H E A L T H
 −1 −1 −1 −1 −1 −1
G D Z K S G

Similarly,
N O R T H
 −1 −1 −1 −1 −1
M N Q S G

Hence, option (d) is correct.

3. As,
C   O   R   D   I   A   L
 +2 −1 +2 −1 +2 −1 +2
E   N   T   C   K   Z   N

Similarly,
S   O   M   E   D   A   Y
 +2 −1 +2 −1 +2 −1 +2
U   N   O   D   F   Z   A

Hence, option (a) is correct.

4. As,
C A L A N D E R

C L A N A E D R

Similarly,
C I R C U L A R
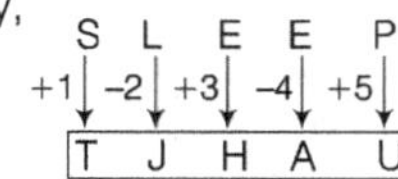
C R I U C A L R

Hence, option (d) is correct.

5. Here, letters are coded by numbers as
From BAKE, we get
B → 5, A → 7, K → 9, E → 6
From FIRE, we get
F → 3, I → 1, R → 4, E → 6
Therefore, FEAR → 3674.
Hence, option (b) is correct.

6. As,
A   M   O   N   G
 +1 −2 +3 −4 +5
B   K   R   J   L

Similarly,
S   L   E   E   P
 +1 −2 +3 −4 +5
T   J   H   A   U

Hence, option (b) is correct.

7. Here, we find that, first and third letters are coded by symbols and second and fourth letters are coded by numbers.
So, the code of T is 8 and for R is 7. Therefore, the code for JRKT will be ★7%8.
Hence, option (b) is correct.

8. Here, numbers are code by letters as
From 1352, we get
$1 \to D, 3 \to E, 5 \to A, 2 \to R$
From 2693, we get
$2 \to R, 6 \to O, 9 \to P, 3 \to E$
Therefore, 9352 is coded as PEAR.
Hence, option (c) is correct.

9. As, 

Similarly,

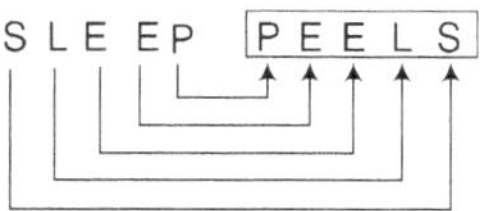

Hence, option (c) is correct

10. Letters are coded by symbols as

Letters	R	A	I	D	P	E
Symbols	%	#	©	$	@	★

Therefore, DEAR is coded as $★ #%.
Hence, option (a) is correct.

11. As,
R E S A N O
+1 +1 +1
S 1 T 2 O 3

Similarly,
M O R A L E
+1 +1 +1
N 3 S 2 M 1

Hence, option (d) is correct.

12. Here, we see that the given word is coded as
G A R D E N
↓ ↓ ↓ ↓ ↓ ↓
M g f v T S

Therefore, the READ will coded as fTgv.
Hence, option (a) correct.

13. Here,
letter's positional value $\times 2$ i.e,
$A \to 1 \times 2 = 2, D \to 4 \times 2 = 8,$
$K \to 11 \times 2 = 22,$
and
T E N
↓ ↓ ↓
40 + 10 + 28 = 78
Therefore, $B = 2 \times 2 \to 4$, $E = 5 \times 2 \to 10$, $L = 12 \times 2 \to 24$
So, code for BEL is $4 + 10 + 24 = 38$
Hence, option (c) is correct.

14. Here, number of letters in the word -1 i.e. MORALE $= 6 - 1 = 5$
and CHARCOAL $= 8 - 1 = 7$
So, GOVERNMENT $= 10 - 1 = 9$
Hence, option (d) is correct.

15. As,

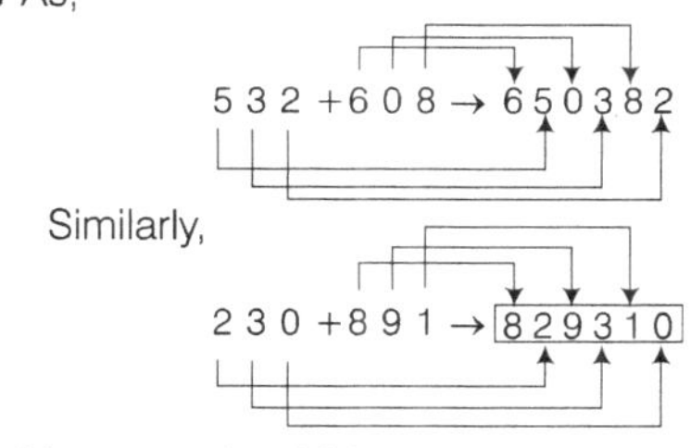

Similarly,

$2 \ 3 \ 0 + 8 \ 9 \ 1 \to 8 \ 2 \ 9 \ 3 \ 1 \ 0$

Hence, option (d) is correct.

16. We know that, colour of milk is white. But in the given code white is coded as blue. So, the colour of milk is blue.
Hence, option (c) is correct.

17. We know that fruits grow on 'tree' and here 'tree' is called 'sky'.So, the fruits grow on the 'sky'.
Hence, option (c) is correct.

Solution (Q. Nos. 18-19)
ho (na) ta $\longrightarrow$ food is (good) ... (i)
Sa ta la $\longrightarrow$ eat food regularly ... (ii)
da (na) ja $\longrightarrow$ keep (good) health ... (iii)

18. From Eqs. (i) and (ii), food is common in both (i) and (ii) and code ta is also common in both (i) and (ii).
So, code for food is ta.
Hence, option (b) is correct.

19. From statements (i) and (ii), 'ta' is common and also word 'food is common. From statements (i) and (iii), 'na' is common and also word 'good' is common.
So, 'ta' means food and 'na' means good. Therefore, from statement (i), food is good will be coded as 'ta ho na'.
Hence, option (a) is correct.

20. According to the question,
2 5 6 $\longrightarrow$ you are (good) ...(i)
6 3 7 $\longrightarrow$ we are bad ...(ii)
3 5 8 $\longrightarrow$ (good) and bad ...(iii)

It is clear that, in first and third statements the common digit is 5 and the common word is 'good'.
In second and third statements,the common code digit is 3 and the common word is bad.
So, '5' means good and '3' means bad.
Therefore, from the third statement 'and means '8'.
Hence, option (c) is correct'.

5 *Jumbled Words*

1. On rearranging the words, we get option (a) MOUSE, option (b) BANANA, option (c) PURPLE and option (d) ELEVEN.
Among all these words, only 'ELEVEN' is a number.
Hence, option (d) is correct.

2. On rearranging the words, we get option (a) TWICE, option (b) THRICE, option (c) SQUARE and option (d) DOUBLE.
Among all these words, only 'THRICE' means the same as 'three times'.
Hence, option (b) is correct.

3. On rearranging the words, we get option (a) MANGO, option (b) RADISH, option (c) BEAR and option (d) ORANGE.
Among these, only 'RADISH' is a vegetable.
Hence, option (b) is correct.

4. On rearranging the words, we get option (a) GRAM, option (b) HOUR, option (c) METRE and option (d) BYTE.
Among these, only 'GRAM' is a unit of measurement for weight.
Hence, option (a) is correct.

5. On rearranging the words, we get option (a) SUNDAY, option (b) SILVER, option (c) BRAIN and option (d) DOLLAR.
Among these, only 'BRAIN' represents a body part.
Hence, option (c) is correct.

6. On rearranging the words, we get option (a) PAPER, option (b) RUBBER, option (c) SCALE and option (d) GLUE. Among these, 'GLUE' is a substance used for sticking objects.
Hence, option (d) is correct.

7. On rearranging the words, we get option (a) TABLE, option (b) MOUSE, option (c) TOFFEE and option (d) PEN.
Among these, only 'MOUSE' is a part of computer.
Hence, option (b) is correct.

8. On rearranging the words, we get option (a) S3HIP, option (b) TRAIN, option (c) PLANE and option (d) TRUCK.

Among these, only 'SHIP' is a means of water transport.
Hence, option (a) is correct.

9. On rearranging the words, we get option (a) HIDF, option (b) WHITE, option (c) BRIGHT and option (d) BLACK. Among these only, 'BRIGHT' is the opposite of dark.
Hence, option (c) is correct.

10. On rearranging the words, we get option (a) CRICKET, option (b) HOCKEY, option (c) CHESS and option (d) TENNIS.
Among these, only 'CHESS' is an indoor game.
Hence, option (c) is correct.

11. On rearranging the words, we get option (a) MUMBAI , option (b) FRANCE, option (c) LONDON, and option (d) PARIS. Among all these words, only 'FRANCE' is a country.
Hence, option (b) is correct

12. On rearranging the words, we get option (a) DIAMOND, option (b) CHINA, option (c) JUPITER and option (d) BOARD.
Among all these , only 'JUPITER' is a planet.
Hence, option (c) is correct.

13. On rearranging the words, we get option (a) UGLY, option (b) WEAK, option (c) FOOLISH and option (d) BRILLIANT.
Among all these words, only 'BRILLIANT' is the synonym of intelligent.
Hence, option (d) is correct.

14. On rearranging the words, we get option (a) BANANA, option (b) DARK, option (c) YELLOW and option (d) BLANK.

Among these, only 'YELLOW' is a name of a colour.
Hence, option (c) is correct.

15. On rearranging the words, we get option (a) MARCH, option (b) SUNDAY, option (c) ORANGE and option (d) LIGHT.
Among these only 'MARCH' is a name of a Month.
Hence, option (a) is correct.

16. On rearranging the words, we get option (a) OCTOBER, option (b) RAINY, option (c) SQUARE and option (d) SHIMLA.
Among these, only 'RAINY' is a kind of season.
Hence, option (b) is correct.

17. On rearranging the words, we get option (a) NURSE, option (b) TEACHER, option (c) PEON and option (d) DOCTOR.
Among all these, only 'TEACHER' is a person who teaches.
Hence, option (b) is correct.

18. On rearranging the words, we get option (a) SCALE, option (b) PENCIL, option (c) CIRCLE and option (d) WHITE.
Among all these, only CIRCLE, is a geometrical shape.
Hence, option (c) is correct.

19. Only 'GUAVA' can be formed from the letters given in square.
Hence, option (d) is correct.

20. Only 'GOA' can be formed from the letters given in square.
Hence, option (b) is correct.

6 *Mathematical Reasoning*

1. In each row, middle number = (sum of the two outer numbers)/2
In row I, $(6 + 8)/2 = 7$
In row II, $(10 + 22)/2 = 16$
Similarly, in row III, $(8 + 6)/2 = 7$
Hence, option (a) is correct.

2. In figure I, $(10 + 15 + 5)/10$
$= 30/10 = 3$
In figure II, $(18 + 11 + 11)/10$
$= 40/10 = 4$
Similarly, in figure III,
$(19 + 20 + 21)/10 = 60/10 = 6$
Hence, option (b) is correct.

3. Here, the number written on the left side of the line is the square of the of the number written on right side.
As, $1^2 = 1$ and $5^2 = 25$
Similarly, $9^2 = 81$
Hence, option (b) is correct.

4. In figure I,

$16 + 20 = 36$ and $36 + 4 = 40$

In figure II,

$25 + 21 = 46$ and $46 + 4 = 50$

Similarly, in figure III,

$$32 + 23 = 55$$

and $\quad 55 + 4 = 59$

Hence, option (d) is correct.

5. In figure I,

$(2 \times 9) - (3 \times 6) = 18 - 18 = 0$

In figure II,

$(2 \times 11) - (5 \times 4) = 22 - 20 = 2$

Similarly, in figure III.

$(7 \times 7) - (8 \times 6) = 49 - 48 = 1$

Hence, option (c) is correct.

6. Here, the addition of the numbers written in circles gives the positional value of the letter written in square as shown below

$1 + 3 = 4(D), 5 + 4 = 9(I)$

Similarly, $11 + 10 = 21$

So, 'U' is the missing letter.

Hence, option (d) is correct.

7. In figure I,

$(2 \times 4) + (5 \times 3) = 8 + 15 = 23$

In figure II,

$(1 \times 6) + (8 \times 4) = 6 + 32 = 38$

Similarly, in figure III,

$$(3 \times 7) + (11 \times 2) = 21 + 22$$
$$= 43$$

Hence, option (a) is correct.

8. In each figure, the numbers inside the box are multiplied to give the number outside.

Box 1 : $2 \times 6 \times 5 \times 1 = 60$

Box 2 : $3 \times 5 \times 2 \times 4 = 120$

Similarly,

Box 3 : $5 \times 5 \times 4 \times 4 = 400$

Hence, option (b) is correct.

9. Here, the letters follow the pattern given below

Considering exercise

In row I, A $\xrightarrow{+6}$ G $\xrightarrow{+6}$ M

In row II, C $\xrightarrow{+6}$ I $\xrightarrow{+6}$ [O]

In row III, E $\xrightarrow{+6}$ K $\xrightarrow{+6}$ Q

Considering columnwise in column I,

$$A \xrightarrow{+2} C \xrightarrow{+2} E$$

In column II,

$$G \xrightarrow{+2} I \xrightarrow{+2} K$$

In column III,

$$M \xrightarrow{+2} [O] \xrightarrow{+2} Q$$

So, 'O' will replace the question mark.

Hence, option (a) is correct.

10. The letters A, B and C appear once in each row and column.

Also, in each row, addition of 1 to the product of the first and the third number gives the second number.

So, the missing letter is 'B' and the missing number is 33, so that

$$(33 \times 1) + 1 = 34$$

Therefore, the middle number in the third row is 34.

The missing entry is thus 33B.

Hence, option (d) is correct.

11. In figure I, $(9 \times 3) + 3 = 30$

In figure III, $(7 \times 8) + 4 = 60$

Similarly, in figure II,

$(8 \times 2) + 4 = X \implies X = 20$

$\therefore X^2 - 1 = 20^2 - 1$

$$= 400 - 1 = 399$$

Hence, option (b) is correct.

12. In left semi-circle, moving anti-clockwise starting from 7 and in right semi-circle, moving clockwise starting from G, each number represents the postitional value in english alphabetical order of the coressponding letter.

So, the positional value of Q i.e. 17 will be the missing number.

Hence, option (b) is correct.

13. Here,

In row I, Z $\xrightarrow{-2}$ X $\xrightarrow{-2}$ V

In row II, A $\xrightarrow{+2}$ C $\xrightarrow{+2}$ [E]

In row III, T $\xrightarrow{-2}$ R $\xrightarrow{-2}$ P

So, 1st column,

$$2 \xrightarrow{+1} 3 \xrightarrow{+1} 4$$

In column II,

$$19 \xrightarrow{-1} 18 \xrightarrow{-1} 17$$

In column III $66 \xrightarrow{+1} [67]$

$$\xrightarrow{+1} 68$$

So, the missing number is E_{67}.

Hence, option (c) is correct.

14. As,

$(2 \times 2) - 1 = 3, \qquad (3 \times 2) - 1 = 5$

$(5 \times 2) - 1 = 9$

Similarly, $(9 \times 2) - 1 = 17$

Here, option (b) is correct.

15. We have, $24 + 2 \times 4 \div 6 - 3$

On substituting the signs, we get $\quad 24 \times 2 - 4 + 6 \div 3$

Simplify the above expression using BODMAS rule,

$$24 \times 2 - 4 + 6 \div 3$$
$$= 24 \times 2 - 4 + 2 = 48 - 4 + 2$$
$$= 50 - 4 = 46$$

Hence, option (b) is correct.

16. We have, $92 \times 12 + 7 - 4 \div 21$

On substituting the signs, we get $= 92 - 12 \times 7 \div 4 + 21$

Simplify the above expression using BODMAS rule,

$$92 - 12 \times 7 \div 4 + 21$$
$$92 - 12 \times \frac{7}{4} + 21$$
$$= 92 - 12 \times 1.75 + 21$$
$$= 92 - 21 + 21 = 113 - 21 = 92$$

Hence, option (b) is correct.

17. We have, $5 \times 4 \div 6 + 5 - 4$

On substituting the signs, we get $5 - 4 + 6 \times 5 \div 4$

Simplify the above expression using BODMAS rule,

$$5 - 4 + 6 \times 5 \div 4$$
$$= 5 - 4 + 6 \times \frac{5}{4} = 5 - 4 + 6 \times 1.25$$
$$= 5 - 4 + 7.5 = 12.5 - 4 = 8.5$$

Hence, option (c) is correct.

18. We have, 12d 8c 10a 14b 7

On substituting the mathematical operators for the given signs, we get

$$12 + 8 \times 10 - 14 \div 7$$

Simplify the above expression using BODMAS rule,

$$12 + 8 \times 10 - 14 \div 7$$
$$= 12 + 8 \times 10 - 2$$
$$= 12 + 80 - 2 = 92 - 2 = 90$$

Hence, option (d) is correct.

19. We have,

$1 \uparrow 41 \leftarrow 5 \uparrow 37 \downarrow 91 \rightarrow 7$

On substituting the mathematical operators for the given signs, we get

$1 + 41 \times 5 + 37 - 91 \div 7$

Simplify the above expression using BODMAS rule,

$$1 + 41 \times 5 + 37 - 91 \div 7$$
$$= 1 + 41 \times 5 + 37 - 13$$
$$= 1 + 205 + 37 - 13 = 243 - 13$$
$$= 230$$

Hence, option (c) is correct.

20. Here, the rule applied is
$$x * y = x^y$$
As, $2 * 3 = 2^3 = 8$, $3 * 2 = 3^2 = 9$
and $5 * 1 = 5^1 = 5$
Similarly, $4 * 3 = 4^3 = 64$
Hence, option (b) is correct.

21. Here, '#' means $\div$, $x \# y = x \div y$
As, $56 \# 14 = 4 = 56 \div 14$
and '~' means '−', $x \sim y = y - x$
As, $34 \sim 54 = 20 = 54 - 34$
Therefore, $98 \# (90 \sim 139)$
$= 98 \div (139 - 90) = 98 \div 49 = 2$
Hence, option (a) is correct.

22. As, $6 \times 5 = 6 \times 5 + 1 = 31$
$7 \times 8 = 7 \times 8 + 1 = 57$
and $3 \times 4 = 3 \times 4 + 1 = 13$
similarly, $9 \times 10 = 9 \times 10 + 1 = 91$
Hence, option (b) is correct.

23. Given, $18 + 6 = 3$
So, $18 \div 6 = 3$
which means '+' stands for '$\div$'.
$34 \div 14 = 20$
So, $34 - 14 = 20$
which means '$\div$' stands for '−'.
$23 - 4 = 92$ So, $23 \times 4 = 92$
which means '−' stands for '$\times$'
$13 \times 14 = 27$.
So, $13 + 14 = 27$
which means '$\times$' stands for '+'.
Therefore, $4 \times 9 + 3 - 6 \div 10$
$= 4 + 9 \div 3 \times 6 - 10$
$= 4 + 3 \times 6 - 10$
$= 4 + 18 - 10 = 22 - 10 = 12$
Hence, option (d) is correct.

24. Here, the rule applied is
$$x \bullet y = x - y$$
As, $27 - 19 = 8$ and $43 - 29 = 14$
Therefore, $54 \bullet 56 \bullet 55$
$= 54 - 56 - 55 = -2 - 55 = -57$
Hence, option (c) is correct.

25. From option (b), after interchanging the signs the equation will be
$$25 \times 5 + 50 \div 2 - 10$$
$= 125 + 25 - 10 = 150 - 10 = 140$
Hence, option (b) is correct.

26. From option (a), applying the interchanges, the equation will be
$4 \times 2 + 5 \implies 8 + 5 = 13$
Hence, option (a) is correct.

27. From option (b), applying the interchanges, the equation will be
$$\text{LHS} = 66 \div 3 \times 11 - 12$$
$$= 22 \times 11 - 12$$
$$= 242 - 12$$
$$= 230 = \text{RHS}$$
Hence, option (b) is correct.

28. On applying the interchanges given in option (a), we get
$$\text{LHS} = 52 + 38 - 88$$
$$= 90 - 88$$
$$= 2 = \text{RHS}$$
Hence, option (a) is correct.

29. Given, $P \times Q + R \div S$
Now, on putting the value of the letters, we get
$$8 \times 5 + 14 \div 7 = 8 \times 5 + 2$$
$$= 40 + 2$$
$$= 42$$
Hence, option (c) is correct.

7 Puzzle Test

Solution (Q. Nos 1-2) As per the given information, the data will arrange as shown below.

	Intelligent	Hard-working	Honers	Ambitions
Kailash	✓	✓	✗	✓
Govind	✓	✗	✗	✓
Harinder	✓	✗	✓	✗
Rajesh	✗	✓	✓	✗
Jitendra	✗	✓	✓	✗

1. From the above table, we find that Harinder is neither hardworking nor ambitious.
Hence, option (c) is correct.

2. From the above table, we find that Govind is neither honest nor hard working, but is ambitious.
Hence, option (b) is correct.

Solution (Q. Nos. 3-5) As per the given information, the data will arrange as shown below

Teachers Subjects	A	B	C	D	E
Hindi	✓	✓	✗	✓	✗
English	✓	✓	✓	✗	✗
Mathematics	✓	✗	✗	✓	✗
History	✗	✓	✗	✗	✓
French	✗	✓	✗	✗	✓
Geography	✗	✓	✓	✗	✗

3. From the above table, it is clear that B is teaching maximum number of subjects.
Hence, option (b) is correct.

4. From the above table, it is clear that Hindi and English are taught by more than two teachers.
Hence, option (d) is correct.

5. From the above table, it is clear that teachers D, B and A teach the Hindi subject only.
Hence, option (c) is correct.

Solution (Q. Nos. 6-8) As per the given information, the data will arranged as shown below.

6. From the above arrangement, it is clear that Rani is in the middle position on the bench.
Hence, option (b) is correct.

7. From the above arrangement, it is clear that Seema is second from the left end of the bench.
Hence, option (d) is correct.

8. From the above arrangement, it is clear that Reeta is second from right end.
Hence, option (c) is correct.

Solution (Q. Nos. 9-10) As per the given information, circle will arranged as show below

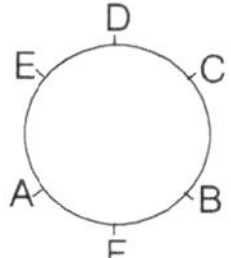

9. From the above figure, it is clear that the neighbours of B are C and F.
Hence, option (b) is correct.

10. From the above figure, it is clear that F is second to the right of E.
Hence, option (c) is correct.

8 Number, Ranking and Alphabet Test

1. Here, first we consider the first letter of each word and then arrange the words in the order, in which the letters appear in the dictionary.
War, Wasp, Waste, Wrist
It is clear that, war comes first.
Hence, option (d) is correct.

2. The words can be arranged as
Afford, After, Answer, Avoid
Here, we see that, answer will come on second position from right side.
Hence, option (c) is correct.

3. Clearly, the given letters when arranged in the order of 4, 2, 1, 6, 5, 3, form a word 'HANDLE'.
Hence, option (b) is correct.

4. Clearly, the given letter when arranged in the order of 4, 2, 6, 5, 3, 1 from a word 'THRONE'.
Hence, option (b) is correct.

5. As per the question, the letters are arranged in reverse order as shown below

```
        ←——16——→
ZYXWVUTSRQPONMLKJIHGFEDCBA
   ←———12———→
```

It is clear that, W is at 12th position from left of the sixteenth letter from left end.
Hence, option (c) is correct.

6. ZYXWUTSRQPONMLKJIHGFED CBA
From the above series, we can see that the thirteenth letter to the right end is M.
Hence, option (a) is correct.

7. 8 9 7 6 3 4 2 8 9 7 6 4 5 9 2 9 7
From the given number sequence, it is clear that there are two 7's which are preceded by 9 and followed by 6.
Hence, option (a) is correct.

8. 8 9 7 6 3 4 2 8 9 7 6 4 5 9 2 9 7
There are three 9's which are preceded by even numbers.
Hence, option (d) is correct.

9. On interchanging the positions of numbers we get,
913, 904, 814, 917
It is clear that, 418 is the least number.
Hence, option (c) is correct.

10. The logical sequence of the words are
Seed, Plant, Tree, Wood, Table
i.e. 5   4   3   2   1
Hence, option (b) is correct.

11. The logical sequence of the words are
infancy, childhood, puberty, Adulthood, senescence.
i.e. 2   4   1   3   5
Hence, option (a) is correct.

12. ∴ Total number of students
= (Position from the top)
+ (Position from the bottom) − Sohan itself
= 7 + 26 − 1
= 32
∴ The total number of students in class = 32
Hence, option (b) is correct.

13. After shifting two places towards left Rohan become 7th from the left end, it means Rohan's earlier position from the left end
= 7 + 2 = 9 th
So, Rohan's earlier position from the right end = 10 − 9 + 1 = 2nd

From left ⊢———2nd ←——⊣ 1st From right
        ⊢———→ 9th
     1st

Hence, option (b) is correct.

14. Rohit obtained more marks than Tarun, but less than Kabir.
Kabir > Rohit > Tarun
Raj obtained more than Vansh, but less than Harshit i.e. Harshit > Raj > Vansh
Now, Kabir obtained less than Vansh i.e.
Harshit > Raj > Vansh > Kabir > Rohit > Tarun

Clearly, Harshit obtained the highest marks.
Hence, option (b) is correct.

15. Mohit is older than Rajesh and Raman i.e.

Mohit > Rajesh/ Raman   ...(i)

Namit is older tahn Rajesh, but younger than Rajeev. Raman is older than Rajeev i.e.

Raman > Rajeev > Namit
      > Rajesh ... (ii)

From Eqs. (i) and (ii), we get

Mothi > Raman > Rajeev > Namit > Rajesh
Clearly, Mohit is oldest.
Hence, option (c) is correct.

9   *Direction Sense Test*

1. 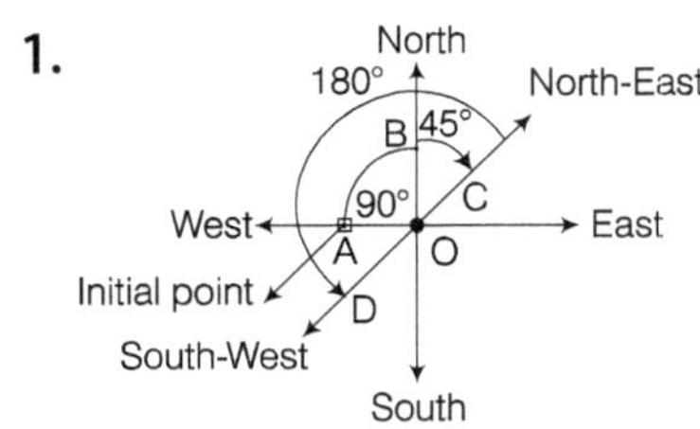

From the above figure, it is clear that Vikas initially faces in direction West. On moving 90° clockwise, he faces in the North direction.

On further moving 45° clockwise, he faces in the North East direction. Finally, on moving 180° anti-clockwise, he faces in the South-West direction.

Hence, option (b) is correct.

2. 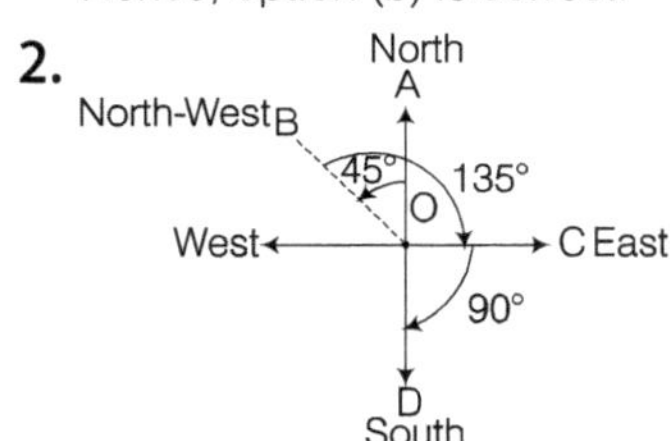

From the above figure, it is clear that Kamal initially faces in the North direction. On moving 45° anti-clockwise, he faces in North-West direction. On further moving 135° clockwise, he faces in the East. Finally, on moving 90° clockwise, he faces in the South direction .

Hence, option (d) is correct.

3. 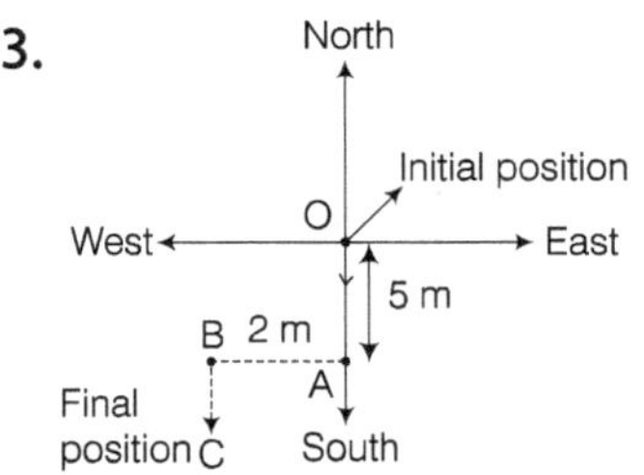

From the above figure, it is clear that Seema initially faces in the South direction.

On moving right, she walked 2 m from A to B i.e. West. Finally, she took left turn and is facing South.

Hence, option (a) is correct.

4. 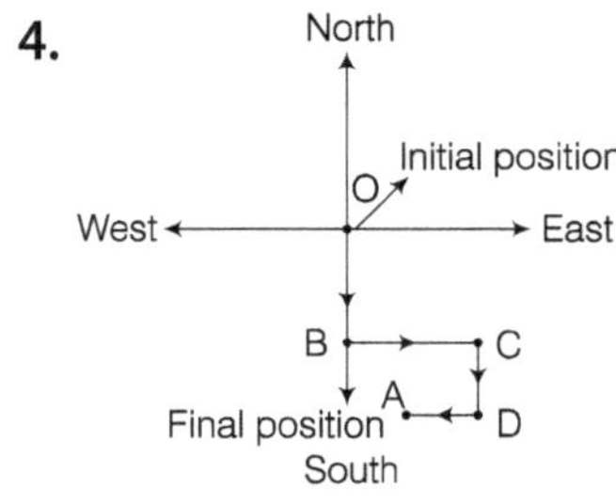

From the above figure, it is clear that initially you are moving from O to B i.e. South. On turning left you are moving in the direction B to C i.e. East.

On further turning right you are moving in the direction C to D i.e. South. Finally, on turning right, you are moving in the direction D to A i.e. West.

Hence, option (b) is correct.

5. Each direction moves 45° anti-clockwise direction. So, East is called South-East.

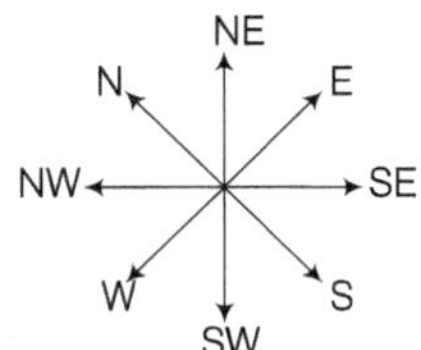

Hence, option (c) is correct.

6. 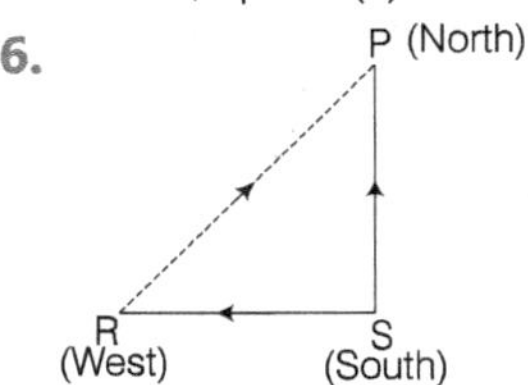

Clearly, P is in North-East direction with respect to R.
Hence, option (b) is correct.

7. 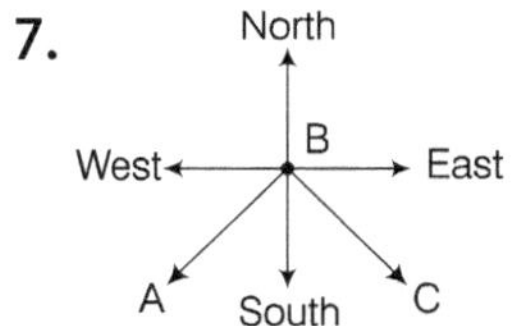

Clearly, C is to the East of A.
Hence, option (b) is correct.

8. 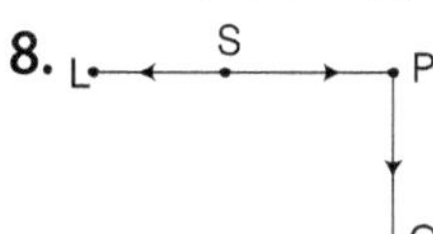

Clearly, L is in the West direction with respect to P.
Hence, option (b) is correct.

9. 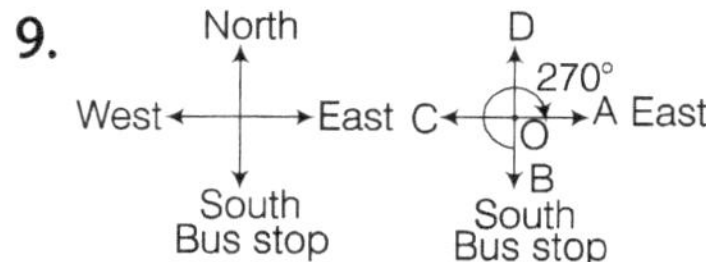

In the above figure, it is clear that, Kavita faces initially to OB i.e. South direction. To face East i.e. OA she initially moves to 90° clockwise i.e. OC, then next move to 90° clockwise i.e. OD and finally to 90° clockwise i.e. OA. So, to reach the East direction she moved, 90° + 90° + 90° = 270° Hence, option (c) is correct.

10. 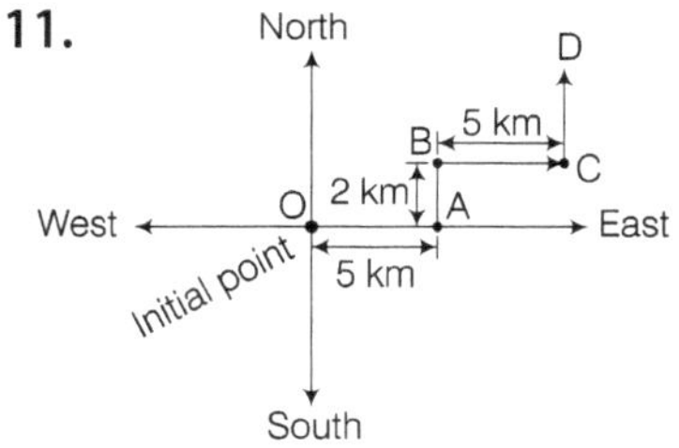

From the above figure, it is clear that ship initially is sailing in South-East. On turning 135° anti-clockwise, it is sailing in the North. Finally, on turning 225° clockwise, it is sailing in South-West.
Hence, option (c) is correct.

11. 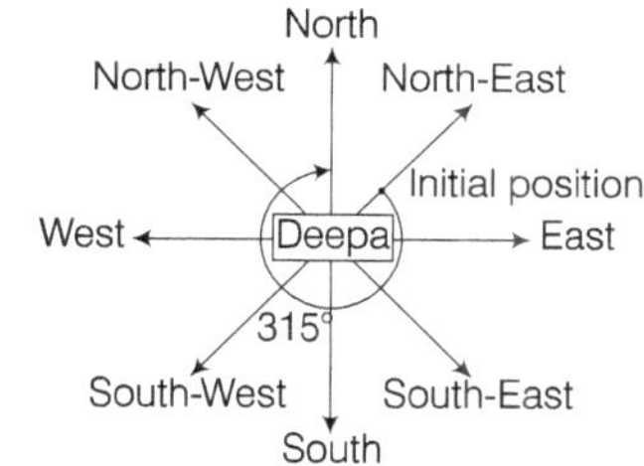

From the above figure, it is clear that the initial position of Raju is O and he walked 5 km towards East. On moving A to B, he walked 2 km. On further moving from B to C, he walked. 5 km. Finally, he turns to left facing the North direction.
Hence, option (c) is correct.

12. To know the starting position of Deepa, we turned back to 315° clockwise from North-East.

So, Deepa was facing North at the start.
Hence, option (c) is correct.

13. 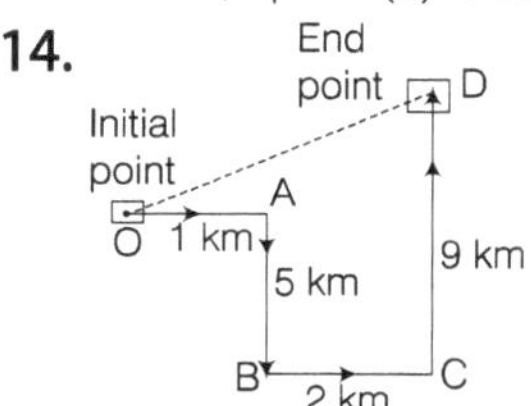

So, after turning 225° anti-clockwise, Amar will be facing towards Nirula's.
Hence, option (d) is correct.

14. 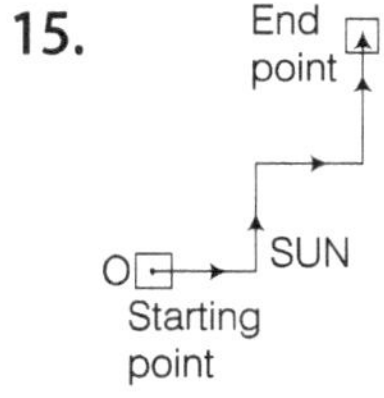

On comparing the above shown direction graph with the standard direction graph, we find that the man is in North-East direction from his initial point O.
Hence, option (b) is correct.

15. 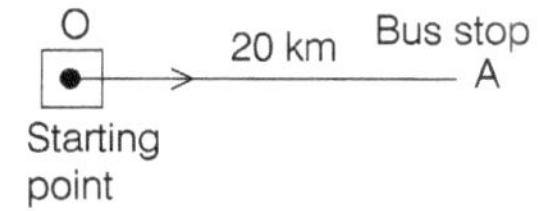

On comparing the above drawn direction graph with the standard direction graph, it is clear that Ram is facing North direction.
Hence, option (c) is correct.

16. Initially, she walked 20 m to East,

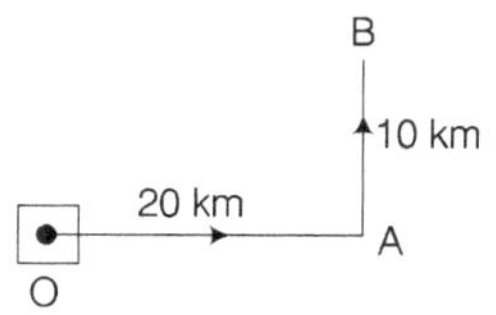

Now, she took turn left

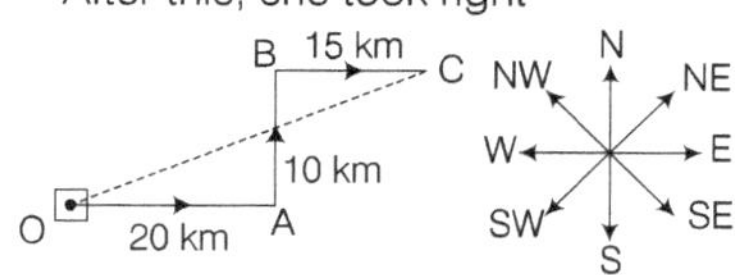

After this, she took right

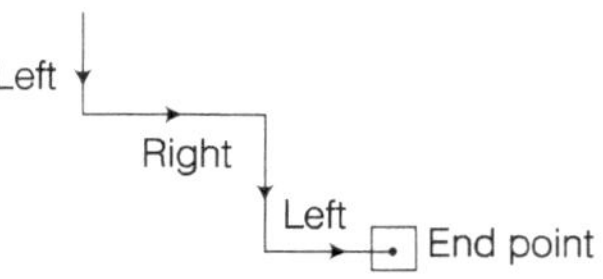

Now, comparing the above drawn direction diagram with the standard direction diagram, we see that Suhani is in North-East direction form her initial position O.
Hence, option (a) is correct.

17. According to the question, the direction diagram is drawn as

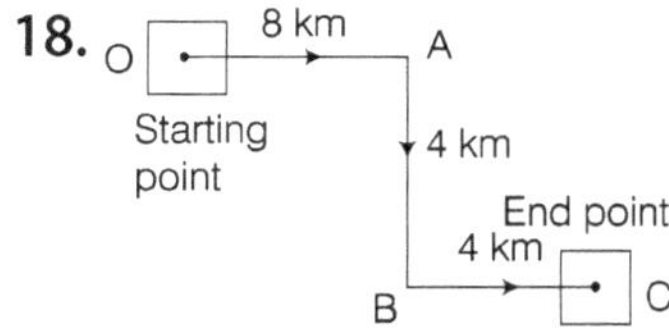

Clearly, he is moving in East direction.
Hence, option (c) is correct.

18. 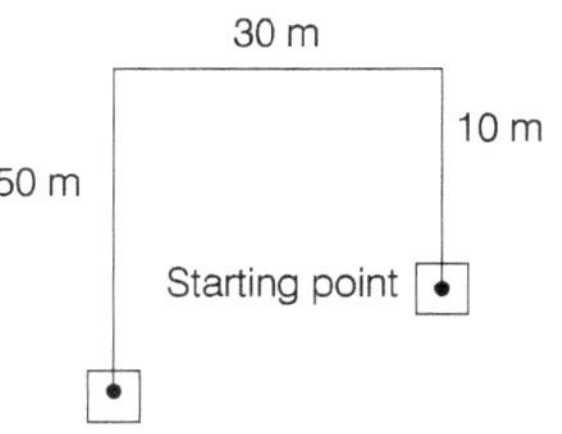

So, the total distance
= OA + AB + BC
= 8 + 4 + 4 = 16 km
Hence, option (b) is correct.

19. According to the question, the direction diagram is drawn as

∴ Total distance = 10 + 30 + 50
= 90 m
Hence, option (d) is correct.

20. 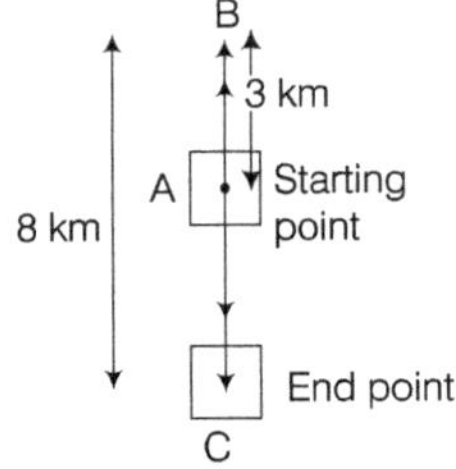

Here, we see that, the position of man at the end of the walk is towards South.

$\therefore$ Total required distance
$$= BC - BA = 8 - 3 = 5\,km$$

Hence, option (d) is correct.

21. 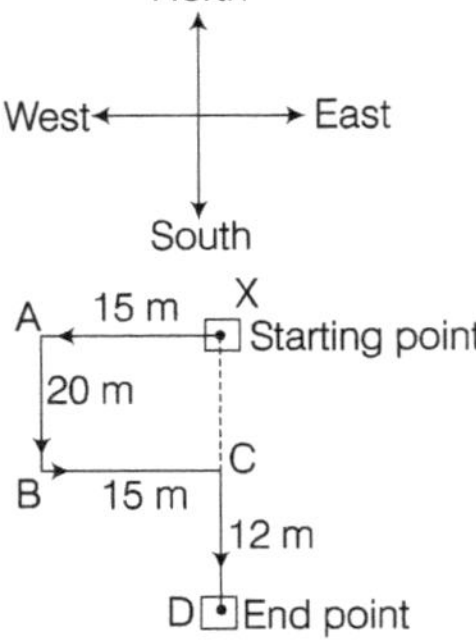

Now, comparing the above drawn direction graph with standard direction graph we see that, Sweta is in South direction from point X.

$\therefore$ Total required distance
$$= XC + CD = 20 + 12 = 32\,m$$

So, Sweta is 32 m far and in South direction from point X.

Hence, option (a) is correct.

10 Venn Diagram

1. Nothing is common between aeroplane, ship and train.
This can be represented as

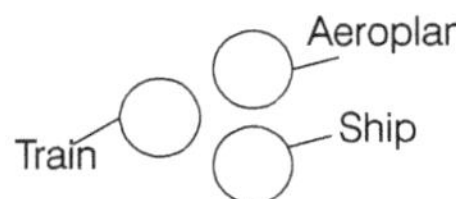

Hence, option (d) is correct.

2. Petals are part of flowers and bunch of flowers is called bouquet.
This can be represented as

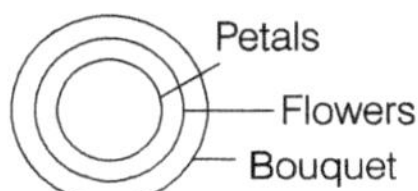

Hence, option (d) is correct.

3. All three classes are related to each other.
This can be represented as

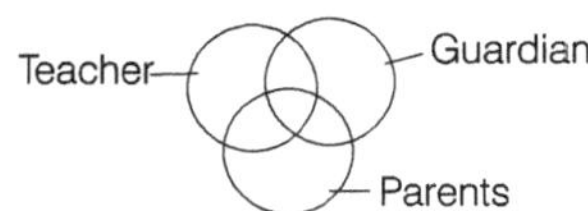

Hence, option (b) is correct.

4. All parrots are birds, but cat is in a separate category.
This can be represented as

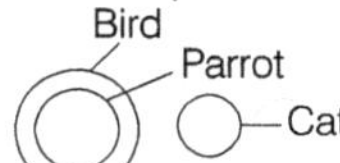

Hence, option (b) is correct.

5. All diamond ring comes under the category of rings and rings come under the category of ornaments.

Hence, option (a) is correct.

6. All the three items are different types of crops.
This can be represented as

Hence, option (a) is correct.

7. Blackboard is in classroom and classroom is in school.
This can be represented as

Hence, option (d) is correct.

8. Some houses are made of bricks. Some bridges are also made of bricks.

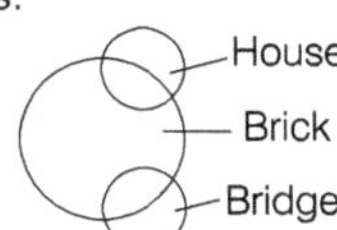

Hence, option (c) is correct.

9. Both paper and pen are stationery items but they are different.

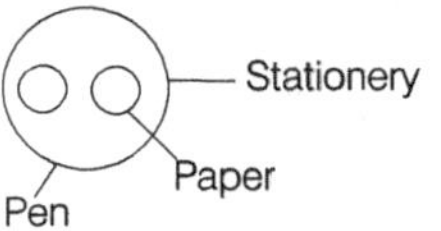

Hence, option (b) is correct.

10. Lips and eye are parts of body but they are different.

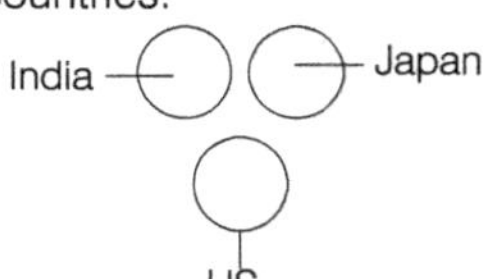

Hence, option (b) is correct.

11. All the three are different countries.

India — Japan — US

Hence, option (d) is correct.

12. Both apple and mango are fruit but they are different.
This can be represented as

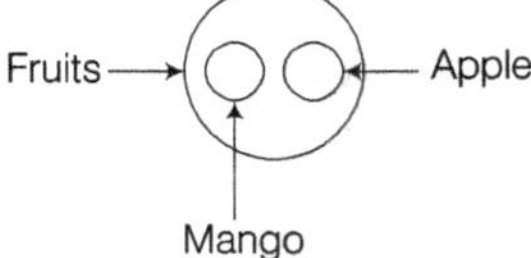

Hence, option (b) is correct.

13. All the three games are different from each other. This can be represented as

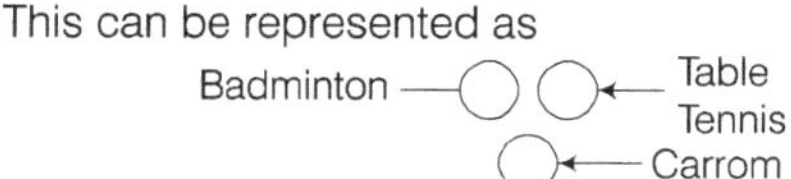

Hence, option (d) is correct.

14.

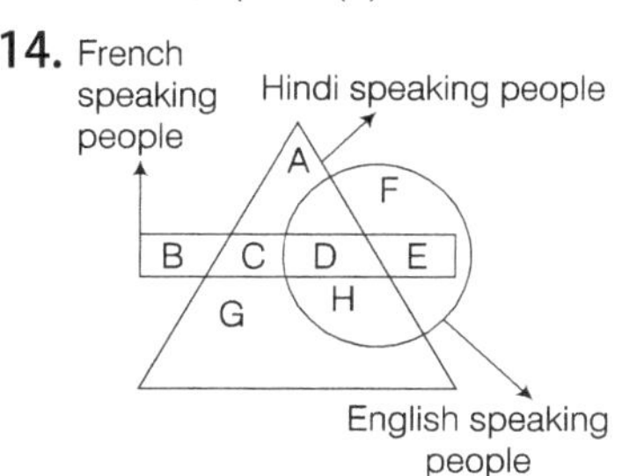

Here, we find that letter 'C' represents both Hindi speaking and French speaking people.
Hence, option (b) is correct.

15. We know that,

ZERO and NATURAL → WHOLE
NUMBER NUMBER
[0] [☐] ☐

So, it represents as ⊙☐

WHOLE NUMBER
⊙☐

and NEGATIVE → INTEGERS
NUMBER
▷ ✏

So, number system will represents as ⊙☐✏ .
Hence, option (a) is correct.

11   *Blood Relation*

1. My father's father is my grandfather i.e. Mr. Rakesh. Meena is my sister. So, my grandfather is also Meena's grandfather. Therefore, Meena is the granddaughter of Mr. Rakesh.
This can be represented as

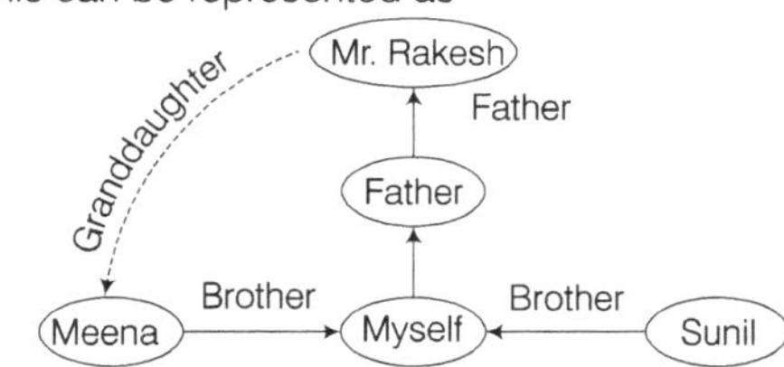

Hence, option (c) is correct.

2. My father's real brother is my uncle i.e. Ramu. So, my real uncle is the son of my grandmother.
This can be represented as

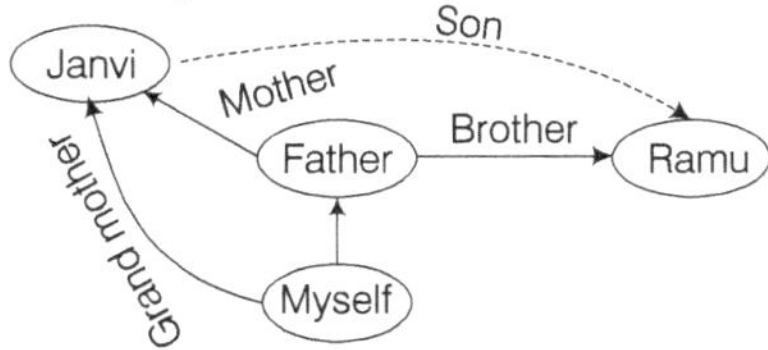

Hence, option (d) is correct.

3. Seema is the daughter of Radhika and Mohan is her brother. Kirti is the wife of Mohan. So, Kirti is the aunt of Seema.
This can be represented as

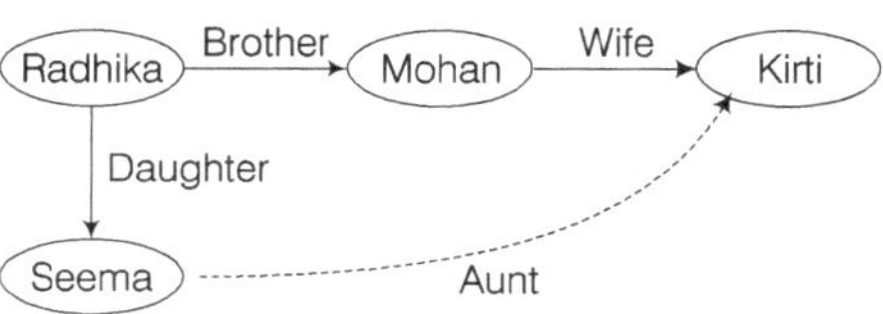

Hence, option (b) is correct.

4. A is the sister of B, B is the brother of C and C is the father of D. Father's sister will be aunt. Therefore, A is the aunt of D.
This can be represented as

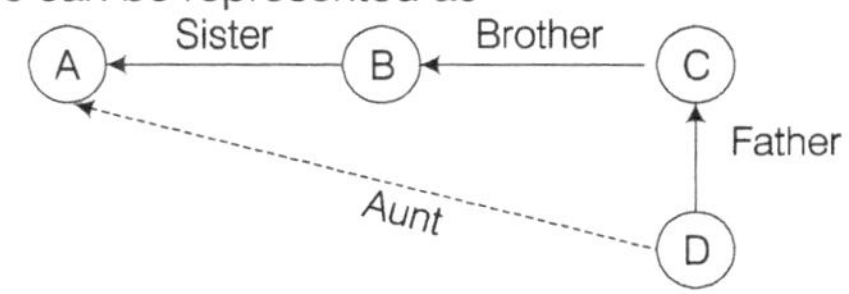

Hence, option (d) is correct.

5. Radhika's sister's father is father of Radhika and the man in the photograph is the son of Radhika's father. So, Radhika is the sister of that man.
This can be represented as

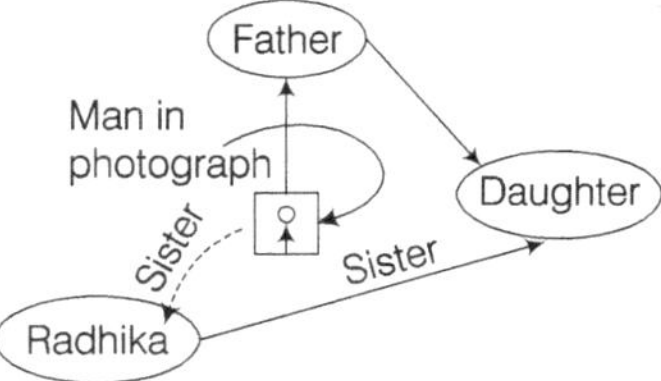

Hence, option (b) is correct.

6. The only daughter of boy's mother's father is his mother herself. So, the boy is the son of that woman.
This can be represented as
Hence, option (d) is correct.

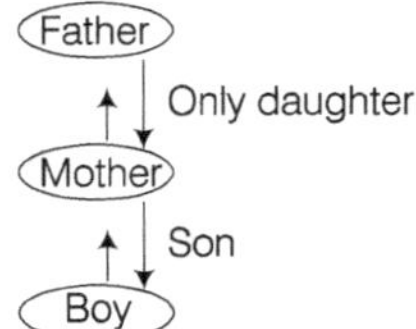

7. Only daughter of Kunal's mother-in-law means she is the wife of Kunal and daughter of Kunal's wife means Ayushi is the daughter of Kunal.
This can be represented as

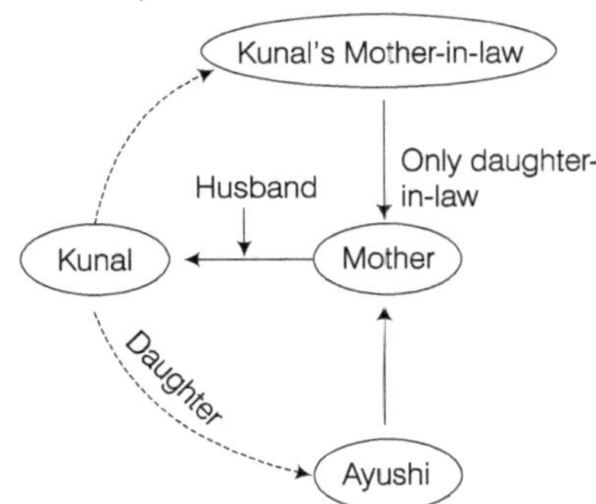

Hence, option (d) is correct.

8. Vimal's mother's husband is father of Vimal. Brother-in-law of Vimal's father is Vimal's uncle.
This can be represented as

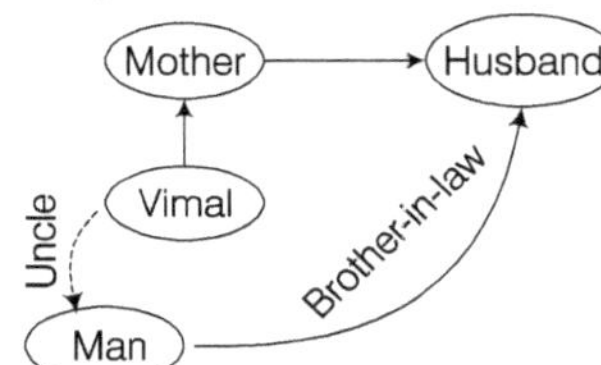

Hence, option (a) correct.

9. Mother of Karan's son is the wife of Karan. Wife's sister is the sister-in-law. So, woman is the sister-in-law of Karan.
This can be represented as

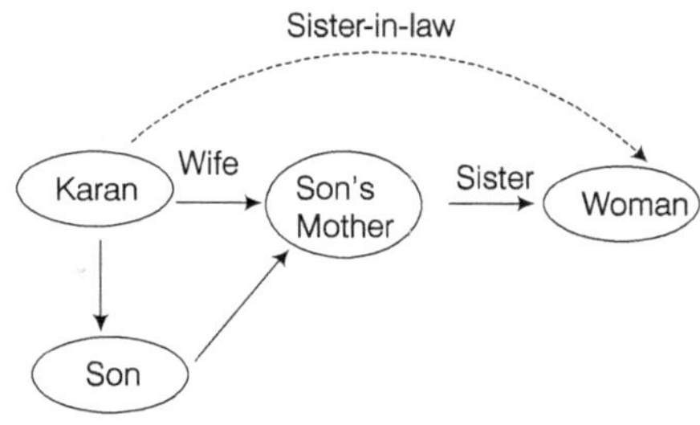

Hence, option (c) is correct.

10. C's mother is also the mother of D and their mother is A's wife, so A is their father. B is A's brother, so he is their uncle. Therefore, D is B's nephew.
This can be represented as

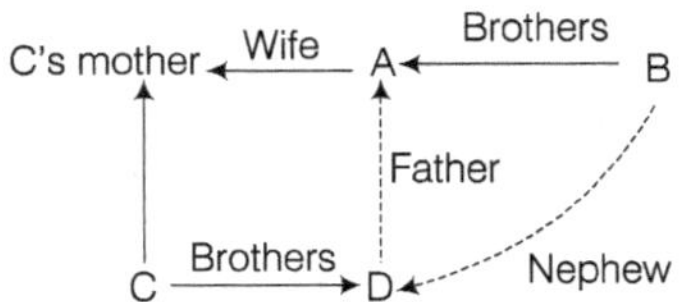

Hence, option (b) is correct.

11. Esha is Bhavi's mother and Aditya is Bhavi's brother Jayant is Aditya's brother, so Jayant is also Bhavi's brother. So, Esha is mother of Jayant, Bhavi and Aditya.
Now, Bharat is father of Jayant, so he is husband of Esha. Therefore Esha is Bharat's wife.
This can be represented as

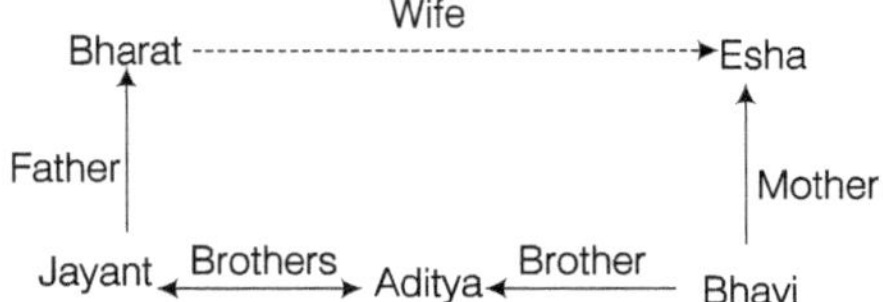

Hence, option (d) is correct.

12. Varun is Sarika's brother, so he is Rahul's Maternal uncle and Ritesh is Rahul's maternal uncle's son, so he is his cousin.
This can be represented as,

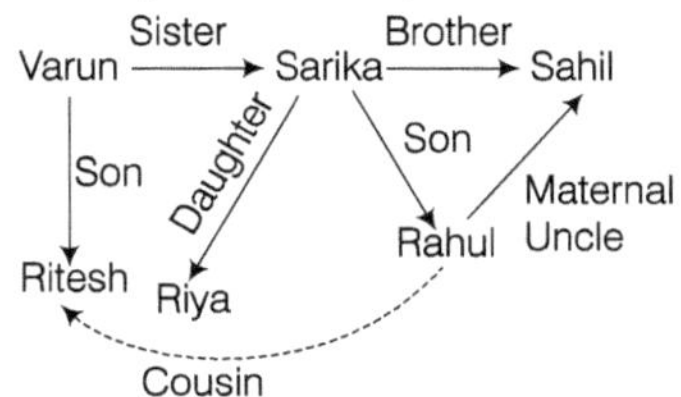

Hence, option (b) is correct.

Solution (Q. Nos. 13-16) The diagram can be drawn as

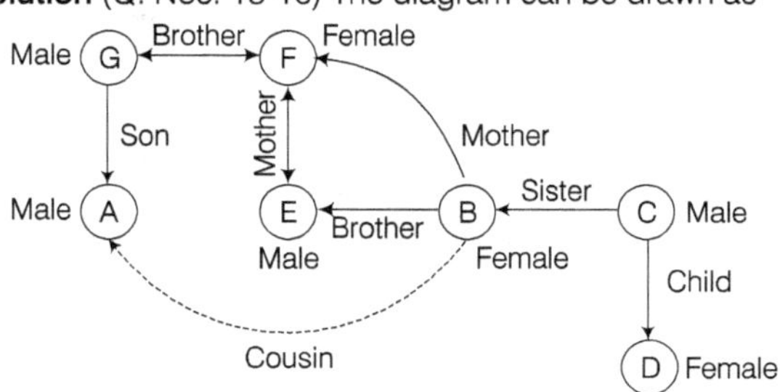

13. According to the question, G is the brother of F and F is the mother of B, C and E. So, G is the uncle of B, C and E. A is the son of G. So, uncle's son i.e. A is the cousin of B, C and E.
Hence, option (a) is correct.

14. When we observe the given options, we see except option (d) all options i.e. (a), (b) and (c) have one male and one female. In option (d), both F and B are females.
Hence, option (d) is correct.

15. From question,
A → A is the son of G.   [male]
→ B is the sister of C.   [female]
→ Male   [given in question]
D → Female   [given in question]
E → E is the brother of B.   [male]
F → F is the mother of E, B and C.
          [female]

→ G is the brother of F.   [male]
Therefore, 4 male members are in the family.
Hence, option (d) is correct.

16. From the above diagram, it is clear that G is the brother of F and F is the mother of B, C and E. Therefore, G is the uncle of C.
Hence, option (c) is correct.

12 *Similar Pairs*

1. Here, as cow gives milk, similarly hen gives egg. So, figure (a) will complete the second pair.
Hence, option (a) is correct.

2. Here, as glasses are wear on eyes, similarly shoes are wear on feet. So, figure (d) will complete the second pair.
Hence, option (d) is correct.

3. Here, as the shape of the Sun is circular, similarly the shape of cylinder is cylindrical.
So, figure (c) will complete the second pair.
Hence, option (c) is correct.

4. Here, the eyes are rotating 180° and smiley remains same. On following this pattern figure (b) will complete the second pair.
Hence, option (b) is correct.

5. Here, in first pair laterally inverted image of first figure is given.
On following this pattern, figure (b) will complete the second pair.
Hence, option (b) is correct.

6. Here, each figure i.e. the upper and lower figure is rotating 180°.
On following this pattern, figure (a) will complete the second pair.
Hence, option (a) is correct.

7. Here, the inner figure becomes the outer figure and outer figure becomes the inner figure.
On following this pattern, figure (c) will complete the second pair.
Hence option (c) is correct.

8. Here, the number of triangles figure reduces from four to one.

On following this pattern, figure (a) will complete the second pair.
Hence, option (a) is correct.

9. Here, the whole figure rotates 90° in anti-clockwise direction and circle becomes double and also one line each at upper part and lower part is added.
On following this pattern, option figure (b) will complete the second pair.
Hence, option (b) is correct.

10. Here, the whole figure rotates 90° in clockwise direction.
On following this pattern, figure (d) will complete the second pair.
Hence, option (d) is correct.

11. Here, the shaded figure becomes unshaded. On following this pattern, figure (b) will complete the second pair.
Hence, option (b) is correct.

12. Here, the upper portion of the figure is removed. On following this pattern, figure (c) will complete the second pair.
Hence, option (c) is correct.

13. Here, the inner most figure comes at lower left position after rotating 90° in anti-clockwise direction, the middle figure comes at top right position and the outer most figure comes at middle position.
On following this pattern, figure (d) will complete the second pair.
Hence, option (d) is correct.

14. Here, the same figure is added to the previous figure. On following this pattern, figure (b) will complete the second pair.
Hence, option (b) is correct.

15. Here, the whole figure is rotating 90° in clockwise direction after adding a line in the middle of the figure.
On following this pattern figure (a) will complete the second pair.
Hence, option (a) is correct.

16. Here, the arrow of the inner figure is rotating 180° and the dot is moving one position ahead in clock-wise direction to get the next position.
On following this pattern, figure (b) will complete the second pair.
Hence, option (b) is correct.

17. Here, in first pair the dots change their position from left slant to right slant and the black dots become white. On following this pattern, figure (b) will complete the second pair
Hence, option (b) is correct.

18. In first pair, both the shapes are laterally inverted and joined together. On following this pattern, figure (c) will complete the second pair.
Hence, option (c) is correct.

19. Here, the ends of the line are joined together and the lines are removed to get the second figure. On following this pattern, figure (d) will complete the second pair.
Hence, option (d) is correct.

20. Here, the shaded portion is taken forward after rotating 90° clockwise. On following this pattern, figure (d) will complete the second pair,
Hence, option (d) is correct.

Series Completion

1. Here, each time one vertical line and one horizontal line is removed to get the next figure.
On following this pattern, option figure (c) will complete the series. Hence, option (c) is correct.

2. Here, a square is removed from the line in each successive step moving in anti-clockwise direction 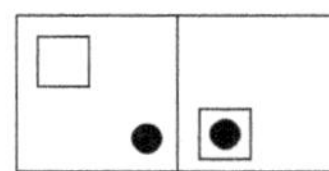.

On following this pattern, option figure (b) will complete the series. Hence, option (b) is correct.

3. Here, in this series, every alternate figure is same. So, the required figure will be same as figure (1) and figure (3).
Hence, option (b) is correct.

4. Here, square is moving from one corner to another in anti-clockwise direction in each step but triangle changes its position diagonally in each alternate step.
On following this patten, option figure (a) will complete the series. Hence, option (a) is correct.

5. Here, each shape/symbol is moving one block from left to right in each step. On following this pattern, figure (a) will complete the series.
Hence, option (a) is correct.

6. Here, both the arrows are rotating 90° in anti-clockwise direction.
On following this pattern, option figure (c) will complete the series. Hence, option (c) is correct.

7. Here, in every group, each letter is rotating 90° in clockwise direction.
On following this pattern, option figure (b) will complete the series. Hence, option (b) is correct.

8. As we move from figure (1) to figure (2), two line segments move one step in anti-clockwise direction and one line segment is added. While we move from figure (2) to figure (3), one line segment is deleted. Following the similar pattern, we observe that figure (d) will be the next figure.
Hence, option (d) is correct.

9. Here, in each step the figure is rotating 45° in clockwise direction and the upper shape is changed and decreased by one.
On following this pattern, option figure (b) will complete the series. Hence, option (b) is correct.

10. The circle shifts half block downward in each successive step and becomes half shaded. This process will be repeated for square. So, the next figure will be same as option figure (a).
Hence, option (a) is correct.

11. Here, vertical and horizontal line segments are added to the figure, alternately.
On following this pattern, option, figure (d) will complete the series.
Hence, option (d) is correct.

12. Here, in each step the number of stair is increased by one.
On following this pattern, option figure (a) will complete the series. Hence, option (a) is correct.

13. Here, the shaded portion is moving one step in anti-clockwise direction and dot changes its position diagonally in each successive step.
On following this pattern option figure (c) will complete the series. Hence, option (c) is correct,

14. Here, in first step a column of squares is removed and in second step a row of squares is removed. This pattern follows in every alternate step.

On following this pattern, option figure (a) will complete the series. Hence, option (a) is correct.

15. Here, square is moving anti-clockwise from one corner to another and dot is moving clockwise from one corner to another.
On following this pattern, the next two figures are shown as below

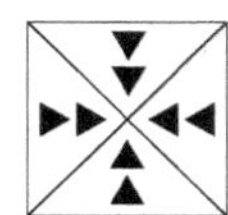

Hence, option (b) is correct.

Figure Matrix

16. The square can be completed as

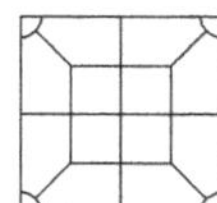

From the above figure, we see that, option figure (a) will complete the large square.
Hence, option (a) is correct.

17. The square can be completed as

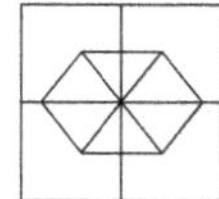

From the above figure, we see that, option figure (a) will complete the large square.

18. The square can be completed as

From the above figure, we see that, option figure (b) will complete the grid.
Hence, option (b) is correct.

19. If we see columns, the shaded symbols become unshaded and *vice-versa* and inverted horizontally.

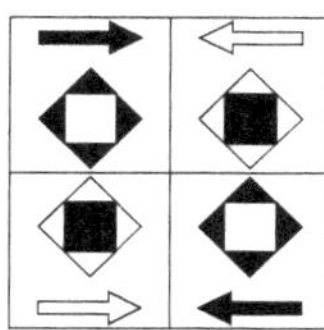

From the above figure we see that, option figure (c) will complete the grid.
Hence, option (c) is correct.

20. Here, a dot is increasing in each block in clockwise direction.
So, the square can be completed as

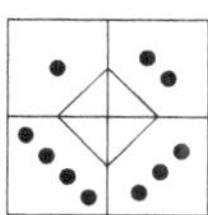

From the above figure we see that, option figure (c) will complete the square.
Hence, option (c) is correct.

21. Here, the shaded portion of the figure in second column is taken forward to third column.
On following this pattern, option figure (b) will complete the grid.
Hence, option (b) is correct.

22. Here, the designs in column (i) and column (ii) are combined to get the design in column (iii).

On following this pattern, option figure (b) will complete the grid.
Hence, option (b) is correct.

23. Here, each row and column contains three different figure. So, the figure in last block of third column will be same as option figure (c).
Hence, option (c) is correct.

24. Here, if we see rows the star is rotating 45° in clockwise direction in each block.
On following this pattern, option figure (d) will complete the grid.
Hence, option (d) is correct.

14 *Odd One Out*

1. In all the figures except figure (a), the lower right quarter is shaded, but in figure (a), the upper right quarter is shaded.
So, figure (a) is odd one.
Hence, option (a) is correct.

2. In all the figures except figure (c), the two shaded squares are at the upper half body of the figure. But in figure (c) the two shaded squares are at the lower half body of the figure. So, figure (c) is odd one.
Hence, option (c) is correct.

3. In all the figures except figure (d), two identical shapes are intersecting one another. But in figure (d) the shapes are not identical.
So, figure (d) is odd one.
Hence, option (d) is correct.

4. In all the figures except figure (b), the arrow head is pointing towards the black dot. But in figure (b) it points towards the white circle.
So, figure (b) is odd one.
Hence, option (b) is correct.

5. All the figures, except figure (d) are divided in equal parts. But in figure (d) is not divided equally.
So, figure (d) is odd one.

Hence, option (d) is correct.

6. In all the figures except figure (c), all the arrow heads lie on different lines but in figure (c) the two arrow heads lie on a same line.
So, figure (c) is odd one.
Hence, option (c) is correct.

7. In all the figures except figure (c), the middle shape is an arc, but in figure (c) it is a complete circle. So, figure (c) is odd one.
Hence, option (c) is correct.

8. All the figures except figure (b), are same when rotated. But figure (b) is different.
So, the figure (b) is odd one.
Hence, option (b) is correct.

9. In all the figures, except figure (d), the arrows are moving in anti-clockwise direction. But in figure (d) the arrows are moving in clockwise direction. So, figure (d) is odd one.
Hence, option (d) is correct.

10. In all the figures except figure (b), the inner most and the middle shapes are same but in figure (b) these two shapes are different. So, figure (b) is odd one.
Hence, option (b) is correct.

11. In all the figures except figure (c), the three white dots lie outside the main figure and one dot lies inside the main figure. But in figure (c) all the dots lie outside the main figure. So, figure (c) is odd one.
Hence, option (c) is correct.

12. In all the figures except figure (d), the bent line and pin are on opposite sides of the object . But in figure (d) both are on same side.
So, figure (d) is odd one.
Hence, option (d) is correct.

13. In all the figures, except figure (c), the two arcs are facing inward and two arcs are outwards. But in figure (c) three arcs are facing outward and one is facing inward.
So, figure (c) is odd one.
Hence, option (c) is correct.

14. Here, except figure (b) all other figures have four shaded squares. But in figure (b) only three squares are shaded.
So, figure (b) is odd one.
Hence, option (b) is correct.

15. All the figures, except figure (a) are same when rotating. But figure (a) is different.

So, figure (a) is odd one.

Hence, option (a) is correct.

16. In all the figure, except figure (c) the shapes at the ends of the line are same. But in figure (c) both the shapes are different. So, figure (c) is odd one.

Hence, option (c) is correct.

17. Except figure (b), all other figure have same number of black dots

as that of number of lines. But in figure (b) the number of lines is 6 and black dots are 8. So, figure (b) is odd one.

Hence, option (b) is correct.

18. In all the figures, except figure (c), the two shaded portions are the part of a common triangle. But in figure (c) the shaded portions are the part of different triangles.

So, figure (c) is odd one.

Hence, option (c) is correct.

19. In all the figures except figure (a). The small white circle lies outside

from both the shapes, but in figure (a) it lies inside the circle.

So, figure (a) is odd one.

Hence, option (a) is correct.

20. Here, all the figures, except figure (d), have two upper and two lower waves on the line. But in figure (d), there are three upper and two lower waves. So, figure (d) is odd one.

Hence, option (d) is correct.

15 Mirror and Water Images

1. The correct mirror image is as shown below

DL4C   Ɔᔕｄ⅃ꓷ

Hence, option (c) is correct.

2. The correct mirror image is as shown below

TRAIN   ИIΛЯT

Hence, option (a) is correct.

3. The correct mirror image is as shown below

3681   ƚ86Ɛ

Hence, option (b) is correct.

4. The mirror image of the given figure is as shown below

 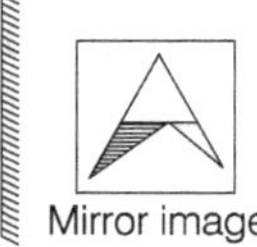

Object   Mirror image

Mirror

Hence, option (d) correct.

5. The mirror image of the given figure is as shown below

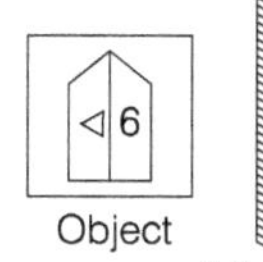 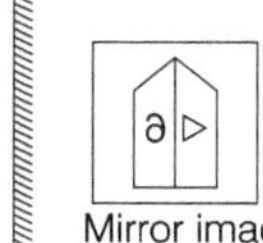

Object   Mirror image

Mirror

Hence, option (d) is correct.

6. The mirror image of the given object is shown as below

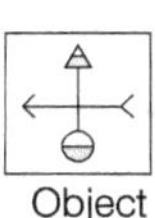 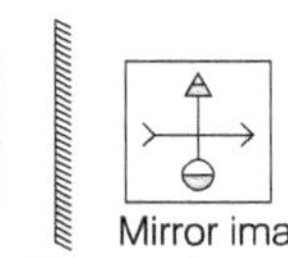

Object   Mirror image

Mirror

Hence, option (b) is correct.

7. The mirror image of the given object is shown as below

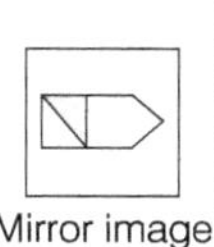 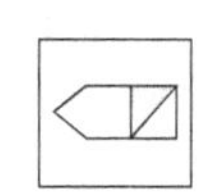

Mirror image   Object

Mirror

Hence, option (a) is correct.

8. The mirror image of the given object is shown as below

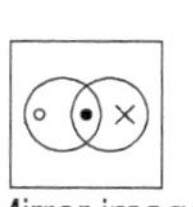 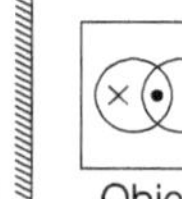

Mirror image   Object

Mirror

Hence, option (c) is correct.

9. The mirror image of the given object is shown as below

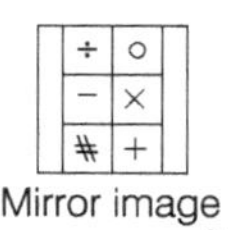 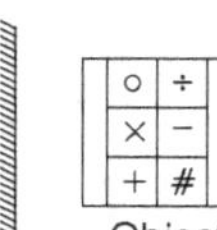

Mirror image   Object

Mirror

Hence, option (b) is correct.

10. The mirror image of the given object is shown as below

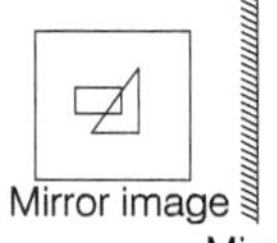 

Mirror image   Object

Mirror

Hence, option (d) is correct.

11. The mirror image of the given object is shown as below

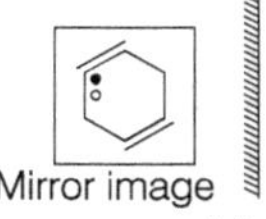 

Mirror image   Object

Mirror

Hence, option (c) is correct

12. The mirror image of the given object is shown as below

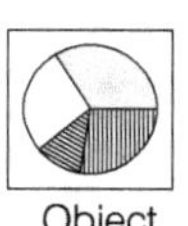 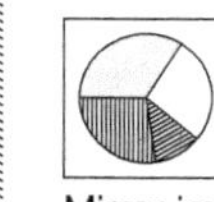

Object   Mirror image

Mirror

Hence, option (a) is correct

Note Unless it is specified the mirror is assumed to be on the right hand side of the object in such problems.

13. The mirror image of the given clock is shown as below

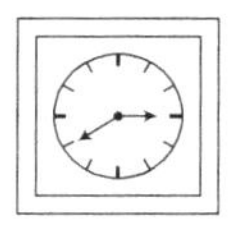 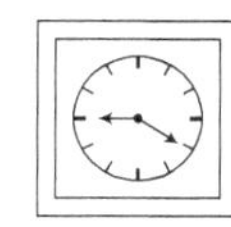

Mirror

Hence, option (b) is correct.

14. The water image of the given letters is shown as below

CODE

Water

CODE

Hence, option (a) is correct.

15. The water image of the given letter is shown as below

TAMNCZ

Water

Hence, option (c) is correct.

16. The water image of the given numbers is shown as below

43867

Water

Hence, option (d) is correct.

17. The water image of the given object is shown as below

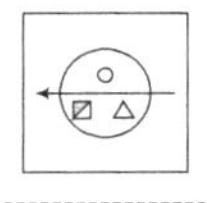 Object

Water

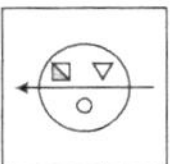 Water image

Hence, option (d) is correct.

18. The water image of the given object is shown as

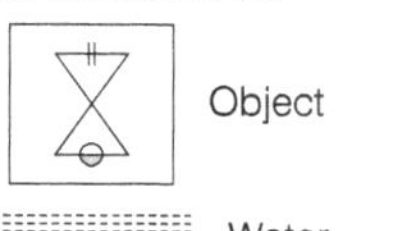 Object

Water

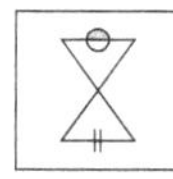 Water Image

Hence, option (b) is correct.

19. The water image of the given object is shown as below

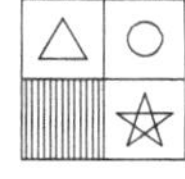 Object

Water

 Water image

Hence, option (d) is correct.

20. The water image of the given object is shown as below

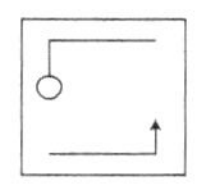 Object

Water

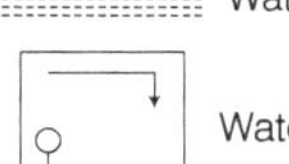 Water image

Hence, option (a) is correct.

21. The water image of the given object is shown as below

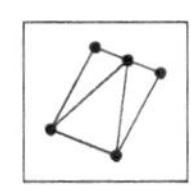 Object

Water

 Water image

Hence, option (c) is correct.

22. The water image of the given object is shown as below

 Object

Water

 Water image

Hence, option (b) is correct.

23. The water image of the given object is shown as below

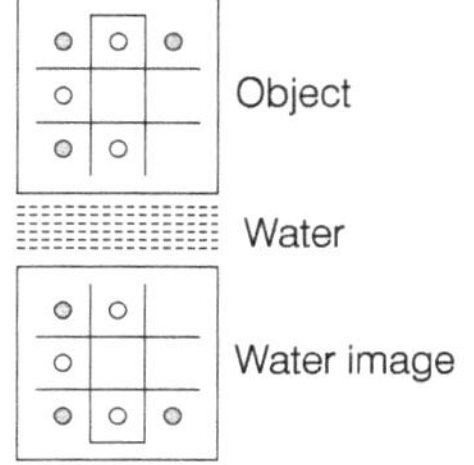 Object

Water

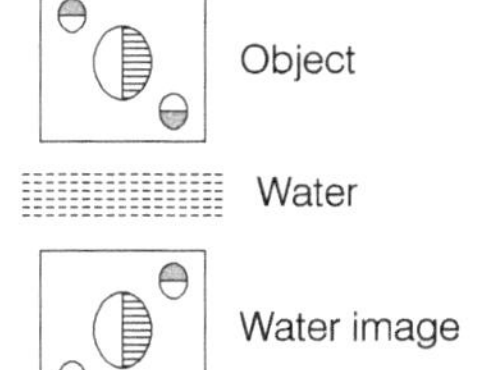 Water image

Hence, option (d) is correct.

24. The water image of the given object is shown as below

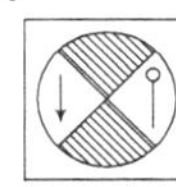 Object

Water

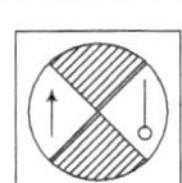 Water image

Hence, option (a) is correct.

25. The water image of the given object is shown as below

Object

Water

Water image

Hence, option (b) is correct.

16 Paper Folding and Paper Cutting

1. The folded transparent sheet will appear as

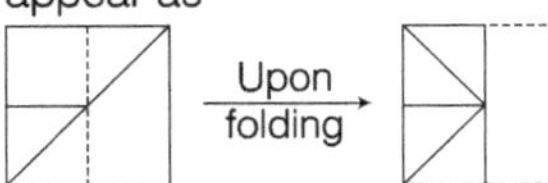

Hence, option (c) is correct.

2. The folded transparent sheet will appear as

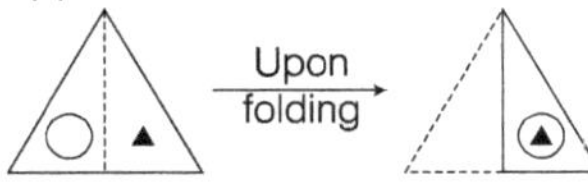

Hence, option (b) is correct.

3. The folded transparent sheet will appear as

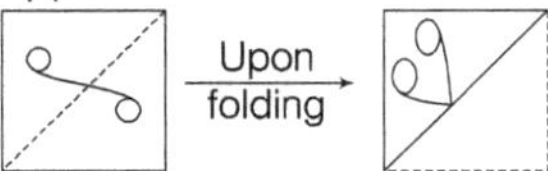

Hence, option (c) is correct.

4. The folded transparent sheet will appear as

Hence, option (a) is correct.

5. The folded transparent sheet will appear as

Hence, option (c) is correct.

6. The folded transparent sheet will appear as

Hence, option (a) is correct.

7. The folded transparent sheet will appear as

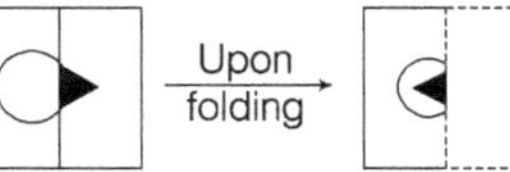

Hence, option (b) is correct.

8. Upon unfolding the folded paper, represented by fig. (Z) will look like as

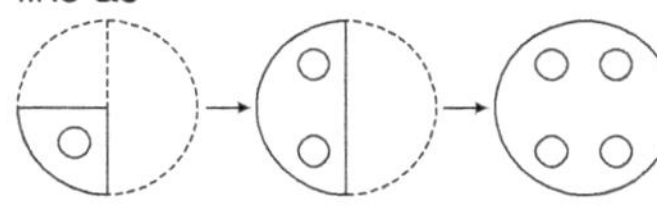

Hence, option (c) is correct.

9. Upon unfolding the folded paper represented by fig (Z), it will look like as

10. Upon unfolding the folded paper represented by fig. (Z), will look like as

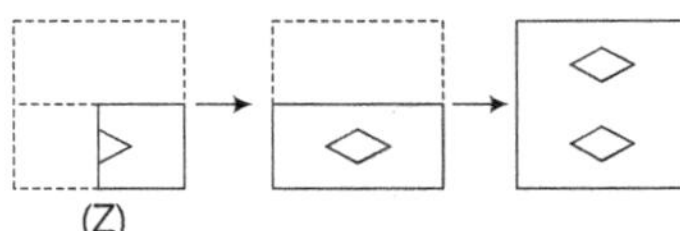

Hence, option (a) is correct.

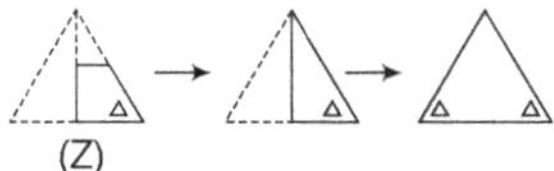

Hence, option (d) is correct.

11. Upon unfolding the folded paper represented by fig. (Z), will look like as

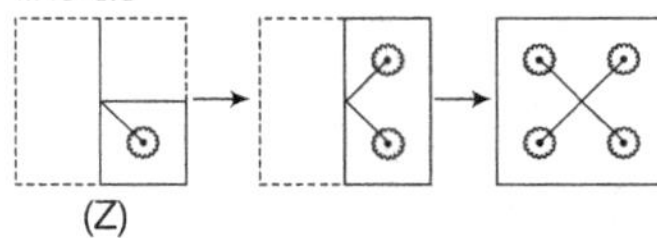

Hence, option (a) is correct.

12. Upon folding the paper sheet represented by fig. (Z) will look like as

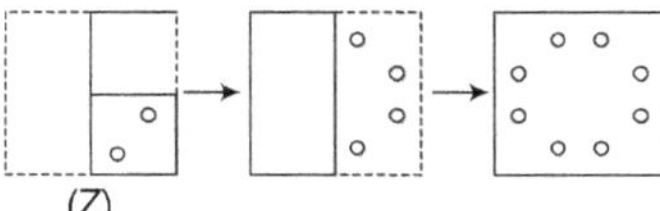

Hence, option (c) is correct.

17 Cubes and Dice

1.

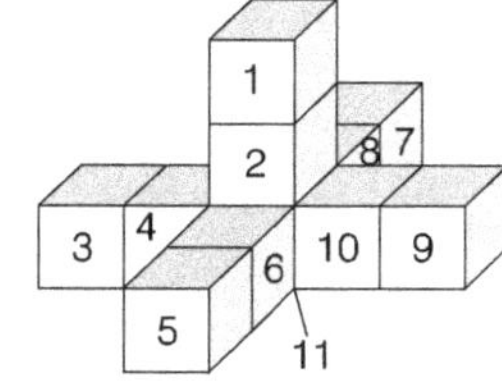

It is clear from the above figure that, there are 10 visible cubes and 1 hidden cube below the cube number 2.

∴ Total number of small cubes = 10 + 1 = 11

Hence, option (c) is correct.

2.

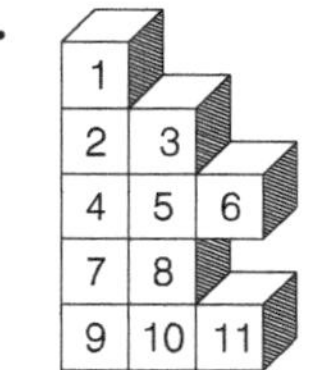

It is clear from the above figure, that there are 11 small cubes.

Hence, option (a) is correct.

3.

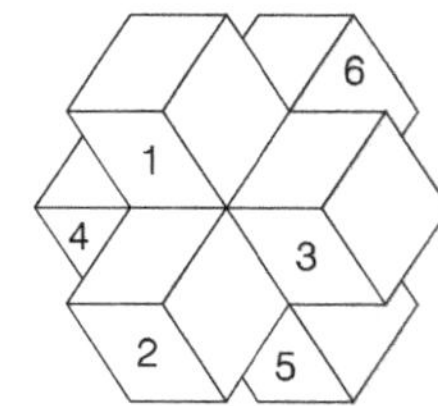

It is clear from the above figure, that there are 6 visible cubes and 1 is invisible cube below cube number 1.

∴ Total number of cubes = 6 + 1 = 7

Hence, option (b) is correct.

4.

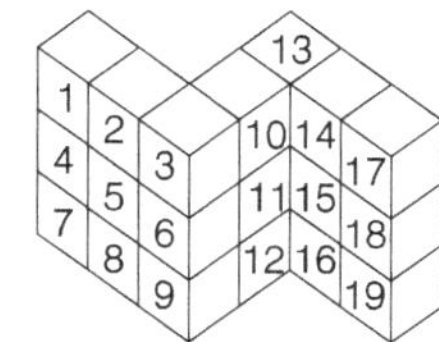

It is clear from the above figure that, there are 19 visible cubes and 2 hidden cubes below the cube number 13.

∴ Total number of cubes

$$= 19 + 2 = 21$$

Hence, option (c) is correct.

5.

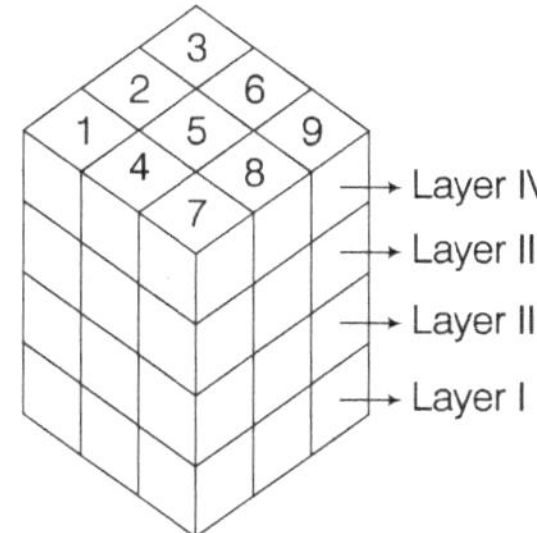

It is clear from the above figure that, there are four layers and in each layer there are 9 cubes.

∴ Total number of small cubes

$$= 9 + 9 + 9 + 9 = 36$$

Hence, option (a) is correct.

6. Here, we see that one digit is common in both the positions i.e. 2. So, the adjacent faces of 2 are 3, 5, 4 and 1. Now, the remaining face having 6 will be opposite to 2.

Hence, option (a) is correct.

7. Here, we find that '2' dots are common at the same faces in both the positions of a dice.

Now, we move in clockwise direction, starting from 2 in both position to find the opposite faces, as shown below

Position (i)	2		1		5
Position (ii)	2		6		3
	Common		Opposite		Opposite

Therefore, the opposite face of '1' is 6.

Hence, option (d) is correct.

8. Here, we find that, letter 'C' is common in both the positions of a dice.

Therefore, on moving in clockwise direction from C, the opposite faces are

Position (i)	C		B		A
Position (ii)	C		D		E
	Common		Opposite		Opposite

So, it is clear that the opposite face of 'A' is 'E'.

Hence, option (b) is correct.

9. Here, we find that, digit '3' is common in both the positions of a dice.

So, the adjacent faces of 3 are 1, 5, 4 and 2. Now, the remaining face having number 6 will be opposite to the face having '3'.

Hence, option (b) is correct.

10. From the figures (ii) and (iii), it is clear that faces having 1, 3, 4 and 6 dots cannot be appeared opposite to the face having 5 dots. So, the remaining face having 2 dots lies opposite to the face having 5 dots.

Hence, option (c) is correct.

11. Here, 2 is common in both positions, so the adjacent faces of 2 are 5, 6, 3 and 4. So, the remaining face having number '1' will be opposite to the face having '2'.

Hence, option (b) is correct.

12. From the figure, the parts of opposite faces are

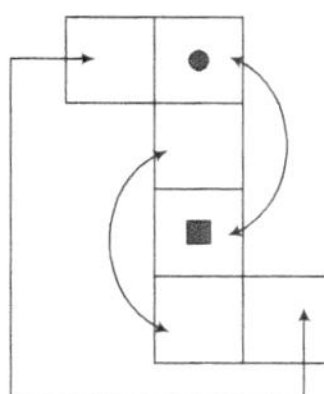

i.e. (•) opposite to (■), □ opposite to □ and □ opposite to □ .

Except figure (d), in all other figures both the opposite faces are appear adjacent to each other.

So, only the figure (d) can be formed from the given net.

Hence, option (d) is correct.

13. From the given figure, the pairs of opposite faces are

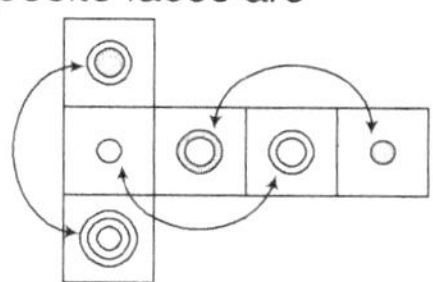

i.e.

◎ Opposite to ⊚

○ Opposite to ◉

◉ Opposite to ○

Here, in cubes (b) and (c), faces (◉ and ◎) are shown on adjacent faces, in cube (d) faces (◉ and ○) are shown on adjacent faces, so these cubes are not possible only the cube given in option (a) can be formed.

Hence, option (a) is correct.

14. From the figure the pairs of opposite faces are

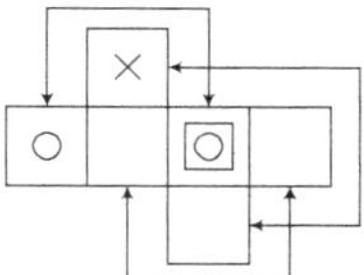

i.e.

○	opposite to	◙
×	opposite to	
	opposite to	

In cube (ii), × and □ are shown on adjacent faces, in cubes (iii) and (iv) ○ and ◙ are shown on adjacent faces. So, these cubes are not possible. Only the cube given figure (i) can be formed.

Hence, option (a) is correct.

15. If the given figure, the pair of opposite faces are

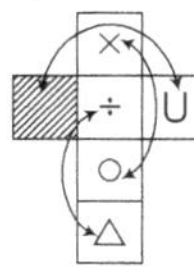

i.e.

×	opposite to	○
▨	opposite to	U
÷	opposite to	△

In cube (a) 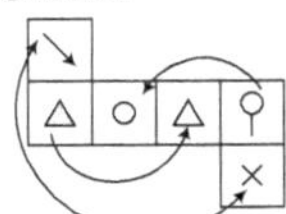 and ☐U☐ are shown on adjacent faces, in cube (b) ☐÷☐ and ☐△☐ are shown on adjacent faces and in cube (d) ☐△☐ and ☐÷☐ are shown in adjacent faces. So, these cubes cannot be formed. Only the cube (c) can be formed because all the three faces appear in this cube can be on faces adjacent.
Hence, option (c) is correct.

16. It is clear from the given options, that only the net given in figure (b) will form the dice as given in question figure. The opposite faces are as shown

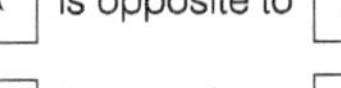

So,

☐↘☐ is opposite to ☐×☐

☐△☐ is opposite to ☐△☐

☐○☐ is opposite to ☐♀☐

In the given cube no above opposite faces are shown adjacent to each other.
Hence, option (b) is correct.

17. The adjacent faces of 2 are 6, 4, 3 and 1.
Now, it is clear that only 5 is remaining.
So, the opposite face of 2 will be 5.
Hence, option (d) is correct.

18 *Embedded Figures, Figure Formation and Analysis*

1. The given figure (X) can be traced out in figure (b) as shown below

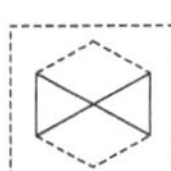

Hence, option (b) is correct.

2. The given figure (X) can be traced out in figure (c) as shown below

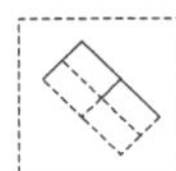

Hence, option (c) is correct.

3. The given figure (X) can be traced out in figure (a) as shown below

Hence, option (a) is correct.

4. From the given options, figure (b) will be formed by joining all the pieces of figure (X), as shown below

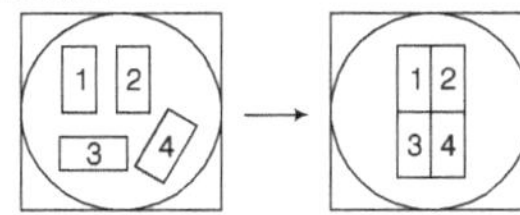

Hence, option (b) is correct.

5. From the given options, figure (c) will be formed by joining all the pieces of figure (X), as shown below

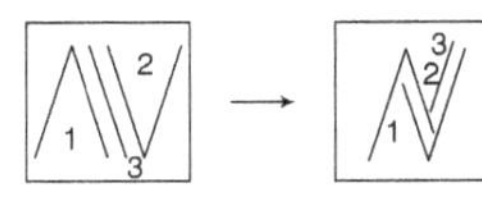

Hence, option (c) is correct.

6. After observation, we see that, figure (d) has the same components as that of the figure (X).

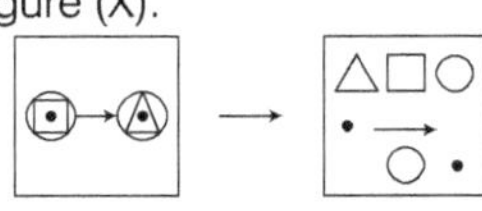

Hence, option (d) is correct.

7. After observation, we see that, figure (d) has the same components as that of the figure (X).

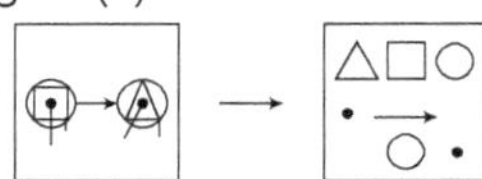

Hence option (d) is correct.

8. After observation, we find that figure (a) exactly fits into figure (X) to form a complete square.

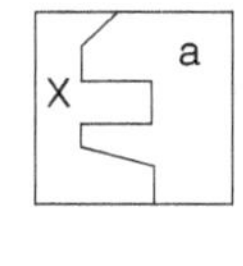

Hence, option (a) is correct.

9. After observation, we find that figure (d) exactly fits into figure (X) to form a complete square.

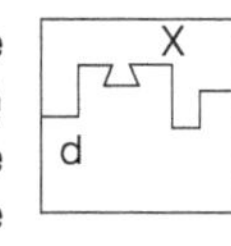

Hence, option (d) is correct.

10. In figures (1), (6) and (8) shapes are divided into two parts and having two black dots. In figures (2), (3) and (9) the shapes are divided by horizontal lines. In figures (4), (5) and (7) same shapes are intersecting each other.
Thus, three group are (1, 6, 8); (2, 3, 9) and (4, 5, 7)
Hence, option (b) is correct.

11. Figures (1), (8) and (6) are composed in circle with different shapes.
Figures (2), (7) and (9) are divided into two equal parts and (3), (4) and (5) are shaded with short lines.
So, three groups are (1, 8, 6); (2, 7, 9) and (3, 5, 4).
Hence, option (c) is correct.

12. Figure (c) will complete the pattern as shown below

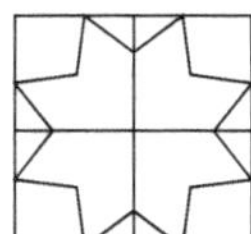

Hence, option (c) is correct.

13. Figure (c) will complete the pattern as shown below

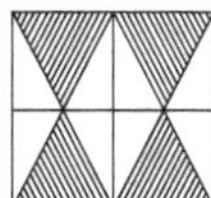

Hence, option (c) is correct.

19 Counting of Figure

1. The figure may be labelled as

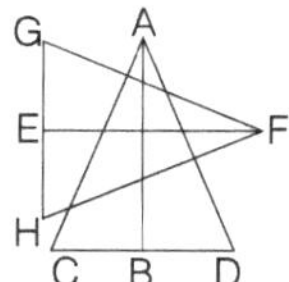

Number of horizontal lines = 2 i.e. EF and CD

Number of vertical lines = 2 i.e. AB and GH

Number of slanting lines = 4 i.e. AC, AD, GF and FH

So, the total number of straight lines = 2 + 2 + 4 = 8

Hence, option (c) is correct.

2. The figure may be labelled as

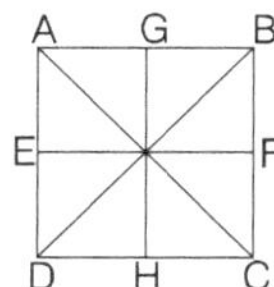

Number of horizontal lines = 3 i.e. AB, EF and DC

Number of vertical lines = 3 i.e. AD, GH and BC

Number of slanting lines = 2 i.e. AC and BD

∴ Total number of straight lines = 3 + 3 + 2 = 8

Hence, option (d) is correct.

3. The figure may be labelled as

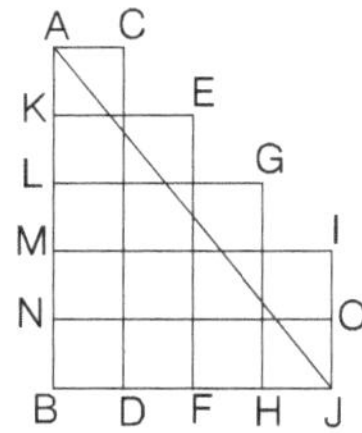

Number of horizontal lines = 6 i.e. BJ, NO, MI, LG, KE and AC

Number of vertical lines = 5 i.e. AB, CD, EF, GH and IJ.

Number of slanting lines = 1 i.e. AJ

∴ Total number of straight lines = 6 + 5 + 1 = 12

Hence, option (b) is correct.

4. The figure may be labelled as

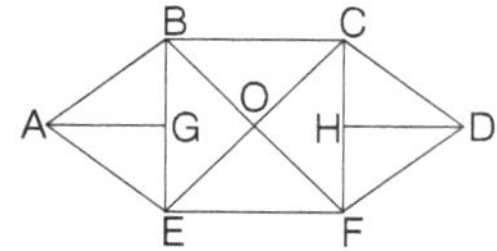

The triangles formed by one component are
ΔBOC, ΔBOE, ΔCOF, ΔEOF, ΔCHD, ΔDHF, ΔAGB, ΔAGE i.e. 8

The triangles formed by two components are
ΔBEF, ΔEBC, ΔEFC, ΔBCF, ΔCFD and ΔBEA = 6 i.e.

∴ Total number of triangles = 8 + 6 = 14

Hence, option (d) is correct.

5. The figure may be labelled as

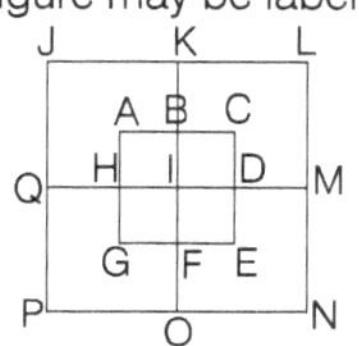

The number of squares formed by one comonent are
☐ABHI, ☐ BCDI, ☐ IDEF and ☐ HIFG i.e 4

The number of squares formed by two components are ☐ JKIQ, ☐ KLMI, ☐ IMNO and ☐ QIOP, i.e. 4. The number of squares formed by more than two components ☐ JLNP and ☐ ACEG i.e. 2

∴ The total number of squares = 4 + 4 + 2 = 10

Hence, option (c) is correct.

6. The figure may be labelled as

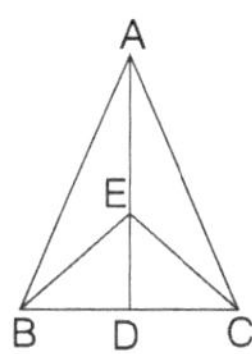

The triangles formed by one component are ΔBED, ΔEDC, ΔAEB, ΔAEC i. e. 4

The triangles formed by two components are
ΔADB, ΔADC, ΔBEC i.e. 3

The triangle formed by four components is
ΔBAC i.e. 1

∴ Total number of triangles = 4 + 3 + 1 = 8

Hence, option (a) is correct.

7. The figure may be labelled as

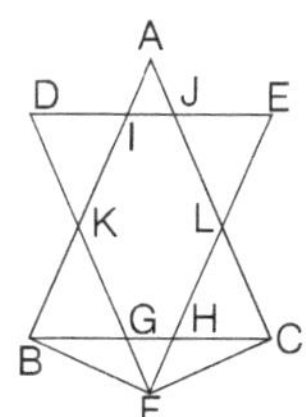

The triangles formed by one component are.
ΔAIJ, ΔDKI, ΔELJ, ΔBKG, ΔLHC, ΔBGF, ΔFHC, ΔGFH i.e, 8

The triangle by two compnents are ΔBHF, ΔGFC, ΔBKF, ΔFLC i.e, 4

The triangles formed by three components are
ΔBCF, ΔDEF, ΔABC i.e. 3

∴ Total number of triangles = 8 + 4 + 3 = 15

Hence, option (a) is correct.

8. The figure may be labelled as

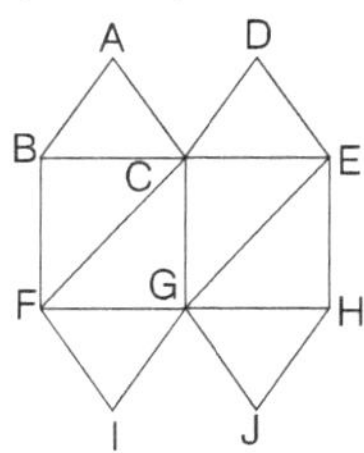

Total number of triangles are
ΔABC, ΔDCE, ΔBFC, ΔFGC, ΔGCE, ΔEGH, ΔFGI, ΔGHJ i.e, = 8

∴ Total number of triangles = 8

Hence, option (c) is correct.

9. The figure may be labelled as

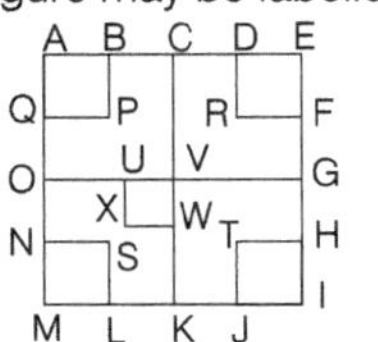

Number of squares formed by one component are ☐ FJMI, ☐ JGKM, ☐ MKHL and ☐ EIML i.e 4 Number of squares formed by more than one component are ☐ FGHE and ☐ ABCD i.e. 2

So, the total number of squares
$= 4 + 2 = 6$

Hence, option (b) is correct.

10. The figure may be labelled as

The number of squares formed by one unit component are ☐ ABPQ, ☐ DEFR, ☐ THIJ, ☐ NSLM and ☐ UVWX i.e.5. The number of squares formed by two units component are ☐ ACVO, ☐ CEGV and ☐ VGIK i.e.3.

The number of squares formed by more than two units component are ☐ OVKM and ☐ AEIM i.e. 2 So, total number of squares $= 5 + 3 + 2 = 10$

Hence, option (a) is correct.

11. There are nine centres i.e. A, B, C, D, E, F, G, H and I in the given figure, as shown below,

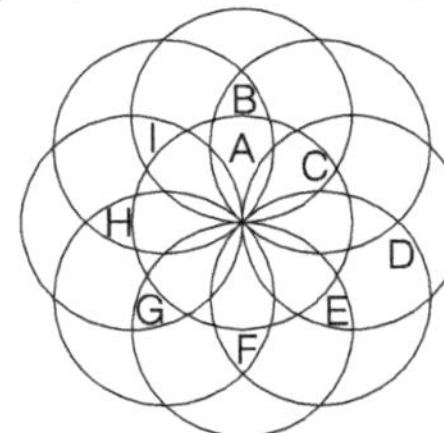

So, the number of circles = 9. Hence, option (a) is correct.

12. The figure may be labelled as

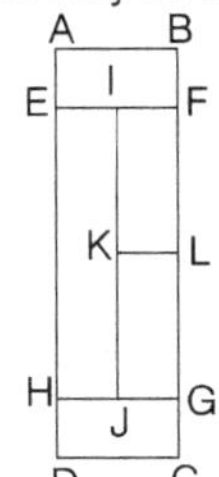

The rectangles formed by one unit component are ☐ ABFE, ☐ HGCD, ☐ IFLK, ☐ KLGJ and units ☐ EIJH i.e. 5

The rectangles formed by two component is ☐ IFGJ i.e.1

The rectangles formed by more than two components are ☐ ABGH, ☐ EFGH, ☐ EFCD, ☐ ABCD i.e. 4

So, the total number of rectangles
$= 5 + 1 + 4 = 10$

Hence, option (b) is correct.

13. The figure may be labelled as

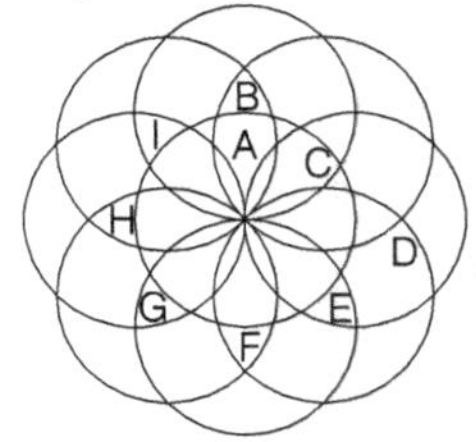

The rectangles formed by one component are ☐ AIKG ☐ IBHK, ☐ KHCJ and ☐ GKJD i.e. 4

The rectangles formed by two component are ☐ ABHG, ☐ HCDG ☐ AIJD and ☐ IBCJ i.e. 4

The rectangles formed by four components are ☐ ABCD i.e. 1

∴ Total number of rectangles
$= 4 + 4 + 1 = 9$

Hence, option (a) is correct.

Practice Set   1

1. The series can be represented as

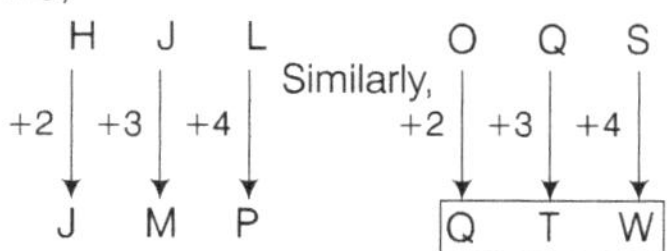

Here, the number to be added is increasing by 2 in each successive step to get the next term.

So, 47 will come next.

Hence, option (b) is correct.

2. AS,

Hence, option (c) is correct.

3. On rearranging the letters given in options, we get

(a) MARCH

(b) TODAY

(c) MONDAY

(d) HOLIDAY

Among all these, only MONDAY is a week day.

Hence, option (c) is correct.

4. In figure I, $8 + 4 = 12$ and $\dfrac{12}{4} = 3$

In figure II, $10 + 10 = 20$ and $\dfrac{20}{4} = 5$

Similarly in figure III, $15 + 9 = 24$

and $\dfrac{24}{4} = \boxed{6}$

Hence, option (a) is correct.

5. Mango is a kind of fruit and vegetable is different from these two.

This can be represented as

Hence, option (d) is correct.

6. The correct mirror image is

NAME25 | ƧƧƎMAИ

Hence, option (b) is correct.

7. We have, $125 \times 25 + 20 - 80$

On substituting the symbols as given in question, we get

$125 \div 25 \times 20 + 80$

$= 5 \times 20 + 80$ $(\because 125 \div 25 = 5)$

$= 100 + 80$ $(\because 5 \times 20 = 100)$

$= 180$

Hence, option (a) is correct.

8. Here, Y is the brother of Z and P is the father of Y and Z. Now, X is the wife of Y,

so she is the daughter-in-law of P. Therefore, P is the father-in-law of X.

This can be represented as

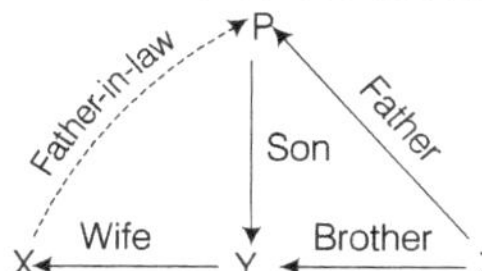

Hence, option (c) is correct.

9. In first pair, the part of the circle is removed from first figure to second figure. On following this pattern (c) will complete the second pair.

Hence, option (c) is correct.

10. In all the figures, except figure (b) the number of lines in outer shape is one less than the number of lines in inner shape. But in figure (b) the number of lines in outer shape is two less than the number of lines in inner shape.

So, figure (b) is odd one.

Hence, option (b) is correct.

11. The information given in question can be represented as

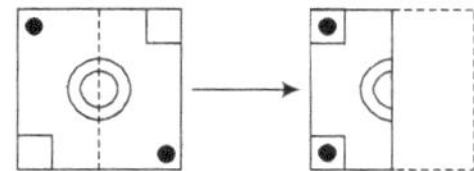

Clearly, P is fourth from the right.

Hence, option (d) is correct.

12. Except, Hale all other are end with ail. So, Hale is odd one.

Hence, option (b) is correct.

13. The circle with shade and two dots, is rotating 90° in clockwise direction and the dot in square is moving one block in anti-clockwise direction in each step.

On following this pattern option figure (b) will come next.

Hence, option (b) is correct.

14. The transparent sheet will appear as

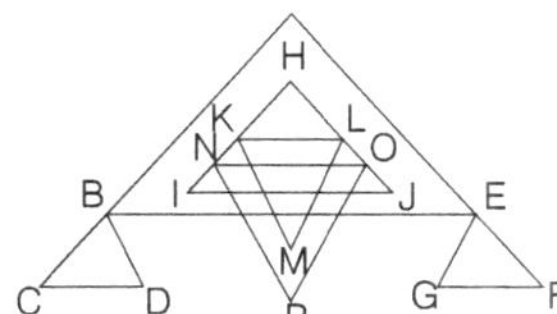

Hence, option (b) is correct.

15. The figure can be labelled as

Number of straight lines are AC, AF, BE, HI, HJ, IJ, KL, KM, LM, NO, NP, OP, BD, CD, GE and FG = 16

Hence, option (b) is correct.

16. When unfolding, the sheet will appear as

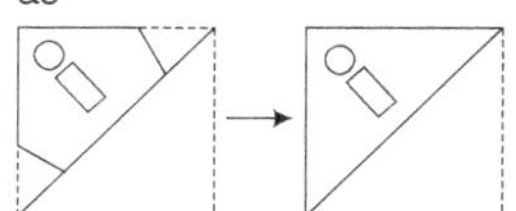

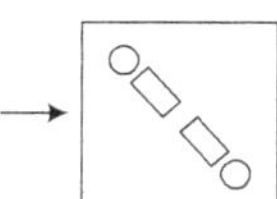

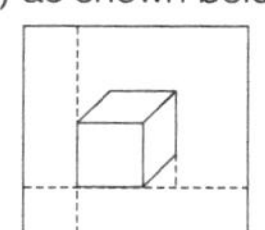

Hence, option (d) is correct.

17. The given figure (X) is embedded in figure (d) as shown below

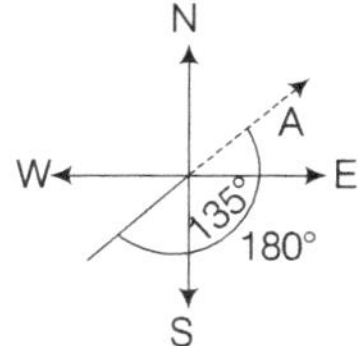

Hence, option (d) is correct.

18.

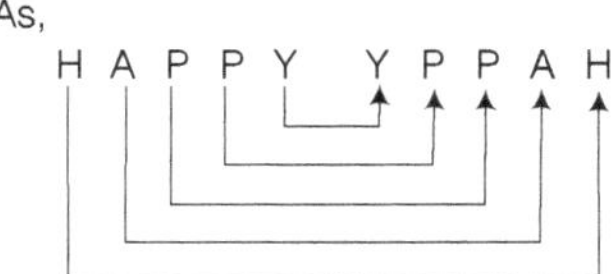

Clearly, he turned 135° clockwise direction and then 180° in anti-clockwise.

So, now he is facing North-East.

Hence, option (c) is correct.

19. As,

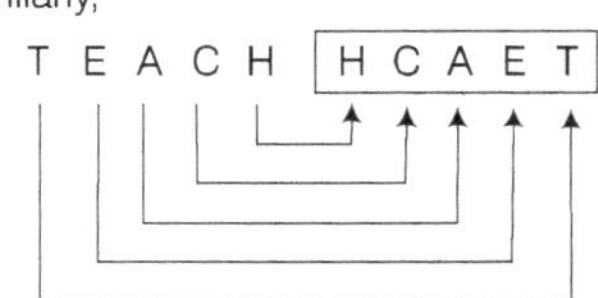

Similarly,

Hence, option (a) is correct.

20. The number '3' is common in both positions, so the adjacent faces of 3 are 6, 4, 5 and 2. So, 1 is opposite to the face having 3.

Hence, option (d) is correct.

Practice Set 2

1. As 'chapter' is a part of the 'book', similarly 'brick' is a part of a 'building'.

Hence, option (c) is correct.

2. The pattern can be represented as

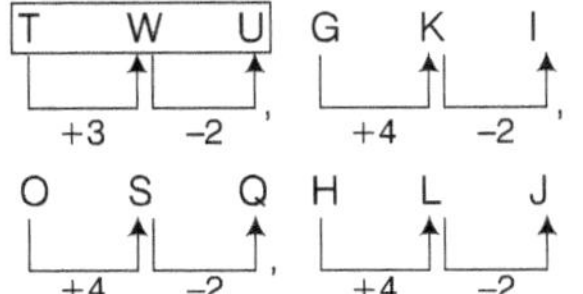

All the groups, except TWU follow similar pattern, but TWU follow different pattern.

So, group TWU is odd one.

Hence, option (a) is correct.

3. The pattern is as follows

$$L \xrightarrow{+2} N \xrightarrow{+3} Q \xrightarrow{+4} U \xrightarrow{+5} \boxed{Z}$$

So, Z will come next.

Hence, option (d) is correct.

4. The letters are coded as

Letters	S	L	O	W	T	A	K	E
Numbers	1	5	9	8	2	4	3	7

Here, L → 5, A → 4, T → 2 and E → 7

So, the code for LATE is 5427.

Hence, option (b) is correct.

5. As, 25 + 15 = 40, 32 + 8 = 40,

28 + 12 = 40 and ? + 2 = 40

∴   ? = 40 − 2 = 38

So, 38 is the missing number.

Hence, option (a) is correct.

6. On rearranging the letters given in option, we get

Option (a) QUICK, option (b) BREAK, Option (c) DAMAGE and option (d) CURE. Among these, only CURE is a synonym of 'Heal'.

Hence, option (d) is correct.

7. As, 7 * 8 = 7 × 8 = 56

6 * 9 = 6 × 9 = 54 and

4 * 6 = 64 × 6 = 24

Similarly, 11 * 5 = 11 × 5 = 55

Hence, option (a) is correct.

8. Pages are the part of book but chair is different.

This can be represented as

Hence, option (d) is correct.

9. The direction graph can be drawn as

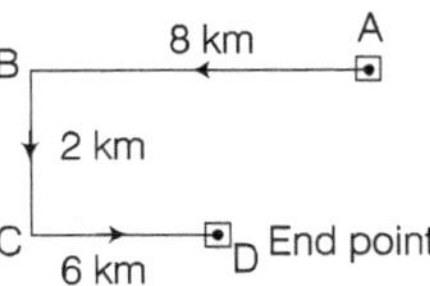

Now, total distance covered by
Akanksha = AB + BC + CD
= 8 + 2 + 6 = 16 km

Hence, option (b) is correct.

10. Ashwini's sister's only brother is Ashwini himself. So, Sachin is the son of Ashwini.

This can be represented as

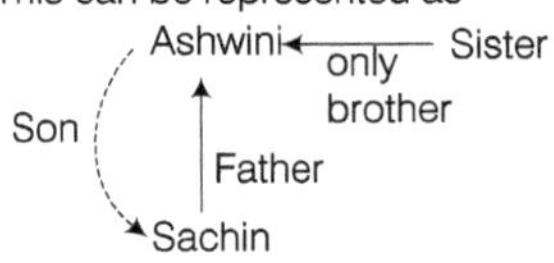

Hence, option (c) is correct.

11. According to English dictionary the correct sequential order of words is 4 → 2 → 1 → 3 i.e. Chitin → Cholera → Hepatitis → Peptidoglycan

Hence, option (b) is correct.

12. The give information can be represented as

Players	Cricket	Hockey	Chess	Swimming
Raghu	✓	✓	✗	✓
Gyan	✓	✓	✓	✗
Sohan	✗	✓	✓	✗
Govind	✓	✗	✗	✓

Clearly, Gyan is a good player in cricket, hockey and chess.

Hence, option (b) is correct.

13. All the figures, except (c) are same when rotated but figure (c) is different.

So, figure (c) is odd one.

Hence, option (c) is correct.

14. The outer arc is rotating 90° in clockwise direction and the inner arc is rotating 90° in anti-clockwise direction in each step. On following this pattern, option figure (a) will complete the series.

Hence, option (a) is correct.

15. The lines used to make the first figure is reduced by one and the new formed figure is enclosed within a circle. On following this pattern, option figure (a) will complete the second pair.

Hence, option (a) is correct.

16. The figure may be labelled as

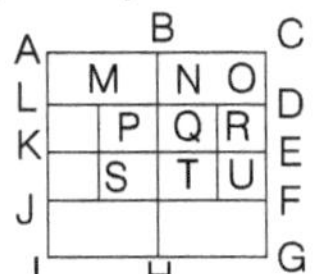

Number of squares formed from one component are

☐LMPK, ☐MNQP, ☐NORQ, ☐ODER, ☐KPSJ, ☐PQTS, ☐QRUT, and ☐REFU i.e. 8

Number of squares formed from three components are ☐ABQK, ☐BCEQ, ☐KQHI, ☐QEGH i.e. 4

Number of squares formed from four components are ☐LNTJ, ☐MOUS and ☐NDFT i.e. 3

Large square is ☐ACGI i.e. 1

∴ Total number of squares
= 8 + 4 + 3 + 1 = 16

Hence, option (b) is correct.

17. On observing the figure, we see that figure (b) will form a complete square when joined with given problem figure as shown below

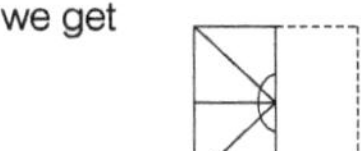

Hence, option (b) is correct.

18. On folding the given transparent sheet, we get

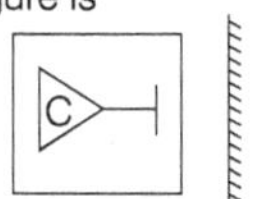

Hence, option (c) is correct.

19. The correct mirror image of the given figure is

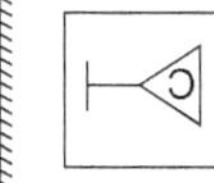

Hence, option (c) is correct.

20. According to the given figure, the opposite faces are

1 opposite to 3,   6 opposite to 5,

2 opposite to 4

In cube (a) 1 and 3 are shown on adjacent to each other, in cube (b) 6 and 5 are shown adjacent to each other and in cube (c) 2 and 4 are shown adjacent to each other, So these cubes are not possible.

Only the cube (d) can be formed because no opposite faces are shown adjacent to each other in this cube.

Hence, option (d) is correct.